Exercises in analysis

Casimir Lewy

Exercises in analysis

ESSAYS BY STUDENTS OF CASIMIR LEWY

Edited by IAN HACKING

The right of the
University of Cambridge
to print and sell
all manner of books
was granted by
Henry VIII in 1534.
The University has printed
and published continuously
since 1584.

CAMBRIDGE UNIVERSITY PRESS
Cambridge
London   New York   New Rochelle
Melbourne   Sydney

Published by the Press Syndicate of the University of Cambridge
The Pitt Building, Trumpington Street, Cambridge CB2 1RP
32 East 57th Street, New York, NY 10022, U.S.A.
296 Beaconsfield Parade, Middle Park, Melbourne 3206, Australia

© Cambridge University Press 1985

First published 1985

Printed in Great Britain at The Pitman Press, Bath

Library of Congress catalogue card number: 84-12082

British Library Cataloguing in Publication Data

Exercises in analysis.
  1. Philosophy
  I. Hacking, Ian
  190   B21

ISBN 0 521 25684 4

Contents

Preface

Casimir Lewy taught each of the contributors to this book. Some were his undergraduate pupils, some were research students, and many were both. An undergraduate supervision occurred weekly. The pupil wrote an essay, posted or delivered it, came at the appointed time to discuss it for an hour, and left with a new topic and reading to do for next week. Research students met less often for longer sessions. It is widely believed that such teaching is a luxury to be afforded by only a few universities. In fact, it means that the teachers work long hours. This book is a token of gratitude for, among other things, those long hours.

We also thank Eleanor Lewy, whose help with the biographical note reminded us once again that we owe a great deal to her also.

Biographical note

Casimir Lewy was born in Warsaw on 26 February 1919 of Ludwik Lewy and Izabela Lewy (née Rybier). His father, a medical doctor, died when Casimir was a child, and he grew up with his mother's family, which was large, warm and talented (especially on the musical side). As a boy he enjoyed and profited from the advantages of living in a charming and lively capital city where the intellectual life was vigorous and tolerant.

From the age of eight he attended the Mikolaj Rej school, a fashionable private school owned by the Lutheran congregation, where he was fortunate to have a number of gifted friends, some now prominent in Poland and the West, who shared his passion for literature, particularly poetry, and history. At the age of 15 his interest in philosophy and logic was aroused by an article in a literary weekly about the philosophy of T. Kotarbiński. He thereupon bought a copy of Kotarbiński's university textbook on the theory of knowledge, logic and scientific method, and found it of such absorbing interest that, besides continuing his reading in philosophy, he attended lectures at Warsaw University.

Lewy came to England in July 1936 a few weeks after leaving school. His primary purpose was to learn English, and he intended to stay for not more than one year. Although he had of course heard of Broad, Moore, Russell and Wittgenstein he wished to return to Poland to read philosophy at Warsaw University, though he was not sure that he wanted to make a career in the subject. But in the meantime he decided that a whole year just learning English would be too boring, and he matriculated at Cambridge with the idea of learning philosophy at the same time, this he then found so congenial that he decided to stay for two more years to take the B.A. degree, which he obtained with First Class Honours in 1939.

In any case, the international situation, as well as the political situation in Poland, was rapidly deteriorating during this period. Lewy spent most of the Long Vacation of 1938 in Poland, returning to Cambridge just before the Munich crisis. But it was not until the defeat of Poland in September 1939 that he realised that he would not be able to go back to his native country.

Lewy now began to work, under the supervision of G. E. Moore, towards the doctorate. His dissertation, on 'Some Philosophical Considerations about the Survival of Death' was accepted and he proceeded to the Ph.D. degree in 1943.

Lewy attended all the lectures given by Wittgenstein between 1938 and 1945 and had a large number of private discussions with G. E. Moore; these discussions were to continue until shortly before Moore's death in 1958. He also assisted Moore for a time during the war in editing *Mind*. He took a vigorous part in the discussions of the Cambridge Moral Sciences Club, a habit which he was to continue for some 15 years after his return to Cambridge. He lectured in the Faculty of Moral Sciences from January 1943 and continued to do so until June 1945.

In these early years at Cambridge Lewy established a friendly personal relationship with all the members of the Faculty's teaching staff, and counted himself particularly fortunate in his friendship with Wittgenstein, Moore and Broad, and latterly with Russell.

In July 1945, Lewy married Eleanor Ford, then a student at the London School of Economics, just before taking up an appointment as Lecturer in Philosophy at the University of Liverpool. This he held until 1952; during this period Eleanor Lewy also held a lectureship, in Economic History, at the same university. In that year he was appointed to a University Lectureship in Moral Sciences at Cambridge. He became Sidgwick Lecturer in 1955, and in 1959 he was elected to a Fellowship at Trinity. It was during the next dozen or so years that the majority of the contributors to this volume passed through his hands. In 1972 he became Reader in Philosophy which post he held until his retirement ten years later.

During his career Lewy three times held Visiting Professorships in the philosophy departments of various universities in the United States: in the University of Illinois in 1951–2, in the University of Texas at Austin in 1967, and at Yale University in 1969. In 1968 he was elected to an Honorary Fellowship of the

Polish Society of Arts and Sciences Abroad, and in 1980 to a Fellowship of the British Academy. From 1962 onwards he was a member of the Advisory Editorial Board of *The Monist*. He and Eleanor have three sons, Nicholas, Sebastian and John Dominic.

Casimir Lewy was an inspiring teacher, both in the privacy of 'supervisions' and in his lectures, where his passion to find and convey the truth of the matter in hand could reach an enthralling intensity without the slightest loss of rigour. By his own example, he taught one to think hard, and above all to think honestly: never to deceive oneself into believing that a half-grasped thought was clear, nor to be content with what was still obscure. The standards he inculcated are as vivid in our minds as is the painful realisation that we usually fall short of them. His pupils, many more than those whose names appear in this book, will always think of his powers of mind with admiration and respect, and of him with warmth and gratitude.

1   *Wicked promises*

J. E. J. ALTHAM

I

When philosophers discuss promising, they frequently concentrate on central cases. Central cases are those where the promisor,
in full possession of all relevant information and subject to no
undue pressure, sincerely promises to perform some action which,
independently of the promise, it is perfectly all right for him to
perform, and where the promisee, also in full possession of all
relevant information and subject to no undue pressure, sincerely
accepts the promise. In a central case, no force, fraud, mistake or
duress is involved, and the promise is not one to do something
that, independently of the promise, one ought not to do. A central
case is one in which it seems most clearly true that the making of a
promise, together with its acceptance, gives rise to an obligation
to perform. A concentration on such cases seems therefore to
allow a philosopher to attend undistractedly to the nature of the
obligation created, and to how it is possible for an obligation to
come about in this way at all. But if he forgets or underestimates
the importance of the peripheral cases, he is liable to produce a
misleading or even an erroneous account. The purpose of this
paper is to attend to what can be learned about promising from a
consideration of one class of peripheral cases in particular, namely
those in which the promise is to do something that ought not to be
done. The example I shall consider is of a promise to do
something that there is a stringent obligation not to do. I call such
promises wicked, thinking mainly of the wicked things that
would be done if they were carried out, but recognising also the
wickedness of making them, where the promisor is in a position
to know what he is about.

Recognition that there are wicked promises provides the clearest way of seeing what is wrong with Searle's purported derivation of 'ought' from 'is'. This is the first lesson I shall draw. The second lesson concerns another kind of attempted refutation of Searle, that put forward by Hare, who is followed in the relevant respect by Mackie. Both argue that in order to conclude from the fact that someone made a promise that he ought to perform, *where the 'ought' is genuinely an evaluative one*, one must subscribe to, or endorse, the institution of promising. I argue that this is at best misleading, because there is no one thing that is *the* institution of promising. An institution is here a set of practices: practices of making and keeping promises, of encouraging their keeping, and criticising and taking sanctions against those who do not perform. There are many such sets of promising practices. There are promises, for example, that it is all right to make in one social group (i.e. that that group treats as all right to make), but that it is not all right to make in another. In one group a promise to do a certain kind of thing may be one a person would be encouraged to keep, and condemned for violating, whereas in another he would be condemned for keeping it. What particular institution of promising there is in a social group is to an important extent determined by the general morality prevailing in that group. A thinking individual may very well partly agree and partly disagree with the general morality prevailing in his social group, and accordingly he may neither wholly endorse nor wholly reject a particular institution of promising. To conclude from the fact that a particular promise was made that it ought to be kept he does not need to endorse any complete institution at all. He needs the moral premiss that this kind of promise, made in these circumstances, ought to be kept. It is true that in the absence of any practice the giving and acceptance of a sign could not create an obligation, so that the existence of a practice is necessary for promising. But that is compatible with the possibility of a variety of practices, and the fact that a claim, about any given promise, that *it* gave rise to an obligation, is never analytic.

Once one has seen the complexity and variability of practices connected with promising, and the falsity of the proposition that all promises voluntarily made ought to be kept (if one is not released from them by the promisee), one may go too far, and reject the fundamental idea that the point of promising is voluntarily to undertake an obligation. This is, unfortunately, what Atiyah (1981) does. Perhaps more than anyone else, Atiyah has recognised and insisted upon the exceptions and qualifications that have to be made to the general idea that to make a promise is voluntarily to undertake an obligation, but he is so impressed by the number and variety of these exceptions and qualifications that he is led to reject the model of the voluntary undertaking of an obligation. Instead, he wishes us to think of promises as at least very like *admissions* of pre-existing obligations. But admissions are so unlike promises that this idea is unhelpful. Fortunately, it is also unnecessary. We can and should both retain the conception of a promise as voluntarily creating an obligation, and acknowledge and give due weight to Hume's point that 'As the obligation of promises is an invention for the interest of society, 'tis warp'd into as many different forms as that interest requires'. (1740: III, V, 524).

II

The first thing to show is that a wicked promise *is* a promise, but does not create any obligation to perform the act promised. I take as my main example a promise to kill someone, and ask the reader to suppose that in the circumstances to carry out the promise would be murder. It is convenient to set down Searle's famous sequence of five propositions, but with the example changed and consequent minor adaptations (1969: 177).

(1) Jack uttered the words 'I hereby promise you, Luigi, that I will kill Harry'.
(2) Jack promised Luigi that he would kill Harry.
(3) Jack placed himself under an obligation to kill Harry.
(4) Jack is under an obligation to kill Harry.
(5) Jack ought to kill Harry.

In his later presentation, Searle clarified his argument by putting forward the following three propositions, and claiming that they are analytic:

(2a) All promises are acts of placing oneself under an obligation to do the thing promised.

    (3a) All those who place themselves under an obligation are (at the time when they so place themselves) under an obligation.

    (4a) If one is under an obligation to do something, then as regards that obligation one ought to do what one is under an obligation to do.

Further, Searle does not think that (2) follows from (1) alone, but does hold that there are purely empirical premisses which, in conjunction with (1), entail (2). For he holds that the conditions under which a man who utters 'I hereby promise' can correctly be said to have made a promise are in a perfectly ordinary sense empirical conditions. He would, therefore dissent from the view that a promise to do something wicked is not really a promise. On this last point he is correct, as we shall see.

Assuming then that the empirical conditions sufficient for Jack's utterance to be a promise are fulfilled, we reach (2). On Searle's view, (5) may be derived from (2) with the help only of the analytic propositions (2a), (3a), and (4a), provided that the sentence (5) is understood to mean 'As regards Jack's obligation to kill Harry, Jack ought to kill Harry'. If it means, 'All things considered, Jack ought to kill Harry', (5) is not claimed to follow.

Searle's view of wicked promises is therefore that if the empirical conditions are fulfilled, a promise to do something wicked *is* a promise, and it *is* true that the promisor ought to perform. However, this 'ought' may be *overridden* by a contrary one arising from the evil nature of the deed.

It is helpful to compare this account with a corresponding account of wicked commands. One who promises, undertakes an obligation, but one who commands, *imposes* an obligation on the person commanded. Command therefore requires authority in the commander. Let us then consider the following sequence:

    (1') The Colonel uttered the words 'I hereby command you, Lieutenant, to drop napalm on the villagers'.

    (2') The Colonel commanded the Lieutenant to drop napalm on the villagers.

    (3') The Colonel placed the Lieutenant under an obligation to drop napalm on the villagers.

    (4') The Lieutenant is under an obligation to drop napalm on the villagers.

(5′) The Lieutenant ought to drop napalm on the villagers.

Corresponding to (2a) one can imagine a philosopher advancing as analytic the following:

(2a′) All commands are acts of placing the addressee under an obligation to do the thing commanded.

A pair of propositions corresponding to (3a) and (4a) might also be put forward. It is not necessary to put them down here.

Just as (2) follows from (1) in conjunction with suitable purely empirical premisses, so (2′) follows from (1′) in conjunction with suitable empirical premisses. But even supposing that a set of such premisses is added, the sequence is still hardly a convincing derivation of 'ought' from 'is'. It is unconvincing even if (5′) is read as 'As regards the Lieutenant's obligation to drop napalm on the villagers, he ought to drop napalm on the villagers'. On the other hand, if the example is changed so that the Colonel's command is one that the Lieutenant shall defend the village against the approaching enemy, then the resulting sequence of five propositions looks *superficially* a more convincing derivation. Similarly, (1)–(5) is superficially a more convincing derivation if the example is different, and one chooses a promise to perform some more or less indifferent action, as in Searle's original case of a promise to pay $5.

In the commanding case, a brief explanation runs as follows. The exercise of authority is part of a practice that proceeds in accordance with rules. The practice includes issuing commands and giving permissions, and on the part of one subject to authority it includes practices of compliance with command, and taking advantage of permissions. It also includes criticism of non-compliance, and often sanctions as well. It includes a number of linguistic ways of insisting on compliance, such as 'You must do it', or 'You've got to do it' (Anscombe 1981a,b: sect. II; sect. II). These expressions and other similar ones are very important. The ordinary point of issuing a command is no doubt to get someone else to do something, but the command achieves this object (where it does achieve it) through the recipient's understanding that, because of the command, he is under a necessity to act, or that he is bound or under an obligation to do it. Recognition of this might lead somebody to espouse (2a′), but wrongly. For the social practice of commanding to be established, there must be commands whose addressees take them as creating an obligation to comply, but once the practice is established, so that 'command' is understood, people can distinguish commands that create an obligation from those that merely purport to do so. Now if we were to think *only* of commands like the Colonel's command to the Lieutenant to defend the village against the approaching enemy, we might be inclined to forget the distinction between a command that does, and one that merely purports to, create an obligation to comply. We might thus erroneously come to think that we had forged a route from 'is' to 'ought'. Examples such as the one about dropping napalm should then remind us that the route does not lead to its imagined destination. Premiss (2a′), then, far from being analytic, is not even true.

The position may be obscured by the thought that the Lieutenant may indeed have a serious conflict. If he does not drop napalm on the villagers, he will be court-martialled and shot. The thought that this may happen may lead one to think that it is true that he ought to drop the napalm, but that this should be weighed against the moral horror of the act itself. This would be a confusion. It is not a necessary truth that disobedience leads to sanctions. The question concerned whether the obligation followed from the fact that the command was given (and received), and this should be considered independently of possible sanctions for disobedience. If it is in any sense true that the Lieutenant ought to drop the napalm, it is not the command in itself that makes it so. This should become clearer in what follows.

A commander normally has a certain sphere of authority. A sphere of authority may be explicitly defined in a table of rules, or it may simply be informally understood what the sphere is. To answer the question whether a particular command imposes an obligation, we must ask first whether the commander was acting within his sphere of authority in giving it. This first question should be understood in a sociological sense, as whether there is in fact an institution in being whose rules involve a commander being able, acting within those rules, to issue that command to that addressee. If the answer is 'Yes', then the second question is whether it is a good thing, or at least acceptable, that there should be such an institution with those particular rules. If the answer to that too is 'Yes', then the addressee is under an obligation to comply. It is then the command that created the obligation to comply, independently of further reasons that there might be, such as those deriving from the consequences of non-compliance. In the case of the command to napalm the villagers, the Colonel either has authority to order the Lieutenant to do it, or he has not. If he has not, his command, being *ultra vires*, creates no obligation to comply (though of course there may be other reasons for doing what is commanded). If he has the authority in the sociological sense, then if it is not acceptable that military authority should encompass the power to order the napalming of civilians, his command still creates no obligation to comply.

The analogue to a command that is *ultra vires* is a promise that 'doesn't count'. The particular promising practice that obtains in a society may be one in which certain promises, made in certain circumstances by certain people, are not taken to create any obligation to do the thing promised. It is outside a person's power to bring about that he has a certain obligation by making a particular promise. His promise is treated as of no effect. An example might be a promise not to exercise an important right. For instance, someone might promise not to defend himself if attacked, but in the practice of his society this promise simply does not succeed in creating an obligation not to defend himself. As such a thing is possible in the law, it is also possible in more informal settings. One should then think of the practice of promising in a given society as having a certain sphere of validity, analogous to the sphere of authority of a commander or the position he occupies. If a given promise does fall within the sphere of validity, that is still not sufficient to establish that it creates an obligation to perform. For there is the further question whether it is acceptable that there should be a promising practice in which that promise, made in those circumstances, should be valid. Before trying to enforce the truth of these points, I shall set out some of the objections to regarding (2a) as analytic, and hence accepting the validity of the derivation (for (3a) and (4a) seem clearly true).

First, it is significant, though admittedly not decisive, that Searle's position is unnatural in relation to what we should normally say. It is hard to envisage circumstances in which one would naturally say that Jack is under an obligation to kill Harry, and still harder to think of ones in which one would naturally say that he *ought* to do so (unless, of course, one shares the underworld ethic, which I am assuming no reader does). Further, the expression 'As regards his obligation to kill Harry, Jack ought to kill Harry' is unnatural in itself, and there seems little reason to believe that the sentence (5) would naturally be used to mean what this unnatural sentence says.

Secondly, there are, of course, cases in which an obligation arising from a promise conflicts with another obligation, but the usual ones are quite unlike the conflict there would be if (2a) were analytic. In the usual cases the promise is to do something it is normally at least all right to do, but some unforeseen event takes place that makes it imperative to do something that would prevent the keeping of the promise. The obligation to do the thing that is, in the circumstances, incompatible with the keeping of the promise, has a source that is independent of the obligation to keep the promise itself. The resulting conflict of obligations is a misfortune that one cannot be sure of avoiding. A wicked promise, on the other hand, purports to create an obligation to do something which is in itself evil. The description of the act given in the promise itself marks it as something not to be done. Because of this difference, it is possible to hold the commonsense position that in some cases a promise creates an obligation that is over-ridden by a contrary one, and yet to deny that wicked promises belong in that class.

Thirdly, where a promise does create an obligation, it also creates a right. The promisee has the right to require that the thing promised be done. But if it is odd to think that Jack is under an obligation to kill Harry, it is still odder to think that Luigi has the right to require that Jack kill Harry.

Fourthly, we must ask what *weight* is supposed to attach to the alleged obligation to keep a promise, where it was to do some-thing it is wrong to do. To say that no weight attaches to it would be tantamount to admitting that there was no obligation. So it must be supposed that the alleged obligation has *some* weight. Now if one has an obligation of a given weight, then all things considered one should do what one has that obligation to do unless there are contrary considerations of at least equal weight. In that case, however, a difficulty arises. For it would then seem that if a man wanted to do something that would normally be just a little bit wrong, he could arrange to promise to somebody that he would do it. He could, in suitable cases, arrange a promissory obligation that would outweigh the normal obligation not to do the act in question, so that, all things considered, he ought to do the thing that, but for the promise, would be wrong. For example, suppose that there is some small lie that it would be in my interest to tell John Doe. Nobody would be harmed by the telling, but it would be an act of deception and leave an unpleasant taste. I find that it would also be in the interest of Janet Roe that I should tell the lie. After a short discussion with her, I solemnly promise to tell Doe the thing that I believe to be false. Reflecting on the seriousness of my promise (after all Janet Roe is relying on me), I conclude that it is now, all things considered, better to tell the lie.

The story is absurd. For it would be a case of somebody using promises to rejig the moral world in his favour, so that normal prohibitions are overridden. To avoid this possibility, the weight given to the obligation to keep a wicked promise must be reduced to something purely nominal. The claim that there always *is* such an obligation is then nugatory.

At this point one might think to try to save the analyticity of (2a) by denying that a wicked promise is really a promise. There would then be no obligation, because there had really been no promise. We have already seen that Searle would disagree with this line, and he would be right. Anscombe has put the main objection (Anscombe 1981c: 16). While a promise to perform an evil deed imposes no necessity to perform it, it does not follow that the promise cannot be invoked at all. If Jack has received money in exchange for his undertaking to kill Harry, then if he does not keep it, Luigi can invoke the promise in demanding that the money be returned. If there was not really a promise, Luigi would have nothing to invoke in demanding his money back.

The right course is to give up the analyticity, and indeed the truth, of (2a). This may seem a reckless thing to do. For it may seem to destroy the very basis of our understanding of what promising is. One thing we must hold fast to is surely that the point of making a promise, what we have the institution for, is to place oneself under an obligation. A second axiom is, or seems to be, that in promising one uses a sign which *signifies* the creation of an obligation. Together these may make it difficult to see how anything more could be needed to bring the obligation into being beyond using the sign which signifies the bringing into being of that obligation. The difficulty can be surmounted, but before saying how, one further piece of evidence is appropriate to show that it must be. This is the fact that some promises made under duress do bind, whereas others do not.

At the end of his discussion of promises in the *Treatise*, Hume makes clear his opinion that if a highwayman forces a traveller to pay him a sum of money, the traveller is not bound to perform (1740: III, V, 525). He seems to mean that the traveller has *no* obligation to pay, as he speaks of force as invalidating contracts, and freeing us from their obligation. But Searle, and others who think like him, must disagree. For if the traveller really *did* make a promise, and the propositions (2a)–(4a) are analytic as claimed, then it is also true that as regards his obligation to pay the highwayman, the traveller ought to pay. One might, as before, try saying that the putative promise is not a real promise, but this route is open to serious objections. Some promises made under duress do bind the promisor. There can be no general doctrine that only a freely made promise binds, and hence no general doctrine that only a freely made promise is really a promise. Parents, for example, may use their authority over their children to require their children to promise to do things, and may on occasion use threats to extract such promises. This would be self-defeating if promises thus extracted were not binding on those making them. Similarly, a judge may require that a man in the dock promise to keep the peace, where the man knows that if he does not so promise he will be sent to prison. Parents and judges will usually be demanding that the promisors promise to do what they ought to do anyway, but there is still point to the promise in that it adds further weight to the obligation. Further, Anscombe's objection holds here also. A man may make a promise under duress but still be paid for it. If he does not perform, the promise can be invoked to demand the money back. For these reasons it should be agreed that a promise a person is forced to make is still a promise.

It would be even more hopeless to make the question whether a forced promise is really a promise turn on whether in the particular circumstances there is some obligation to keep it. For that would be to abandon all pretence of having derived 'ought' from 'is', by making the existence of the promise an overtly evaluative question.

One might instead try following Adam Smith, who surprisingly thought that 'A gentleman who should promise a highwayman five pounds and not perform, would incur some blame' (1759: VII, IV, 331). Smith's own discussion, however, gives support to the opinion of those who think that no obligation attends such a promise. (Smith admits that these opponents will regard his position as superstitious.) His argument appeals to properties of the imagination.

Treachery and falsehood are vices so dangerous, so dreadful, and, at the same time, such as may so easily, and, upon many occasions, so safely be indulged, that we are more jealous of them than of almost any other. Our imagination therefore attaches the idea of shame to all violations of faith, in every circumstance and in every situation. (1759: 332)

The conclusion evidently does not follow from the premiss. We can perfectly well recognise the dangers of treachery, and the possibility of getting away with it, and yet still distinguish in our imaginations and beliefs between circumstances where it is alright to break a promise and those where it is not. But Smith's discussion, though weak, has at least the merit of treating the issue as a matter of casuistry, and not of meaning or logic. He does not claim that it followed from the mere fact that the promise was made that at that time the traveller had some obligation to perform. So if the *moral* argument does not show that there is such an obligation, there is none.

The main objection to thinking that the promise made to the highwayman creates any obligation is, however, similar to the objection to thinking that wicked promises do. If a wicked promise creates an obligation, as we have seen, a bad man would be able to use promises to adjust the moral world in his favour. Similarly, the highwayman would, by unjust threats, be able to adjust the moral world in *his* favour. There is little to be said for a promising institution that enables such things.

The truth is rather this: where a man is induced to make a promise by force or threats, the promise is binding if the person using force or threats had the right to require him to make the promise, and had the right to use force or threats to bring it about that he did so. But if the promise was elicited by force or threats used by someone without the right to do so, then the promise is at least normally not binding. That is, it does not create *any* obligation.

It seems then that there are good reasons for rejecting (2a). It is neither analytic, nor even true. Some promises place one under an obligation, but others do not. It is now time to do a bit more to dispel the puzzlement that rejection of (2a) may cause, by showing that rejection of (2a) is compatible with retaining the axiom that in promising one uses a sign which signifies the creation of an obligation.

III

Hume's treatment of promising provides the main ideas needed to remove this puzzlement. Anscombe has admirably elucidated and expanded upon Hume, and my discussion is heavily in debt to hers.[1] Hume correctly saw that even if there were such an act of the mind as willing an obligation (and he thought that there was no such act), it would not follow that the performance of such an act would result in an obligation. There would be a real question as to whether what was willed did come into existence. Hume indeed claimed that it was 'naturally unintelligible' that an act of willing an obligation should actually bring an obligation into being. We may think of a form of words as expressing such an alleged act of mind, for example, 'I will that I be under an obligation to do A'. Sincere utterance of such a form of words would not make it the case that I *was* under such an obligation. There may be, however, an established social rule according to which, if one says 'I will that I be under an obligation to do A', then one has got to do it. What this amounts to is that there is a general practice whereby if someone says this, he is expected by others to act accordingly, encouraged to do so, criticised and reproached for not doing so, and so on. Children are trained in this practice. It *is* intelligible that there should be such a practice, and the existence and maintenance of such a practice has point in that it facilitates social co-operation. However, a practice that maintained a rigid and unqualified connection between such a form of words and the necessity to act would be subject to various inconveniences. It is much *more* in the general interest to have a

---

[1] Cf. especially Anscombe (1981a).

more complex practice, which if articulated in rules would allow certain classes of exceptions to the connection between the utterance of the words and the necessity to act accordingly. These exceptions would include such cases as where the utterance was made under some grave misapprehension of fact, as well as those where it was extorted unjustly or purported to undertake an obligation to do something wicked.

A promise is of course not an interior act of will. It is an act whereby one communicates an intention to undertake, by that act of communication, an obligation to do a certain action (Finnis 1980: 298). But the Humean point holds when put in these terms also. Just as willing an obligation does not by itself make it the case that there is that obligation, so communicating an intention to undertake an obligation by that act of communication does not by itself make it the case that the intention is fulfilled. Where the communicative act is efficacious, it is so only through its place in a practice of saying, of people who perform such acts, that they must do what they said they would, and of treating them, by way of encouragement and reproach, appropriately to that claim. And while this practice *could* take the form of a rigid connection between the communicative act and treating the utterer as under an obligation to perform, there is no necessity that it should. The practice can take various forms.

Now while 'I promise' would have no use unless there were *some* practice connecting its utterance with treating the utterer as bound, that practice does not give the *meaning* of 'I promise', and the meaning of 'I promise' does not vary with variations in the practice. For in all the different possible practices, 'promise' retains the meaning of communicating an intention to undertake, by that act of communication, an obligation to do some action. The differences in the practices concern differences in the circumstances in which such a communicative act is treated as having brought an obligation into being as intended. For example, practices may vary in how they treat promises which, if kept, would be seriously contrary to the interest of the promisor. In one society such a promise might be treated as just as binding as any other. If the promisor suffers, then that is bad luck, but one makes a promise at one's own risk. Another society might adopt a different practice, according to which such promises were of no effect, thereby perhaps reflecting a more paternalistic attitude. Such a difference, however, would not mean that the word for 'promise' had a different meaning in the two societies. One may say then that it *is* analytic that there are circumstances in which promises are treated as obligatory, since otherwise there would be no practice of promising at all, and no promising sign would have a use. But it is false that there are some circumstances and some particular promises such that it is analytic that in those circumstances those promises are treated as obligatory. For if in any given circumstances a given promise is treated as obligatory, this is so in virtue of a substantive rule that does not give part of the meaning of 'promise'.

As the example given suggests, the particular practice prevailing in a society will reflect its general morality. A person learning how to use a promising sign in a social group must learn, if he is to use the sign effectively, what promises, made in what circumstances, are counted within that group as giving rise to obligations. Initially, as a child, he has to accept what is treated as giving rise to an obligation as actually doing so. For at this stage he has no basis for criticism. But in due course he can come to see that the particular practice reflects moral beliefs, and can come to be able to think about moral beliefs, and hence to assess and to criticise the particular promising practice he has learned. This practice may be unsatisfactory or even bizarre in certain respects, and may quite coherently be judged so, even by one who has grown up with it. He can, that is, judge that certain promises which are taken to create obligations do not really do so, or that others which are not taken to create obligations ought to be taken to do so. The established practice of treating some promises as binding and others as not does not suffice to make it the case that the former are binding and the others not. It is further necessary that that part of the practice according to which a particular promise is taken as binding, as made in particular circumstances, should be morally acceptable. An analogy with commands may again be made. The fact that there is a practice of treating a particular type of command as imposing an obligation to act accordingly does not suffice to make it the case that the person commanded ought really to do so. The fact that a policeman has been ordered to torture a suspect within a society in which there is a practice of treating such commands as imposing an obligation to torture does not prove that the policeman ought to torture the suspect.

Thus 'promise' can have the significance it does and yet a particular promise not give rise to an obligation. There is an obligation only if the promise fits appropriately into a practice, and that practice, or the relevant part of it, is morally acceptable.

IV

It is now time to see what is wrong with the attempt to refute the Searlian derivation by means of an alleged distinction between an external and an internal way of speaking. I shall deal with this in the form presented by Mackie (1977: 64–73), who is to a considerable extent following Hare (1967: 115–27). I continue to use my propositions (1)–(5) about Jack's promise to Luigi that he will kill Harry. This is fair, since the proposed rebuttal of Searle does not depend upon the *content* of the promise. According to Mackie then, when speaking externally one is describing the promising institution and its demands, but one's descriptions carry no implication that one endorses or subscribes to the demands themselves. If one takes (1)–(5) in this way, says Mackie, then the argument goes through as a matter of general logic, but the conclusion is as purely factual as the first premiss; for (5) is short for (roughly) 'The promising institution demands that (in these circumstances) Jack should kill Harry'. On the other hand, if one speaks internally, the crucial transition comes in (3). Without invoking and endorsing the promising institution we can certainly get as far as (2), and indeed to the proposition that Jack purported to place himself under an obligation. But if we wish to conclude that he did succeed in placing himself under an obligation, we must ourselves endorse the rules of the promising institution.

Here the usefulness of considering an example of a wicked promise shows itself. For it is simply not true that the rules of 'the promising institution' demand that Jack kill Harry. So even if there is an external way of speaking, the argument (1)–(5) does not go through in that way of speaking, whether by general logic or in any other way (if there is another way). There is, however, within the underworld group to which Jack and Luigi belong, a sub-institution of promising. In their practice, Jack will indeed be severely taken to task if he does not kill Harry. An advocate of the external reading might then propose to read (5) as 'The underworld's promising institution demands that Jack kill Harry'. To read it thus would, however, reveal the artificiality of the idea of an external reading. Nobody not in pursuit of a philosophical thesis would naturally understand (5) in this way. Even if it is so understood, it still does not follow without an extra premiss saying what the underworld's promising institution is.

Mackie says that if one speaks internally, then (5) follows from (1) and other unstated factual premisses by a special logic that involves appeal to and endorsement of the rules of the promising institution. This is at best highly misleading: there is no such special logic. What Mackie's claim amounts to is that one who speaks internally uses as a rule of inference the synthetic principle that one who makes a promise places himself under an obligation. It would be much clearer and more accurate to drop reference to a special logic and state the synthetic principle as a needed extra *premiss*. It would then be seen that what someone endorses or fails to endorse is entirely irrelevant. The question concerns what follows from what, and is a matter of logical relations, the holding of which cannot be affected by what someone endorses or fails to endorse. Mackie's mistake is to hold that the meaning of 'promise' is such as to embody the synthetic claim that promises ought to be kept (1977: 72). So he thinks that if one uses 'promise' with its *full* meaning, no additional premiss is needed in the argument (1)–(5); the move from (2) to (3) is licensed by the full meaning of 'promise', and using 'promise' in its full meaning involves endorsing the promising institution. His reply to Searle is weak because he shares a mistake with Searle. Both think that the meaning of 'promise' is such that promises ought to be kept. I have argued that this is not so, and that one can accept that it is not so while still accepting the idea that where a promisor places himself under an obligation by his promise it is through the fact that 'promise' signifies the undertaking of an obligation that he does so. The crucial point is that it is not only through this fact; other conditions must be satisfied for what is signified to be the case.

Mackie misidentifies the evaluative element that needs to be added to make the derivation work. We can now see what it is. It is a proposition of disheartening banality, namely 'Jack's promise that he would kill Harry placed him under an obligation to do so'. This is synthetic, evaluative, and in the example, false.

V

Atiyah has recently put forward an account of promising very different from those with which philosophers have been most familiar (Atiyah 1981: see especially chapter VII). In place of the conception of a promise as an act that creates, or at least purports to create, an obligation, he expounds a theory according to which the paradigm of an explicit promise is an *admission* by the promisor of the existence and extent of a pre-existing obligation. It differs from a mere admission mainly in being more or less conclusive and difficult to withdraw. Among the more plausible examples given in support of this account are the following. First, if one person has caused injury to another in a traffic accident, a promise by the former to pay a certain sum of money to the latter is an admission of a pre-existing obligation to compensate the other for his injury. Secondly, people very often promise to pay their debts. Here there are pre-existing obligations, and the promises should be seen as (more or less) conclusively admitting them.

Even in these relatively favourable cases, however, it is not correct to regard a promise as *being* an admission. In the case of the traffic accident, one party may well make the promise to pay without admitting any prior obligation to do so. He may, for example, believe and continue to maintain that he was not in the least at fault, and under no obligation. He may promise to pay purely in order to avoid the matter's being brought to court, with the risk that judgment will go against him and his financial liability become far larger than in an out-of-court settlement. Atiyah says 'the promise is not made in order to create an obligation; it is made in order to settle a dispute'. This may be true, but that is quite compatible with the fact that it settles the dispute *by* creating the obligation. When a man promises to pay a debt, there is of course a pre-existing obligation, if he really had a debt. Also, if he says 'I promise to pay my debt', he is implicitly admitting the debt, and hence the obligation. But the function of a promise is not the same as that of an admission. It may be absolutely clear that the obligation to pay exists prior to the promise. If the promise were an admission, it would have little point in such circumstances. One does not bother to admit what is in any case common knowledge. A promise in such circumstances *can* still have point. It *adds* the obligation arising from it to the one that already exists. Since both are obligations to do the same thing, its effect is to make the obligation weightier. A kind of dishonour attaches to a breach of *promise* to pay that does not attach to a merely admitted debt.

In dealing with some other sorts of promise, Atiyah is led to say things so odd that they reveal the weakness of his position. For example, he proposes that a father's promise of a treat to his children be taken as an admission by the father that this is the best way to discharge his duties. Similarly, promising a donation to a charity is treated as an admission that one recognises a duty to it (Atiyah 1981: 212). These propositions will seem to many sufficient by themselves to expose the falsity of the idea of promises as admissions, but it may be worthwhile to add a further objection. An admission is true or false according as the state of affairs admitted obtains or not. In particular, if the state of affairs admitted does not obtain, admitting that it does cannot make it do so. Now suppose that I have at present no obligation to take my children on an outing to Wicksteed Amusement Park, but I never the less promise to do so next Saturday. If promises are admissions, I still have no obligation to take the children there. On Saturday morning I can explain to them that my admission–promise was false, and go off to play golf with a clear conscience. If the children understand promising they too will realise that they have nothing to reproach me with. But of course this is just not how things are with promising, whether in the family or elsewhere. Atiyah might be thought to have forestalled this objection through his claim that a promise is a (more of less) *conclusive* admission, but the claim does not really help. The idea of a conclusive admission is in fact mysterious. If the source of an obligation is independent of whether the obligation is admitted, the admission cannot be conclusive that one has it, any more than an admission that I have ?20 in my pocket is conclusive that I do. If the source is not independent of the admission, then the admission can be conclusive, by bringing the obligation into being, but then it is not an admission of anything pre-existing, and is better not described as an admission at all.

Why should so intelligent a writer as Atiyah embrace so strange a theory? He is greatly impressed by the changes that have taken place over the past century and a half in social and legal attitudes towards promissory obligation. There has been a large movement away from 'the ideology of liberalism'. (Liberalism here has its English, not its American sense.) According to that ideology, an individual is as far as possible free to create obligations for himself, and free from the imposition of obligations by others without his consent. A man's obligations result from things he voluntarily does. The idea of a promise as creating an obligation is an important part of that social morality. But social morality today has moved far from that position. It is paternalistic, and does not leave it to the individual to choose his obligations. It restricts his ability to create obligations for himself in the light of its own view of his and others' interests, and lays upon him numerous obligations by virtue of his position in, or mere membership of, his society. Where such a morality prevails, the conception of a promise as freely creating an obligation is out of date. The idea of promises as admissions is then brought in to replace it. It reflects the idea that our obligations are there independently of our choice, socially imposed rather than individually undertaken. Promising then cannot *change* the moral situation; it can only acknowledge it.

The erosion of the ideology of liberalism is indisputable as social fact. It has been compellingly charted, together with its effects on the law of contract, by Atiyah himself in another work (Atiyah 1979). But, at least in the sphere of personal relations and their morality, the erosion has not gone nearly as far as he claims, and if it had the right conclusion to have drawn would have been not that our theory of promising is obsolete, but that promises themselves no longer had any serious function. But it remains obvious that promises are made every day to do things that the promisors had no previous obligation to do, but that they ought to do as a result of having promised. It is possible that Atiyah implicitly shares with those he criticises the erroneous assumption that if the function of promising is voluntarily to undertake obligations, then it belongs to the promising institution that every voluntarily made promise does create some obligation. Since he sees that social morality has evolved in such a way as to show the consequent to be untenable, he is led to reject the antecedent. But the broadly Humean position I have described here allows for great flexibility in the practice of promising. Changing moral views may lead to widespread restriction on what promises, made in what circumstances, create obligations, without requiring any change in the general framework for understanding promising, and without requiring us to abandon the conception of promising as creating, *in appropriate circumstances*, an obligation to do what we said we would.

VI

Consideration of a blatantly wicked promise provided reason to believe that some promises put the promisor under no obligation to do what he promised. If we are to conclude that a particular promise put the promisor under an obligation, we need a moral premiss, that what he promised to do is not morally prohibited. Promising then provides no route from 'is' to 'ought'. Hume provided the materials necessary to explain the correct connection between promising and obligation, and to show its compatibility with the fact that only some promises oblige. Mackie shares with Searle the view that the proposition 'All promises ought to be kept' is a principle embodied in the meaning of 'promise'. Unlike Searle, he regards that proposition as synthetic, but his holding it still prevents his criticism from being other than weak, and leads to his confusing questions of logical relations with matters of personal endorsement. Atiyah correctly rejects the proposition, but is wrongly led by his rejection to proffer an erroneous alternative theory.

The Humean view according to which promises purport to create obligations, some succeed in doing so, and the institution is widely adjustable to fit the interests of society, is tenable in itself, and enables us to avoid the errors this paper has sought to expose.[2]

REFERENCES

Anscombe, G. E. M. 1981a. 'Rules, Rights and Promises' in *Ethics, Religion and Politics* by G. E. M. Anscombe, Oxford: Blackwell.
  1981b. 'On the Source of the Authority of the State' in *Ethics, Religion and Politics* by G. E. M. Anscombe, Oxford: Blackwell.
  1981c. 'On Promising and its Justice, and Whether it Need be Respected *in foro interno*' in *Ethics, Religion and Politics* by G. E. M. Anscombe, Oxford: Blackwell.
Atiyah, P. S. 1979. *The Rise and Fall of Freedom of Contract*, Oxford: Clarendon Press.
Atiyah, P. S. 1981. *Promises, Morals and Law*, Oxford: Clarendon Press.

---

[2] In preparing this paper, I have been helped by discussions with Diane Proudfoot.

Finnis, John 1980. *Natural Law and Natural Rights*, Oxford: Clarendon Press.

Hare, R. M. 1967. 'The Promising Game' in *Theories of Ethics*, ed. Philippa Foot, London: Oxford University Press.

Hume, David 1740. *A Treatise of Human Nature*, book III, ed. L. A. Selby-Bigge, 1888. Oxford: Clarendon Press.

Mackie, J. L. 1977. *Ethics*, Harmondsworth: Penguin.

Searle, John R. 1969. *Speech Acts*, Cambridge: Cambridge University Press.

Smith, Adam 1759. *The Theory of Moral Sentiments*, eds. D. D. Raphael and A. L. Macfie, 1976. London; Oxford University Press.

2   *Ethical non-naturalism*

THOMAS BALDWIN

All students of G. E. Moore's ethics are indebted to Casimir Lewy
for his incisive lecture 'G. E. Moore on the Naturalistic Fallacy'
(1968). Lewy not only showed how Moore's 'open question'
argument should be formulated; he also expounded Moore's own
later thoughts about the 'Naturalistic Fallacy', and thereby provided the best introduction available to the tangled doctrines of
Principia Ethica. My aim here is to discuss what Moore's ethical
non-naturalism amounts to and to assess this theory critically. I
shall show that although Moore surrounds his presentation of
ethical non-naturalism in *Principia Ethica* with a rhetoric that leads
one to associate the theory with a conception of values as abstract
objects of rational intuition, that rhetoric does no work in the
actual argumentation of *Principia Ethica*, and ethical non-naturalism turns out to be defined by reference to some rather less
abstract, though nonetheless strange, propositions. These propositions admit of a modest reinterpretation which raises the hope
that ethical non-naturalism can be reformulated in a metaphysically acceptable way. I shall discuss in detail how such a revised
non-naturalism should be characterised, and in particular whether
it can be presented in such a way as not to lead directly to ethical
anti-realism. Since Moore was himself strongly committed (except for one brief period) to ethical realism, it certainly seems
worth trying to present a realist ethical non-naturalism. I shall
argue, however, that although some familiar short routes from
non-naturalism to anti-realism can be obstructed, it is in the end
impossible to sustain a realist ethical non-naturalism.

I

It is useful to start in an indirect way by considering the appropriate analogy within the philosophy of mind for ethical non-naturalism, if one focuses simply on the way in which the relationship between 'values' and 'facts' is conceived within ethical non-naturalism, and then asks what position within the philosophy of mind provides a similar account of the relationship between minds and bodies. The analogy here is to be no more than illustrative, but I think that the question of what analogy is appropriately highlights a central interpretative issue. The obvious answer might seem to be Cartesian dualism, with the real distinction between mind and body occupying a position similar to Moore's claim that moral properties are non-natural. Now although this analogy is in some respects appropriate, I think it draws upon a picture of ethical non-naturalism which is seriously misleading, and I shall later suggest that there is a different position within the philosophy of mind which provides a better analogy for ethical non-naturalism. That different analogy, however, can wait; I want first to articulate the picture of ethical non-naturalism which makes the analogy with Cartesian dualism seem appropriate, and to discuss why it is misleading. The picture is one of values subsisting, along with the natural numbers, in a heavenly realm of non-natural being, but also associating, in no very clear way, with certain natural states of affairs such as 'the pleasures of human intercourse' (Moore 1903: 188). Warnock gives a particularly clear expression to this picture of ethical non-naturalism (1967: 14):

The picture presented is that of a realm of moral qualities, *sui generis* and indefinable, floating, as it were, quite free from anything else whatever, but cropping up here and there, quite contingently and for no reason, in bare conjunction with ordinary features of the everyday world.

Substitute 'minds' here for 'moral qualities', and 'human bodies' for 'ordinary features of the everyday world', and the result is something at least akin to Cartesian dualism. When thus pictured, ethical non-naturalism cannot but appear a strange doctrine, so strange that it must be mistaken (this is part of Mackie's 'Argument from Queerness' against it (1977: 38)). This picture of ethical non-naturalism, which I shall henceforth call the 'Cartesian picture', does receive some justification within *Principia Ethica*, and certainly Moore's views there are, in many respects (including some not represented in this picture), very strange. Nonetheless, if one looks sympathetically at the argument of *Principia Ethica* one can find within Moore's ethical non-naturalism doctrines to which this Cartesian picture is inappropriate. Cox pointed out some years ago (1970) that Warnock's Cartesian picture of ethical non-naturalism was inappropriate to Moore's later ethical writings (especially the paper 'The Conception of Intrinsic Value' (1922)); I want to take Cox's argument back into *Principia Ethica* itself.

I begin with a few remarks about the structure of Moore's position in *Principia Ethica*. As one reads the first chapter it seems that Moore wants to put forward as fundamental two independent propositions: that goodness is unanalysable, and that it is non-natural. It would have been tidy if these had been Moore's fundamental claims. They bear witness to the separate and opposed influence upon Moore of his teachers Sidgwick and McTaggart and, *via* McTaggart, other idealists such as T. H. Green. On the one hand Sidgwick had maintained that the fundamental ethical properties are unanalysable (1901: 32), and on the other Green had maintained that the applicability to us of ethical properties shows that in some respects we are not merely natural beings (1883: 9–11). In fact, however, Moore typically merges these two propositions into the single proposition that goodness is not analysable in terms of properties that are natural or 'metaphysical', in a sense to be defined below. It is the denial of this complex proposition that Moore usually describes as the commission of the 'Naturalistic Fallacy'; and it follows that the reasons he gives for supposing that there is a 'Naturalistic Fallacy' are not necessarily arguments for ethical non-naturalism, understood as requiring only the proposition that goodness is non-natural. For arguments, such as the famous 'open question' argument, which purport to show that goodness is unanalysable do not thereby show that it is not natural. I shall not here attend to these arguments, and shall concentrate on the natural/non-natural distinction itself. Moore's account of this distinction is far from straightforward. He begins (1903: 40) by suggesting that that which is natural is 'that which is the subject-matter of the natural sciences and also of psychology', and in the revised preface to *Principia Ethica* (cf. Lewy 1968: 137) he says that this is the best he could offer by way of elucidation of the distinction. However, an account of this kind is unsatisfactory by itself, since it defines what is natural in terms of the natural sciences, and a bare list of the natural sciences will not explain why ethics is not a natural science.

I shall later suggest that there is, indeed, some point to this initial account of the natural/non-natural distinction. But in *Principia Ethica* (pp. 40–1) Moore moves quickly beyond it to an ontological distinction. He begins by distinguishing between those objects which are natural and those which are not: natural objects, he says, are just those that exist in time. Objects which are not natural, therefore, do not exist in time, and these fall into two classes. First, there is the class of objects such as the natural numbers and intrinsic value. Moore holds that these objects do not literally exist at all, but still in a certain sense *are*. At any rate this class is non-empty. Then there is the class which Moore believes to be empty, of objects that exist but not in time, such as God, the Absolute, the Pure Will, and all the other fictions of idealist metaphysics. The former of these is the class of non-natural objects, the latter that of metaphysical objects (where 'meta-physics' is a term of abuse in Moore's early philosophy). So we have here a tripartite distinction between natural objects, meta-physical objects, and non-natural objects. This distinction bears witness to Moore's previous commitment to, and then disaffec-tion from, the idealism of Kant and Bradley. Moore had at one time accepted a Kantian appearance/reality distinction, and, hav-ing accepted Bradley's arguments for the unreality of time, had committed himself to the timelessness of reality. Since reality was to include ethical values, it followed that these values could not exist in time – hence the thought that goodness is not a natural object. Moore soon turned against this idealism; but since he still accepted for a short time their arguments for the unreality of time, he could not show his rejection of idealist metaphysics by simply placing ethical values among the objects which exist in time: instead, he distinguished between the timeless existence of the puta-tive metaphysical realities which he rejected, and the bare being of the abstract objects – natural numbers and values – which he accepted. Hence the tripartite distinction one finds in *Principia Ethica*.

Yet by 1903 Moore no longer believed in the unreality of time. So he no longer needed to insist that goodness was not a natural object, not something that exists in time, in order to secure its reality. Nonetheless he persisted in his belief that goodness was non-natural; but both the nature of this belief, and his reasons for it, changed in an important way. What lies behind this change is not so much his new belief in the reality of time, as his recognition that general properties quite generally do not exist in time (1901: 115). For once this general claim about properties is accepted, it follows at once that insofar as goodness, and other values, are properties, they do not exist in time and are therefore non-natural objects. But, equally, once this general claim about properties is accepted it follows that the distinctive thesis of ethical non-naturalism cannot be expressed simply by saying that goodness is a non-natural object. For the properties of being yellow, and being a state of pleasure will then be just as much non-natural objects as goodness is.

Moore does not state this point in *Principia Ethica* as clearly as one might wish, and much of his rhetoric remains tied to the 'ontological' conception of ethical non-naturalism (cf. pp. 110–11). Nonetheless, in the crucial passage in which he tries to explain his natural/non-natural distinction (pp. 40–1), he moves from his distinction between natural *objects* and others, to the question of a similar distinction among *properties*: 'which among the properties of natural objects are natural properties and which are not?'. This question, he says, 'is more difficult'. Despite his difficulty in answering it, Moore is certainly here raising the right question; for the switch from a question about objects to one about properties is indeed an acknowledgment that the distinctive thesis of ethical non-naturalism can only be stated by means of a natural/non-natural distinction within the class of properties.

One distinction between properties which might be introduced here is that between those properties whose instances are natural objects, those whose instances are 'metaphysical' objects, and those whose instances are non-natural objects. On this proposal, the property of being a property, or being a proposition, would be a non-natural property. But though Moore had once contemplated something of this sort (1899: 186), in *Principia Ethica* he rules it out as irrelevant: 'I do not deny that good is a property of certain natural objects: certain of them, I think, *are* good'. But, then, when is a property natural or non-natural? Moore's answer is strange, and I will give it in full (p. 41; cf. p. 124):

Well, my test for these [sc. natural properties] too also concerns their existence in time. Can we imagine 'good' as existing *by itself* in time, and not merely as a property of some natural object? For myself I cannot so imagine it, whereas with the greater number of properties of objects – those which I call the natural properties – their existence does seem to me independent of the existence of those objects. They are, in fact, rather parts of which the object is made up than mere predicates which attach to it. If they were all taken away, no object would be left, not even a bare substance: for they are in themselves substantial and give the object all the substance it has. But this is not so with good.

This passage suggests two reasons why goodness is not a natural property: first, it cannot exist by itself in time, and, secondly, it is not a part of anything of which it is a property. The connection between these two reasons appears to be that since natural objects, which exist in time, only have parts which can exist by themselves in time, goodness, which cannot exist by itself in time, cannot be a part of a natural object of which it is a property. Given the bizarre nature of these claims, it may seem strange to suggest that Moore is here moving towards a different, and more fruitful, account of the natural/non-natural distinction. Nevertheless, this is just what I do want to suggest. To understand this new account, one must appreciate some features of the metaphysics implicit in the passage I have quoted. It is not difficult to grasp roughly what Moore has in mind when he talks of properties as parts: it is a part/whole theory of predication, according to which, in the case of most properties, for an object to have a property is for a particular instance of that property to be a part of that object. Behind this theory there lies the connected treatment of most predicates as sortal predicates (e.g. colour predicates are treated this way) with simple particulars as instances, and of material objects as 'composite existents' whose identity is determined by that of the simple particulars that constitute them by congregating in space and time (for these views cf. Moore 1901; 1902; they are also manifest in chapter 6 of *Principia Ethica*).

Now I mention all this not in order to present it for critical discussion: we are not likely to find much to attract us in the thought that the whiteness of this piece of paper is a part of it which could exist by itself. Instead I present it so that we can grasp the sense of Moore's natural/non-natural distinction for properties – between properties that have particular instances that can exist by themselves in time, and properties for which this is not so, even though they have instances that exist in time. For when we come at it this way, we can see why, in the thought that natural properties are those whose instances can exist by themselves in time, the stress is on the phrase 'by themselves', and not on the phrase 'in time'. That is, what is distinctive about non-natural properties is not, despite Moore's opening remark that the test for natural properties 'concerns their existence in time', anything about their existence or not in time; it is that the instances of non-natural properties cannot exist 'by themselves'.

Since this distinction is enmeshed within Moore's early atomist metaphysics, it may seem that there is little of interest in it once that metaphysics is rejected. But that is too quick. For what lies behind Moore's distinction between natural and non-natural properties is, as Moore implies at one point (*ibid.*), a distinction between independent and dependent properties. Moore contrasts the properties of being yellow and being good by saying that something which is yellow has a part which is yellow and nothing else, whereas something which is good lacks a part which is good and nothing else. The contrast he has in mind here is better expressed by the thought that the fact that something is yellow is independent of that thing's other properties, whereas the fact that something is good is dependent upon its other properties. This latter distinction is obviously still problematic, but one modification to it is essential: non-natural properties must be dependent without being reducible to the properties on which they depend. Otherwise the reduction of ethics to a discipline such as psychology would not be ruled out, and it is clear that Moore's ethical non-naturalism must be interpreted to rule out any such reduction. Correlatively, then, natural properties are to be either those which are independent of all properties not analysed in terms of them, or those which are wholly analysable in terms of independent properties; this ensures that logically complex properties, such as being yellow or brown, are natural if their constituent properties are natural. The result of this modification is that an unanalysability claim is, after all, built directly into ethical non-naturalism itself. As I remarked before, this is in fact wholly characteristic of Moore's position in *Principia Ethica*; it does not, of course, show that ethical naturalism is refuted by arguments to the effect that goodness is unanalysable.

Before attempting to take ethical non-naturalism any further, I want to close my interpretative remarks about *Principia Ethica* with two comments. First, I should acknowledge that in proposing my interpretation, I am enjoying the benefits of Moore's hindsight. In his 'Reply to My Critics' (1942: 588) Moore wrote:

> It is true, indeed, that I should never have thought of suggesting that goodness was 'non-natural', unless I had supposed that it was 'derivative' in the sense that, whenever a thing is good (in the sense in question) its goodness (in Mr Broad's words) 'depends on the presence of certain non-ethical characteristics' possessed by the thing in question: I have always supposed that it did so depend.

Moore is not always in his autobiography and 'Reply' a reliable witness to his early self. What he says here is certainly not a full and fair account of what he said in *Principia Ethica*. Still, if my interpretation of *Principia Ethica* has been correct, he does, at the crucial point, suggest the account of ethical non-naturalism which he was later to say that he had always had in mind. To this extent, therefore, these later remarks confirm my interpretation. Another place in which he proposes roughly the position I have been describing is in his paper 'The Conception of Intrinsic Value' (1922: 274), where he suggests that 'predicates of intrinsic value' can be distinguished from 'intrinsic properties' by virtue of the fact that the former, unlike the latter, can be properly omitted from a 'complete description' of a thing which has these properties. For in his 'Reply' (1942: 585) he confirms that that distinction is indeed that which, in *Principia Ethica*, he had described as the non-natural/natural distinction.

Secondly, if what I have proposed is correct, then the Cartesian picture of ethical non-naturalism is inappropriate. That picture is based, understandably enough, on Moore's ontological distinction between natural and non-natural objects. I have argued, however, that although this distinction is indisputably a feature of Moore's thought in *Principia Ethica*, it cannot be central to ethical non-naturalism since it fails to distinguish ethical properties from any others. Furthermore, since the distinction which in fact seems crucial, that between natural and non-natural properties, is not an ontological, but, roughly speaking, a logical distinction, some of the familiar criticisms of Moore's ethical non-naturalism (such as Mackie's 'Argument from Queerness' (1977)) turn out to attend to Moore's rhetoric, but not to his argument.

II

At this point I turn away from the interpretation of Moore's ethics to the task of fashioning ethical non-naturalism into a presentable ethical theory. In undertaking this task, obviously, I shall take as fundamental the thought that in some sense moral properties are non-natural because they are dependent but not reducible to the properties on which they depend. The alternative to the analogy with Cartesian dualism which I want to propose is an analogy with epiphenomenalism, in particular with the currently favoured form of this general philosophy of mind, Davidson's anomalous monism (1980: essay 11); I should perhaps add that my use of anomalous monism does not carry any commitment to its truth. Davidson himself explicitly compares his account of the relation between the mental and the physical with Moore's account of the relation between the moral and the natural (1980: 214, 253); and the feature he picks on is that of dependence without reducibility. This, by itself, shows the appropriateness of the Davidsonian analogy; but what Davidson's theory suggests further is that ethical non-naturalism can be viewed, in respect of its ontology, as a monist doctrine, involving the view that all objects are, in some sense, natural, although some of them possess dependent moral properties which cannot be reduced to purely natural properties. Manifestly, to take ethical non-naturalism in this way is to give up some of its Moorean connections, those which concern non-natural objects; but these, if my previous discussion was correct, are not in fact central to Moore's position in *Principia Ethica*.

This is also an appropriate point to shed some further Moorean baggage with which I do not wish to encumber my discussion of ethical non-naturalism. First, I want to shed any commitment to the intrinsicality of moral properties. Moore's thought that the fundamental values of goodness and beauty are intrinsic, or, as we would now say, essential properties is an interesting one to which I shall briefly return. But it raises many problems – for example, it requires a very extensive essentialism – and since the issues it raises are to some extent separable from those of ethical non-naturalism they are best treated separately. Secondly, I want to shed any commitment to ideal utilitarianism, or consequentialism, at least where this is understood as Moore understood it, as the claim that the answers to all deontic questions depend only upon the results of action (1912: chapter 5). Ross famously argued that the property of being a *prima facie* duty was not consequential in this sense, but that it was dependent in the sense in which Moore held that intrinsic value was dependent (1930: chapter 2); and ethical non-naturalism need embody no commitments in this area.

Having detached ethical non-naturalism from these Moorean claims, I return to the task to fashioning it into a presentable theory. An essential requirement here is that of making the thought that moral properties are non-natural because dependent more precise. There are two issues here: first, that of the 'base' upon which moral properties are dependent, and, secondly, the nature of this relation of dependence, in the absence of reducibility. First, then, the 'base': Moore's line of thought in *Principia Ethica* suggests that it be possible to characterise some absolutely independent properties (those whose particular instances can 'exist by themselves in time'), and that these constitute the base upon which moral properties depend. But once one sheds atomist prejudices, it is very hard to see by what criterion absolutely independent properties can be identified, and it is certain that this criterion will end up with unwanted results. For example, the colour of an object, being a secondary quality, is dependent on the object's primary qualities; but it is not reducible to these primary qualities. So colours would seem to be classified as non-natural, if one relies solely on the condition of dependence without reducibility.

Once this line of thought is rejected, it follows that the 'base' has to be identified in some other way. One proposal is that non-moral properties form it. But this has two defects: first, it makes use itself of the moral/non-moral distinction which, it might be hoped, ethical non-naturalism would do something to elucidate. Secondly, it turns the non-reducibility thesis into the trivial truth that moral properties are not reducible to non-moral ones. By thus, in effect, taking the 'natural' to be the non-moral, it leaves no space for ethical naturalism, ruling it out *a priori* in the manner of Moore's worst formulations of the 'Naturalistic Fallacy'. The result, therefore, is that ethical non-naturalism requires that the concept of the natural, that on which moral properties are supposed to depend, be given some content; and with this we are back with Moore's problem in *Principia Ethica*.

The concept of 'nature' is a notoriously contested one. Even within the context of the present discussion I doubt whether a non-question-begging account of the natural can be given. As I mentioned above, at one point (1922: 274) Moore suggested in effect that to be natural was to be descriptive. This entails that to be moral a property must be non-descriptive, since moral properties cannot belong to the class upon which they depend. This proposal, I think, begs too many questions, for it collapses the contrast between ethical naturalism and non-naturalism into one between ethical realism and anti-realism. Although I shall argue that there are connections here, they are not to be secured by a simple definitional *fiat*. After all, despite this suggestion of Moore's, his ethical thought is predominantly marked by a forthright commitment to realism concerning values; so it would be excessively uncharitable to define ethical non-naturalism as an anti-realist theory.

An alternative view is that the natural is the empirical, a proposal which makes the natural/non-natural distinction into an epistemological one. Such a proposal would be deeply alien to Moore's thought at the time of *Principia Ethica*, since he was then deeply hostile to the philosophical pretensions of epistemology, which he regarded simply as a branch of empirical psychology (1903: 133). But this fact is not a sufficient reason for dismissing this proposal as the best way of making sense of ethical non-naturalism; when Broad later put it forward (1942: 32), Moore did not repudiate it, though he did not endorse it either (1942: 592). The difficulty with this proposal, as I see it, is that by taking the natural to be the empirical, it compels the non-natural to be the non-empirical; and this seems to leave the non-naturalist who wanted to be a realist with an unattractive choice between rational intuitions of moral facts and ethical anti-realism after all. It may be that in the end the non-naturalist does face this choice; but, as before, one would like to find a definition of the natural which does not yield it immediately.

One way round this difficulty would be to strengthen the epistemological requirements placed on the natural, taking it to be that which is verifiable from the relatively disinterested point of view of strict science. For this would not condemn the non-natural to be verifiable, if at all, only by non-empirical means. Instead it would be verifiable from within a point of view which was informed by interests and concerns other than those of strict science, such as friendship, understanding, self-expression, and humour. The trouble with this move, in the present context, however, is that the non-natural would here include much more than the moral: it would include the psychological and all descriptions of the world which characterised it in more than strictly scientific terms. As a result, nothing very distinctive would be here proclaimed for moral properties by the claim that they are not natural, and the dependence of moral properties on natural properties requires some very substantive assumptions about the dependence of everything that matters to morality on the strictly scientific which are no feature of Moore's philosophy. For these reasons this approach does not seem likely to result in a satisfactory formulation of ethical non-naturalism. Indeed, by grouping together the moral with the psychological and the human 'life-world', this proposal might well be viewed as a form of ethical naturalism.

The proposals I have just been considering, to the effect that to be natural is in some sense to be empirical, can be viewed as arising out of Moore's original thought that there is a connection between the natural and the natural sciences. I want to suggest that there is a different way of developing that thought which is more fruitful than these epistemological proposals. But before presenting my proposal directly, I want to consider a particular dispute which I take to exemplify the dispute between ethical naturalists and non-naturalists, that between natural law theorists (such as Fuller (1963)) and legal positivists (such as Hart (1961)). Central to this dispute is the question as to whether the concept of law which figures in explanatory sociological theories is also normative, as natural law theorists insist, or whether, as legal positivists object, we must sharply separate the law as it is (the explanatory concept) from the law as it ought to be (the normative concept). This seems to me an interesting dispute, whose resolution is not obvious, and one which provides a paradigm of the naturalist/non-naturalist issue. On my understanding, ethical naturalists claim that fundamental moral concepts are explanatory, and ethical non-naturalists deny this. Thus further examples of ethical naturalism will be political theories, such as those of Aristotle and Hegel, which seek to explain politics by reference to a teleology whose goal is strongly normative; psychological theories, such as those of Plato and Kant, which propose that our psychic structure is in some sense moral; and metaphysical theories such as that of Leibniz, insofar as he held that whatever happens happens because it is for the best that it should happen. Opposed to all these theories stands a positivist scepticism, which denies that evaluation, and moral judgment, has any proper place within a purely explanatory theory. Ethical naturalism is the secular child of natural theology; ethical non-naturalism is the companion of natural theology's deadly enemy – positivism.

My proposal is, then, that to be natural is to be explanatory. But this proposal must now be qualified in three ways. First, it may be objected that ethics indisputably provides ethical explanations, in which particular moral propositions are explained by reference to more general moral principles. It can be doubted whether these explanations ever really achieve much (cf. Bradley 1927: 194). But in the present context, the important point is that these explanations are in no way causal or teleological. No connection in things themselves is invoked in such explanations. The best way to rule out this sort of trivial counter-example to ethical non-naturalism is to say that the explananda of the moral concepts which the naturalist claims to be explanatory should include facts which are not obviously moral, because they are primarily psychological, sociological, or whatever (one cannot say here that the explananda must be non-moral, because it is precisely the naturalist's claim that psychology or politics, etc. is both moral and descriptive).

The second qualification is more serious. Although it does seem plausible to say that deontic claims do not explain the situations to which they apply, what may be said nonetheless is that they help to explain the behaviour of those who acknowledge them; as where my behaviour is explained by reference to my belief that I ought to keep a certain promise, and this belief is in turn explained by my recognition of this moral feature of my situation. Clearly, important epistemological issues are raised by this last thought; but I want to steer clear of epistemology, if possible. In order to do so, I shall say that a property is not natural where its only explanatory role is that by virtue of applying in a particular case, it enters into an explanation of the fact that someone comes to believe that it applies in that case. This may seem an *ad hoc* move, but unless one introduces it, all objective concepts will count as explanatory and thus, on my present suggestion, natural, with the consequence that the natural/non-natural distinction collapses back into the realism/anti-realism distinction.

The third problem arises from virtues, such as humility, and motives, such as the sense of duty. It is manifest that these are explanatory concepts, but it would be silly for an ethical non-naturalist to deny that they are moral (despite Moore's scepticism about their moral significance (1903: 171ff)). In order, therefore, to prevent the immediate refutation of ethical non-naturalism by such cases, the non-naturalist has to hold that the explanatory role of virtues and moral motives is independent of their moral content, and can be subsumed under more general connections between dispositions and motives of any kind, on one side, and human actions, on the other. He can then allow that virtues and moral motives are explanatory, but only derivatively so, by virtue of the fact that they are dispositions and motives with a moral content. In this way, the non-naturalist will say, the moral concepts that define virtues and moral motives are not themselves explanatory.

It may be felt that with all these qualifications the natural/non-natural distinction is here being whittled away to nothing. But it seems to me that ethical non-naturalism is informed by an idea which is, at least from a distance, reasonably clear: it is that of moral properties attaching only at the periphery to other properties. They are dependent, but nothing non-moral depends on them (remember the general analogy with epiphenomenalism in the philosophy of mind). Where this picture is too simple is that it takes no account of our judgments concerning these moral properties, and of our actions which are influenced by these judgments. It is because of these latter elements that an ethical non-naturalist cannot maintain that moral concepts are never explanatory, without committing himself to ethical anti-realism; for if moral properties are objective, then moral knowledge, and therewith moral action, is to be explained by reference to situations in which these properties are present. This may now seem an adequate argument for supposing that ethical non-naturalism is, indeed, inconsistent with ethical realism. But my feeling is that the issue should be taken further by the restrictions I have suggested on what is natural, which block this short route from ethical non-naturalism to anti-realism. As I mentioned before, Moore's ethical non-naturalism is usually regarded as a realist theory; hence it would be unsatisfactory to give an account of the natural which immediately produced the result that ethical non-naturalism was an anti-realist theory.

This account of the natural deals with the first issue raised by ethical non-naturalism – that of the 'base' upon which, it is held, moral properties depend, without themselves belonging to this base. I have tried to provide an account which ensures that the natural/non-natural distinction is neither identical with, nor does it immediately collapse into, the realist/anti-realist distinction. In doing this my aim has not only been to protect the realist aspirations of Moore's ethical non-naturalism, but also to articulate what I take to be the controlling thought of ethical naturalism: that values are natural in the sense that they affect our lives by their substantive connections with aspects of human psychology, social relations, political institutions or whatever. I have not attempted to fill out my account of ethical non-naturalism with a realist epistemology, and this remains a serious gap. It might be hoped that this gap could be plugged through an account of the relation of dependence without reducibility which, the ethical non-naturalist believes, holds between the moral and the natural; for if this relation could be interpreted to yield an account of moral reasoning, the epistemological issue would be resolved. Unfortunately, however, it seems to me that it is here that the realist aspirations of a Moorean non-naturalism cannot be satisfactorily sustained. For the realist position turns out to demand that we can have a grasp of synthetic entailments of the moral by the natural, and this, though not a self-contradictory requirement, engenders an unacceptable sense of mystery.

III

In his paper 'The Conception of Intrinsic Value' (1922) Moore suggests an account of the relation of dependence without reducibility which he takes to hold between the moral and the natural in terms of 'supervenience' (though Moore never used this term): no two situations can have all their natural properties in common, but differ in their moral properties. Familiar as this concept now is, its implications are unclear. Consider again anomalous monism: Davidson explicitly accepts the supervenience of the mental upon the physical (1980: 214), and one might suppose that this supervenience is adequately catered for by his thesis of the token identity of mental and physical states (I do not accuse Davidson of thinking this). For if mental states just are physical states, then it seems to follow that if two people differ in their mental state, they must also differ in their physical state. But, in fact, this does not follow: suppose John's present desire for sleep is his physical state of type P_1 and Mary's present desire for a cake is her physical state of type P_1: then Mary and John could be in the same physical condition, but differ in their mental state. Thus the supervenience of the mental upon the physical requires that mental properties be linked in some way with physical properties, and it will help if I state the supervenience claim precisely: suppose the property V is supervenient upon properties of type N (represented as $N_1 .. N_i ..$), then the claim is that though V itself is not of type N the following holds:

(S) $\Box (\forall y)(Va \ \& \ ((N_1a \equiv N_1y) \ \& \ .. \ \& \ (N_ia \equiv N_iy) \ \& ..) \supset V_y)$

from which it follows that, if $N_j'a$ is N_ja, if N_ja, and is $\sim N_ja$ if $\sim N_ja$,

(S') $\Box (Va \ \& \ (N_1'a \ \& .. \& \ N_i'a \ \& ..) \supset$
$(\forall y)(N_1'y \ \& .. \& \ N_i'y \ \& ..) \supset Vy))$

Thus where properties of type N are physical and V is a mental property, supervenience does require some physico–psychical correlation – that specified in the consequent of (S').

Manifestly, the correlation thus required is highly unspecific and does not look like the sort of law Davidson rejects. In particular, nothing so far seems to require that the correlation itself be necessary. One thing which would require this would be the necessity of 'Va' and each 'Na'; interestingly, Moore's use of supervenience in connection with intrinsic value and intrinsic natural properties does therefore require that the connection between the intrinsically natural and the intrinsically valuable be necessary, as Moore claimed that it was. But since I have not taken over Moore's commitment to essential properties, this line of argument is not available; nor would it make any impact on Davidson's position. Nonetheless, it has been argued that super-venience, in both the philosophy of mind and ethics, does require that there be a necessary connection between the supervened and the supervenient. In the philosophy of mind this claim has been forcefully pressed by Kim (1978), but I shall not pursue his argument. Instead I shall concentrate on Blackburn's argument (1971: 110–15),[1] to the effect that supervenience in the moral case requires either necessary connections between the natural and the moral, or ethical anti-realism. So far as I can see, Blackburn's argument should generalise to the philosophy of mind, presenting Davidson with a choice between physico–psychical laws or anti-realism with respect to the mental, neither of which seems likely to commend itself to him.

The heart of Blackburn's argument is that the supervenience claim is a comparative claim (no moral difference without a natural difference) whose truth, at least for a realist, requires the truth of some non-comparative claims. Thus consider the thought that B must be virtuous because he has the same natural properties as A, and A is virtuous: if we now ask what makes B virtuous, the answer must surely be his (B's) natural properties, and not any of A's natural properties. Yet if this is the case, then there must be a necessary connection between B's natural properties and his virtue. To suppose otherwise requires one to suppose that the way in which a moral property depends on natural properties in one case depends on the way in which the former is contingently associated with the latter in another case. If there is no necessary connection between B's natural properties and his virtue, then B could be as he is in all natural respects but not be virtuous. Yet if this is possible, why is it not possible once one takes account of the features of someone else, A, in whom virtue happens to be conjoined with the natural features that A possesses? Though this supposition is not inconsistent, it is sufficiently implausible to make the case.

This seems to me a forceful argument. I want first to comment briefly on its application to anomalous monism. If the argument is right, Davidson cannot retain supervenience and realism about the mental, and yet reject all necessary relations between the physical and the mental: supervenience turns out to require that a person's total physical condition at a time determine his mental state at that time. Clearly, this does not entail reducibility of the mental or psycho–physical determination; nor does it add in any obvious way to the constraint that supervenience already placed upon the

---

[1] It is worth noting in the present context that Blackburn ascribes the argument to Lewy (1971: 105 n1).

interpretation of the mental. For the physico–psychical connection that supervenience requires is completely unspecific; it is quite consistent with there being no specific laws of this kind, no laws by which one might infer a specific mental property from a specific physical one. And it seems to be this which Davidson most wants to reject; he writes (1980: 253–4) that given supervenience, 'if a certain psychological concept applies to one event and not to another, there must be a difference describable in physical terms. But it does not follow that there is a single physically describable difference that distinguishes any two events that differ in a given psychological respect'.

Turning now to ethics, Blackburn's argument leads to the conclusion that, for a realist, supervenience of the moral requires a necessary connection between the natural and the moral. The question that now arises is how it is that an anti-realist can avoid this conclusion, as Blackburn maintains. The argument centres on the thought that the possession of a supervenient property is not fundamentally dependent upon the possession of that property, and other properties, by something else: does an anti-realist deny this with respect to moral properties? That is, does he hold that in some cases his moral attitude to one thing is dependent upon his having the same attitude to another thing which he believes to have the same natural properties? Blackburn seems to suggest not; he writes (1971: 114–15): 'Now moral attitudes are to be held towards things because of their naturalistic properties. Therefore it is not possible to hold a moral attitude to one thing, believe a second to be exactly alike, yet at the same time not hold the attitude to the other.' Blackburn seems to be here inferring supervenience, now expressed as a constraint on relevant attitudes and beliefs (though a constraint which would be better expressed in terms of a commitment to an attitude rather than in terms of the necessity of having it) from an anti-realist rendering of the necessary connection claim – that 'moral attitudes are to be held towards things because of [sc. beliefs about] their naturalistic properties'. This latter claim seems precisely the realist necessary connection claim rephrased as one about a relation between beliefs and attitudes; and it must be this claim if supervenience can be inferred from it in the way Blackburn says that it can.

Anti-realism of this kind, which merely replaces the realist's necessary connections between natural and moral properties by a relation of commitment which holds between beliefs about natural properties and moral attitudes, is an uninteresting doctrine. For it inherits in this relation of commitment all the realist's problems concerning necessary connections between the natural and the moral. But anti-realism does not have to be thus. In particular, the anti-realist can escape the argument from supervenience to necessary connections precisely by maintaining what the realist cannot plausibly maintain, that in some cases the possession of a supervenient property is dependent upon the possession of that property by something else; or rather, to put the point in terms of beliefs and attitudes, the anti-realist can hold that our commitment to a moral attitude to one thing arises only *via* our having the same attitude to something else which we believe to be the same in all natural respects. The philosopher who saw all this years ago was Professor Hare, with his account of supervenience as universalisability (1952: 153; 1963: 16–19); for it is precisely a feature of Hare's view that universalisability is not a derivative feature of our moral attitudes, but is constitutive of them. We admire Jones, and believing Smith to be in respect of all natural properties similar to Jones, we are committed to admiring Smith: our commitment to admiration of Smith is, in this case, dependent upon our admiration of Jones, and the Harean anti-realist believes that there is no way in which such a commitment arises without reference to our attitudes to others. In holding this, the anti-realist is rejecting any analogue of the realist's necessary connections between the natural and the moral. Thus, if supervenience is understood as arising from the universalisability of moral attitudes, the anti-realist can have supervenience without necessary connections. And the difference between anti-realism and realism in this respect is that there is no plausible way in which universalisability can be read back into moral properties in such a way as to ensure that once a contingent association between natural and moral properties has occurred in one instance, then that association must apply to all instances of the natural properties in question.

    This conclusion cannot but favour the thought that ethical non-naturalism combines more easily with ethical anti-realism than with moral realism. For the prospect of explaining how, in the absence of reduction there are necessary connections between the natural and moral looks pretty forbidding. I want, finally, to explore how this task might be undertaken, but my exploration will reveal that the best way of making these necessary connections acceptable points directly back towards ethical naturalism. I begin by reverting, for the last time, to the analogy with anomalous monism. In the case of anomalous monism I stressed that the necessary connections required by the supervenience of the mental were totally unspecific. In theory the same point applies to ethical non-naturalism: supervenience does not require, for a realist, that any specific natural properties be singled out for presentation in a graspable moral principle. Yet there is an important difference between the two cases: in the case of anomalous monism, the ascription to someone of mental properties is to be based upon a holistic interpretation of his behaviour constrained by the requirements of the supervenience of the mental. Nothing plays a role comparable to that of behaviour in the case of ethical non-naturalism: it is our beliefs about natural facts themselves which are to provide reasons for our moral attitudes, and in this case the dependence of the moral on the natural must admit of an epistemological interpretation. Hence it is inadequate for an ethical non-naturalist who is a realist just to treat moral properties as unspecifically determined by the totality of natural facts in each case, since this totality is inaccessible to any human intelligence. Realist ethical non-naturalism must make some space for specific moral principles by reference to which we can begin to get a grasp of the moral significance of things; and if these principles are to help with the problem of explaining how the unspecific necessary connections arise and are grasped by us, they must themselves state specific necessary connections between natural and moral properties. To admit such principles, however, does not require the adoption of an absolutist position in ethics, to the effect that certain courses of action are absolutely right or wrong. The difficulty about absolutist principles is that if there is more than one of them, then, because of the complexity of our lives, we are liable to face moral dilemmas in which we satisfy the antecedents of two such principles which have incompatible consequents. For this reason, ethical non-naturalists such as Ross and Moore who invoked specific necessary principles of this kind maintained that the moral properties thus entailed were only *prima facie* properties, in the sense that their prescriptive implications could be justly overridden.

From the perspective of my present discussion, two difficulties in this familiar version of ethical non-naturalism stand out. One problem arises from the non-absolutist character of the principles proposed; for if no such principles govern one's absolute duty, and this is the intuitionism of familiar ethical non-naturalism, but issues of absolute duty do satisfy the supervenience principle, the problem of the unspecific necessary connection between natural and moral properties has not been banished. In Ross' work, this problem is openly acknowledged – he writes of the concept of absolute duty as 'toti-resultant' (1930: 28) and requiring, for confidence in its application, omniscience (1930: 32). But this just invites moral scepticism. One way round this problem would be to reject intuitionism, and have just one principle of absolute duty; thus Sidgwick's utilitarianism. But this, though formally adequate, seems morally inadequate. Whatever is said about this, I want also to argue that the conception of specific necessary connections between the natural and the moral makes much more sense in the context of ethical naturalism than in that of ethical non-naturalism. This, then, is the second difficulty with the familiar version of realist ethical non-naturalism. The problem is that of explaining how it is possible that there should be necessary connections of this kind, in the absence of analytic reducibility; talk here of 'synthetic entailments' (Moore 1942: 607–8) names a problem, not its solution. I think that the only way to move towards a solution to this problem is to invoke what I have so far avoided: Moore's essentialism with respect to intrinsic value. For if these necessary connections can be presented as arising out of essentialist truths, then perhaps the air of mystery they engender will disappear. Now essentialist claims are notoriously problematic, but in this case it seems to me that an ethical non-naturalist is especially badly placed to render acceptable any essentialist claims of this kind. For an ethical naturalist moral properties are also explanatory, and therefore enter directly into the mesh of concepts by which human life is explained; and since essentialist claims are, at least according to one plausible line of thought, an integral element of explanatory theories (Wiggins 1980: chapter 4), there is some prospect of an ethical naturalist making reasonable sense of moral essentialism. But none of this is available to the ethical non-naturalist, and, if this is right, it indicates that there is a deep tension in Moore's ethical theory between his moral essentialism and his ethical non-naturalism.

44   THOMAS BALDWIN

This result strengthens my previous claim that ethical non-naturalism favours ethical anti-realism; it must now appear that ethical non-naturalism demands anti-realism, for only thus can it be rid of these inexplicable necessary connections with their undesirable epistemological implications. Conversely, ethical naturalism surely favours realism. For if moral properties enter into general explanatory theories, then the price of anti-realism with respect to moral properties will be anti-realism with respect to the explanatory theories into which they enter. And this is a high price to pay. Thus although I attempted in the second section of this paper to steer the natural/non-natural distinction away from the realist/anti-realist distinction, I am bound to admit that in the end the two distinctions coincide. In particular, the price to be paid for maintaining a realist ethical non-naturalism is not worth paying; so in this sense my attempt to breathe life into a refurbished Moorean ethical non-naturalism has failed.

REFERENCES

Blackburn, S. W. 1971. 'Moral Realism' in *Morality and Moral Reasoning*, ed. J. Casey, London: Methuen.
Bradley, F. H. 1927. *Ethical Studies*, Oxford: Clarendon Press.
Broad, C. D. 1942. 'Certain Features in Moore's Ethical Doctrines' in *The Philosophy of G. E. Moore*, ed. P. A. Schilpp, La Salle: Open Court.
Cox, H. 1970. 'Warnock on Moore', *Mind* 79: 265–9.
Davidson, D. 1980. *Essays on Actions and Events*, Oxford: Clarendon Press.
Fuller, L. 1963. *The Morality of Law*, New Haven: Yale University Press.
Green, T. H. 1883. *Prolegomena to Ethics*, Oxford: Clarendon Press.
Hare, R. M. 1952. *The Language of Morals*, Oxford: Clarendon Press.
    1963. *Freedom and Reason*, Oxford: Clarendon Press.
Hart, H. L. A. 1961. *The Concept of Law*, Oxford: Clarendon Press.
Kim, J. 1978. 'Supervenience and Nomological Incommensurables', *American Philosophical Quarterly*, 15: 149–56.
Lewy, C. 1968. 'G. E. Moore on the Naturalistic Fallacy' in *Studies in the Philosophy of Thought and Action*, ed. P. Strawson, London: Oxford University Press.
Mackie, J. L. 1977. *Ethics*, Harmondsworth: Penguin.
Moore, G. E. 1899. 'The Nature of Judgment'; *Mind* 8: 176–93.
    1901. 'Identity' *Proc. Aristotelian Society* 1: 103–27.
    1902. Articles in *Dictionary of Philosophy and Psychology*, ed. J. M. Baldwin, London and New York: Macmillan.
    1903. *Principia Ethica*, Cambridge: Cambridge University Press.

1912. *Ethics*, London: Williams and Norgate.
1922. 'The Conception of Intrinsic Value' in his *Philosophical Studies*, London: Routledge and Kegan Paul.
1942. 'Reply to my Critics' in *The Philosophy of G. E. Moore*, ed. P. A. Schilpp, La Salle: Open Court.
Ross, Sir W. D. 1930. *The Right and the Good*, Oxford: Clarendon Press.
Sidgwick, H. 1901. *The Methods of Ethics*, 6th edn, London: Macmillan.
Warnock, G. 1967. *Contemporary Moral Philosophy*, London: Macmillan.
Wiggins, D. 1980. *Sameness and Substance*, Oxford: Blackwell.

3   *Supervenience revisited*

SIMON BLACKBURN

I

A decade ago, in an article entitled 'Moral Realism' I presented an argument intended to show that two properties, which I called supervenience and lack of entailment, provided together an unpleasant mystery for moral realism (Blackburn, 1971). This argument was originally suggested to me in a discussion with Casimir Lewy, which in turn was directed at the paper of G. E. Moore, entitled 'The Conception of Intrinsic Value' (1922). The intervening decade has provided a number of reasons for revisiting my argument. First of all, it was couched in an idiom which subsequent work on modal logic – particularly the distinctions of various kinds of necessity and the general use of possible worlds as models – has made a little quaint. It would be desirable to see if the new notions allow the argument to stand. Secondly, we have seen a great deal of interest in supervenience, as a notion of importance beyond moral philosophy. Thus in conversation and correspondence I have heard it suggested that my argument must be flawed, because exactly the same combination of properties that I found mysterious occurs all over the place: for example, in the philosophy of mind, in the relationship between natural kind terms and others, in the relation between colours and primary properties, and so on. Since anti-realism in these other areas is not attractive, this casts doubt upon my diagnosis of the moral case. Finally, moral realism is again an attractive option to some philosophers, so that although when I wrote I might have seemed to be shadow boxing, the argument is just now becoming relevant again. In any case, enough puzzles seem to me to surround a proper analysis of supervenience to warrant a fresh look at it.

Suppose we have an area of judgments, such as those involving moral commitments, or attributions of mental states. I shall call these *F* judgments, and I shall also talk of *F* truths and *F* facts: this is not intended to imply any view at all about whether the commitments we express in the vocabulary are beyond question genuine judgments, nor that there is a real domain of truths or facts in the area. Indeed part of the purpose of my argument was to find a way of querying just these ideas. At this stage, all this terminology is entirely neutral. Now suppose that we hold that the truths expressible in this way supervene upon the truths expressed in an underlying *G* vocabulary. For example, moral judgments supervene upon natural judgments, or mental descriptions of people upon physical ones (either of the people themselves or of some larger reality which includes them). This supervenience claim means that in *some* sense of 'necessary' it is necessarily true that if an *F* truth changes, then some *G* truth changes, or necessarily, if two situations are identical in point of *G* facts, then they are identical in terms of *F* facts as well. To analyse this more closely, I shall make free use of the possible worlds idiom. But it must be emphasised that this is merely a heuristic device, and implies no theory about the status of the possible worlds. Let us symbolise the kind of necessity in question by 'N' and possibility by 'P': for the present it does not matter whether these are thought of as logical, metaphysical, physical or other kinds of modalities. We are now to suppose that some truth about a thing or event or state, that it is *F*, supervenes upon some definite total set of *G* truths, which we can sum up by saying that it is *G**. Of course, *G** can contain all kinds of relational truths about the subject, truths about other things, and so on. In fact, one of the difficulties of thinking about all this properly is that it rapidly becomes unclear just what can be allowed in our conception of a totality of *G* states. But intuitively it is whatever it is by way of natural or physical states that bring it about that the subject is *F*. I shall express this by talking of the set of *G* states which 'underlies' an *F* state. Belief in supervenience is then at least the belief that whenever a thing is in some *F* state, this is because it is in some underlying *G* state, or is in virtue of its being in some underlying *G* state. This is the minimal sense of the doctrine. But I am interested in something stronger, which ties the particular truth that a thing is *F* to the fact that it is in some particular *G* state. We can present the general form of this doctrine as characterising, the relation 'U' that holds when one 'underlies' the other:

(S) $N((\exists x)(Fx \ \& \ G^{\star}x \ \& \ (G^{\star}xUFx)) \supset (y)(G^{\star}y \supset Fy))$

The formula says that as a matter of necessity, if something x is F, and $G^{\star}$ underlies this, then anything else in the physical or natural or whatever state $G^{\star}$ is F as well. There is no claim that $G^{\star}$ provides the only way in which things can become F: intuitively something might be, say, evil in a number of different ways, and something in one given physical state might possess some mental property which it could equally have possessed by being in any of a family of related physical states. The supervenience claim (S) is thus in no opposition to doctrines which now go under the heading of 'variable realisation'. To get the claim which these doctrines deny, we would need to convert the final conditional: ... $(y)(Fy \supset G^{\star}y))$. But the resulting doctrine is not one in which we shall be interested.

I now want to contrast (S) with a much stronger necessity:

(N) $N(x)(G^{\star}x \supset Fx)$

Of course, (N) does not follow from (S). Formally they are merely related like this: (S) necessitates an overall conditional, and (N) necessitates the consequence of that conditional. So it would appear there is no more reason to infer (N) from (S) than there would be to infer Nq from $N(p \supset q)$. Hence also there is no inconsistency in a position which affirms (S), but also affirms:

(P) $P(\exists x)(G^{\star}x \ \& \ {\sim}Fx)$

At least, this is the immediate appearance. In my original paper it was the nature of theories which hold both (S) and (P) (which I shall call the (S)/(P) combination) which occupied me. Such a theory would think it possible (in some sense commensurate with that of the original claim) that any given G state which happens to underlie a certain F state, nevertheless might not have done so. In other words, even if some G set-up in our world is the very state upon which some F state supervenes, nevertheless, it might not have been *that* F state which supervened upon it. There was the possibility (again, in whatever modal dimension we are working) that the actually arising or supervening F state might not have been the one which supervened upon that particular G set-up. My instinct was that this combination provided a mystery for a realist about judgments made with the F vocabulary, and that the mystery would best be solved by embracing an anti-realist (or as I now prefer to call it, a projectivist) theory about the F judgments.

To pursue this further, we might question whether there could be any motivation for holding the (S)/(P) combination. Consider the following possible doctrine about 'underlying', and about the notion of the complete specification of an underlying state, $G\star$:

$$\text{(?)} \qquad N((\exists x)(Fx \mathbin{\&} G\star x \mathbin{\&} (G\star x\, U\, Fx)) \supset N(\gamma)(G\star\gamma \supset F\gamma))$$

The rationale for (?) would be this. Suppose there were a thing which was $G\star$ and F, so that we were inclined to say that its being in the G state underlies its F–ness. But suppose there were also a thing which is $G\star$ and $\sim F$. Then would we not want to deny that it was x's being $G\star$ which underlies its being F? Wouldn't it be its being $G\star$ *and* its being different from this other thing in some further respect – one which explains why the other thing fails to be F? We can call that a *releasing* property, R, and then F will supervene only on $G\star$ and $\sim R$. More accurately, $G\star$ would denote a set of properties which do not really deserve the star. We would be wrong to locate in them a *complete* underlying basis for F.

This raises quite complicated questions about the form of these various doctrines. Let me put aside one problem right at the beginning. Since (S) is a conditional and contains an existential clause as part of the antecedent, it will be vacuously true if nothing is $G\star$ and F; the necessitation will likewise be vacuously true if nothing could be $G\star$ and F. So if (S) captured all that was meant by supervenience, we could say, for instance, that being virtuous supervened upon being homogeneously made of granite. Necessarily, if one thing homogeneously made of granite were virtuous, and this underlay the virtuousness, then anything so made would be. But this is just because it is impossible that anything of this constitution should be virtuous. I am going to sidestep this problem simply by confining the scope of F and G henceforwards, to cases where it is possible that something with a set of G properties, denoted by $G\star$, should be F. In fact, we are soon to deal with different strengths of necessity and possibility, and I shall suppose that this thesis is always strong enough to stop the conditional being satisfied in this vacuous way. The next problem of logical form is quite how we construe the denotation of a set of properties made by the term 'G*'. Firstly, we do not want the supervenience thesis to be made vacuously true through it being impossible that any two distinct things should be G^* – it then following that if one G^* thing is F, they all are. And the threat here is quite real. If, for instance, G^* were held to include all the physical properties and relations of a thing – if it were that and nothing less which some property F supervened upon – then assuming the identity of indiscernibles, we would have (S) satisfied vacuously again. To get around this I am going to assume a *limitation* thesis. This will say that whenever a property F supervenes upon some basis, there is necessarily a boundary to the kind of G properties which it can depend upon. For example, the mental may supervene upon the physical, in which case the thesis asserts that necessarily there are physical properties of a thing which are not relevant to its mental ones. A plausible example might be its relations to things with which it is in no kind of causal connection (such as future things). Again, the moral supervenes upon the natural, and the thesis will tell us that there are some natural properties which necessarily have no relevance to moral ones – pure spatial position, perhaps, or date of beginning in time. Given the limitation thesis, (S) will not be trivialised by the identity of indiscernibles. The last problem of form which arises is whether 'G^*' is thought of as a name for some particular set of properties (which form a complete basis for F), or whether it is built into the sense of 'G^*' that any set of properties it denotes is complete. The difference is easily seen if we consider a very strong kind of necessity – say, conceptual (logical or analytic) necessity. It is unlikely to be thought analytic that being made of H_2O underlies being water. One reason is that it is not analytic that being made of H_2O exhausts the kind of physical basis which may affect the kind to which a substance belongs. That is a substantive scientific truth, not one guaranteed in any more *a priori* way. I am going to build it into the sense of 'G^*' that at least in one possible world, the set of properties it denotes is sufficient to underlie F. I do not want it to follow that this is true in all worlds, although that is a very delicate matter. Fortunately, so far as I can see, it does not occupy the centre of the stage I am about to set.

If we accept (?) as a condition on what it is for a set of properties to underlie another, and hence on what it is for a property to supervene upon such a set, the relationship between supervenience and (E) changes. Suppose that there is something whose $G^{\star}$-ness underlies its F-ness:

(E) $(\exists x)(Fx \ \& \ G^{\star}x \ \& \ (G^{\star}x \ U \ Fx))$

then we can now derive (N). In other words, (?) and (E) together entail (N). And as I have already said, (?) is an attractive doctrine. But it does mean that supervenience becomes in effect nothing but a roundabout way of committing ourselves to (N); the *prima facie* simpler doctrine that some set of underlying truths necessitates the F truth. This is in fact the way that supervenience is taken by Kim (1978): it enables Kim to suppose that where we have supervenience, we also have reductionism. Another way of getting at the attractions of (?) would be to cease from mentioning the requirement that there is something which is $G^{\star}$ and F altogether. After all, surely some moral property might supervene upon a particular configuration of natural properties, regardless of whether there actually is anything with that set. Or, some mental property might supervene upon a particular physical make-up which nobody actually has. If we took this course, we would replace (S) by a doctrine:

$$(G^{\star}x \ U \ Fx) \supset (y)(G^{\star}y \supset Fy)$$

and then the doctrine which would give us (N) immediately would be:

$$(G^{\star}x \ U \ Fx) \supset N(G^{\star}x \ U \ Fx)$$

Yet supervenience claims are popular at least partly because they offer some of the metaphysical relief of reductions, without incurring the costs; I want therefore to preserve any gap that there may be for as long as possible. This is particularly important in the moral case, where supervenience is one thing, but reductionism is markedly less attractive. So I am going to stick with the orginal formulation, subject to the caveats already entered, and while we should remain well aware of (?), I do not want to presuppose a verdict on it.

If we put (?) into abeyance we should be left with a possible form of doctrine which accepts both (S) and (P): the (S)/(P) combination. It is this which I originally claim to make a mystery for realism. If there is to be a mystery, it is not a formal one, and I actually think that with suitable interpretations, there are relations between F and G vocabularies which are properly characterised by (S) and (P). It is just that when this combination is to be affirmed, I believe it needs explanation. In the moral case I think that it is best explained by a projective theory of the F predicates. But in other cases, with different interpretations of the modalities, other explanations are also possible. I shall argue this later.

Here, then, is a way of modelling (S) and (P) together. In any possible world, once there is a thing which is F, and whose F-ness is underlain by $G^\star$, then anything else which is $G^\star$ is F as well. However, there are possible worlds in which things are $G^\star$ but not F. Call the former worlds $G^\star/F$ worlds, and the latter, $G^\star/O$ worlds. The one thing we do not have is any *mixed* world, where some things are $G^\star$ and F, and some are $G^\star$ but not F. We can call mixed worlds $G^\star/FvO$ worlds. These are ruled out by the supervenience claim (S): they are precisely the kind of possible world which would falsify that claim. My form of problem, or mystery, now begins to appear. Why should the possible worlds partition into only the two kinds, and not into the three kinds? It seems on the face of it to offend against a principle of plenitude with respect to possibilities, namely that we should allow any which we are not constrained to disallow. Imagine it spatially. Here is a possible world w_1 which is $G^\star/F$. Here is another, w_2 which we can make as much like w_1 as possible, except that it is $G^\star/O$. But there is no possible world anywhere which is just like one of these, except including just one element with its $G^\star$ and F properties conforming to the pattern found in the other. Why not? Or, to make the matter yet more graphic, imagine a time element. Suppose our possible worlds are thought of as having temporal duration. A mixed world would be brought about if w_1 starts off as a $G^\star/F$ world at some given time, but then at a later time becomes a $G^\star/O$ world. For then, overall, it would be mixed and the supervenience claim would be falsified by its existence. This kind of world then cannot happen, although there can be worlds which are like it in respect of the first part of its history, and equally worlds which are like it in respect of the second part of its history.

This is the ban on mixed worlds: it is a ban on inter-world travel by things which are, individually, at home. The problem which I posed is that of finding out the authority behind this ban. Why the embargo on travel? The difficulty is that once we have imagined a $G\star/F$ world, and a $G\star/O$ world, it is as if we have done enough to imagine a $G\star/FvO$ world, and have implicitly denied ourselves a right to forbid its existence. At least, if we are to forbid its existence, we need some explanation of why we can do so. The positive part of my contention was that in the moral case, projectivists can do this better than realists. In the next section I rehearse briefly why this still seems to me to be so, if we make some important distinctions, and then I turn to consider related examples. And in time we have to return to the difficult claim (?), to assess its role in this part of metaphysics.

II

Necessities can range from something very strict, approximating to 'analytically true' through metaphysical and physical necessity, to something approximating to 'usually true'. Then anyone who sympathises a little with the puzzle in a (S)/(P) combination can quickly see that it will remain not only if there is one fixed sense of necessity and possibility involved, but also in a wider class of cases. For whenever the supervenience claim (S) involves a strong sense of necessity, then it will automatically entail any version with a weaker sense of necessity. Hence, we will get the same structure at the lower level, when the possibility is affirmed in that corresponding, weaker, sense. Thus if (S) took the form of claiming that it is metaphysically necessary that ..., and (P) took the form of claiming that it is physically possible that ..., and if we also suppose (as we surely should) that metaphysical necessity entails physical necessity, then we would have the (S)/(P) combination at the level of physical necessity. On the other hand we will not get the structure if the relation is reversed. If the possibility claim (P) is made, say, in the sense of 'possible as far as conceptual constraints go', this does not entail, say, 'metaphysically possible'. And then if (S) just reads 'metaphysically necessary' there is no mystery: we would just have it that it is metaphysically necessary that F supervenes upon $G\star$, but not an analytic or conceptual truth; equally, it would not be an analytic or conceptual truth that any given $G\star$ produces F, and there is no puzzle there. For the puzzle to begin to arise, we need to bring the modalities into line.

I mention this because it affects the moral case quite closely. Suppose we allow ourselves a notion of 'analytically necessary' applying to propositions which, in the traditional phrase, can be seen to be true by conceptual means alone. Denying one of these would be exhibiting a conceptual confusion: a failure to grasp the nature of the relevant vocabulary, or to follow out immediate implications of that grasp. In a slightly more modern idiom, denying one of these would be 'constitutive' of lack of competence with the vocabulary. We may contrast this with metaphysical necessity: a proposition will be this if it is true in all the possible worlds which, as a matter of metaphysics, could exist. Of course, we may be sceptical about this division, but I want to respect it at least for the sake of argument. For the (S)/(P) combination in moral philosophy provides a nice example of a *prima facie* case of the difference, and one which profoundly affects my original argument. This arises because someone who holds that a particular natural state of affairs, $G^\star$, underlies a moral judgment, is very likely to hold that this is true as a matter of metaphysical necessity. For example, if I hold that the fact that someone enjoys the misery of others underlies the judgment that he is evil, I should also hold that in any possible world, the fact that someone is like this is enough to make him evil. Using 'MN' for metaphysical necessity, I would have both:

$$(S_m) \; MN((\exists x)(Fx \, \& \, G^\star x \, \& \, (G^\star x \, U \, Fx)) \supset (y)(G^\star y \supset Fy))$$

and

$$(N_m) \; MN(x)(G^\star x \supset Fx)$$

and I would evade the original argument by disallowing the metaphysical possibility of a world in which people like that were not evil. This, it might be said, is part of what is involved in having a genuine standard, a belief that some natural state of affairs is sufficient to warrant the moral judgment. For, otherwise, if in some metaphysically possible worlds people like that were evil and in others not, surely this would be a sign that we hadn't yet located the natural basis for the judgment properly. For instance, if I did allow a possible world in which some people like that were not evil, it might be because (for instance) they believe that misery is so good for the soul that it is a cause of congratulation and rejoicing to find someone miserable. But then this fact becomes what I earlier called a releasing fact and the real underlying state of affairs is now not just that someone enjoys the misery of others, but that he does so not believing that misery is good for the soul.

Because of this the original puzzle does not arise at the level of metaphysical necessity. But now suppose we try analytic necessity. It seems to be a conceptual matter that moral claims supervene upon natural ones. Anyone failing to realise this, or to obey the constraint would indeed lack something constitutive of competence in the moral practice. And there is good reason for this: it would betray the whole purpose for which we moralise, which is to choose, commend, rank, approve, forbid, things on the basis of their natural properties. So we might have:

$$(S_a)\ AN((\exists x)(Fx\ \&\ G^\star x\ \&\ (G^\star x\ U\ Fx)) \supset (y)(G^\star y \supset Fy))$$

But we would be most unwise to have

$$(N_a)\ AN(x)(G^\star x \supset Fx)$$

For it is not plausible to maintain that the adoption of some particular standard is 'constitutive of competence' as a moralist. People can moralise in obedience to the conceptual constraints that govern all moralising, although they adopt different standards, and come to different verdicts in the light of a complete set of natural facts. Of course, this can be denied but for the sake of this paper, I shall rely on the common view that it is mistaken. So since we deny (N_a) we have:

$$(P_a)\ AP(\exists x)(G^\star x\ \&\ Fx)$$

We then arrive at a $(S_a)/(P_a)$ combination, and my mystery emerges: why the ban on mixed worlds at this level? These would be worlds possible as far as conceptual constraints go, or 'analytically possible' worlds. They conform to conceptual constraints, although there might be metaphysical or physical bars against their actual existence.

Of course, in a sense I have already proposed an answer to this question. By saying enough of what moralising is to make (S_a) plausible, and enough to make (P_a) plausible, I hope to enable us to learn to relax with their combination. It is just that this relaxation befits the anti-realist better. Because the explanation of the combination depended crucially upon the role of moralising being to guide desires and choices amongst the natural features of the world. If, as a realist ought to say, its role is to describe further, moral aspects of morality, there is no explanation at all of why it is constitutive of competence as a moralist to obey the constraint (S_a).

Can this argument be avoided by maintaining (?)? No, because there is no prospect of accepting (?) in a relevantly strong sense. For (?) to help, we would need it to be read so that, necessarily (in some sense) if something is F and $G\star$, and the $G\star$-ness underlies its being F, then it is analytically necessary that anything $G\star$ is F. And this we will not have in the moral case, for we want to say that there are things with natural properties underlying moral ones, but we also deny analyticities of the form (N_a). (?) would not help if the necessity of the consequent were interpreted in any weaker sense. For example, we might want to accept (?) in the form:

$$(?_{MN})\ MN((\exists x)(Fx\ \&\ G\star x\ \&\ (G\star x\ U\ Fx)) \supset$$
$$MN(y)(G\star y \supset Fy))$$

and then there will be metaphysical necessities of the form of the consequent, that is, of the form (N_m), but they will not help to resolve the original mystery, since that is now proceeding at the level of analytical necessity. It is the possibility, so far as conceptual constraints go, of mixed worlds, which is to be avoided.

III

The argument above works because we are careful to distinguish the status of the supervenience claim, and in this case its extremely strong status, from that of the related possibility claim. I have done that by indexing the modal operators involved: we have four different forms of modal claim: (S), (N), (P) and (?), and each of them can involve analytic or conceptual necessity, $(_a)$ metaphysical necessity $(_m)$, and we come now to physical necessity $(_p)$. For now I want to turn to consider non-moral cases of the same kind of shape. These examples are all going to start life as examples of the joint (S)/(P) combination. They may not finish life like that: it may become obvious, if it is not so already, in the light either of the plausibility of (?) or of the difficulty over banning mixed worlds, that either supervenience is to be abandoned, or (N) accepted. But here are some test cases:

1st example   Suppose that in w_1 a physical set-up $G^\star$ underlies some particular mental state F. Suppose $G^\star$ is possession of some pattern of neurones or molecules in the head, and F is having a headache. Nowhere in w_1 is there anything unlike x, in being $G^\star$ but not F. Next door, in w_2 however, there are things which are $G^\star$ but not F. Now we are told that w_1 is acceptable, and that w_2 is acceptable. But nowhere is there a world w_3 which is like w_1 but which changes to become like w_2, or which contains some particular individuals who are like those of w_2.

2nd example   Suppose that in w_1 a particular molecular constitution $G^\star$ underlies membership of a natural kind, F. $G^\star$ consists of a complete physical or chemical breakdown of the constitution of a substance (e.g. being composed of molecules of H_2O) and F is being water. Nowhere in w_1 could there be a substance with that chemistry, which is not water. In w_2 however this combination is found. Once again, although each of these possible worlds exists, there is no $G^\star/FvO$, or mixed world, in which some substances with this chemical constitution are water, and others are not.

3rd example   Suppose that in w_1 a particular set of primary qualities, particularly concerning refractive properties of surfaces, $G^\star$, underlies possession of a colour F. Nowhere in w_1 could there be things with that kind of surface, without the particular colour. However, there are possible worlds where this combination is found: $G^\star/O$ worlds. Again, there are no mixed worlds, where some things with the primary, surface properties are F, and others are not.

In each of these cases we have the (S)/(P) combination. And I hope it is obvious that each case is at least *prima facie* puzzling – enough so to raise questions about whether the combination is desirable, or whether we should make severe distinctions within the kinds of necessity and possibility involved, to end up avoiding the combination altogether. How would this be done?

First example

How should we interpret the supervenience of the mental on the physical? Perhaps centrally as a metaphysical doctrine. So we shall accept (S_m). Should we accept (S_a)? We should if we can find arguments, as strong as those in the moral case, for claiming that it is constitutive of competence in the mental language that we recognise the supervenience of the mental on the physical. But I doubt if we can do this. For whether or not we are philosophically wedded to the doctrine, we can surely recognise ordinary competence in users who would not agree. One day Henry has a headache, and the next day he does not. Something mental is different. But suppose he simply denies that anything physical is different (giving voice to Cartesianism). Is this parallel to the error of someone who makes the same move in a moral case? I do not think so: Henry is not so very unusual, and if his error is shown to be one because of the 'very meaning' of mental ascriptions, then whole cultures have been prone to denial of an analytic truth. In other words, it seems to me to be over-ambitious to claim that it follows, or follows analytically, from change in mental state, that there is change in an underlying physical state. It makes views conceptually incoherent when enough people have found them perfectly coherent (consider, for example, changes in God's mind).

Let us stick then with (S_m). It would seem to me plausible, if we accept this, to accept the correlative necessities, (N_m), and $(?_m)$. We would then be forced to deny (P_m), and we just do not get involved with the problem of banning mixed worlds. (N_m) does the work for us, by disallowing the metaphysical possibility of $G\star$ without F. However there is the famous, or notorious, position of Davidson to consider, which accepts some form of supervenience of the mental on the physical, but also denies the existence of lawlike propositions connecting the two vocabularies (Davidson 1980). Davidson is not very explicit about the strength of necessity and possibility involved in his claims. But it can scarcely be intended to be weaker than joint acceptance of (S_m) and of (P_p). And even if supervenience is taken not as a matter of metaphysical, but just of sheer physical necessity (in our physical world, there is no mental change without physical change, even if there *could* be), it does not matter. For from (S_m) we can deduce (S_p), so we have the $(S)/(P)$ combination, at the level of physical necessity. So according to me the position ought to be odd, and indeed it is. Why is it physically impossible for there to be a world which contains some w_1 characters, with headaches, and some w_2 characters, in the same physical state, but without them? Once we have allowed the physical possibility of the w_2 type, how can we disallow the physical possibility of them mingling with w_1 types?

It does not appear to me that light is cast on this by Davidson's reason for allowing (P_p). This reason is that in some sense the mental and the physical belong to different realms of theory: ascriptions of mental properties answer to different constraints from ascriptions of physical ones, and hence we can never be in a position to insist upon a lawlike correlation of any given physical state with any given mental state (this is *not* just the variable realisation point: here we are told not to insist upon a physically necessary physical-to-mental correlation; *prima facie* we might be allowed to do that in various cases, even if we could never insist upon lawlike connections the other way around). I do not accept that this is a good argument, for there can certainly be interesting laws which connect properties whose ascriptions answer to different constraints: temperature and pressure, or colour and primary properties, for instance. However, I do not want to insist upon that. For there remains the oddity that if Davidson's reasoning is good, it should equally apply to the supervenience claim. How can we be in a position to insist upon anything as strong as (S_p), let alone as strong as (S_m)? The freedom which gives us (P_p) is just as effective here. I may coherently and effectively 'rationalise' one person as being in one mental state, and another as being in another, obeying various canonical principles of interpretation, regardless of whether they are in an identical $G^\star$ state: I might just disclaim interest in that. Of course, if (N_p) were true, it would be different, but it is precisely this which the anomalous character of the position denies.

So if the mental reality is in no lawlike connection with the physical, as (P_p) claims, I can see no basis for asserting that nevertheless it supervenes upon it. But, again, the word 'reality' matters here. *One* way of thinking that the mental just has to supervene upon the physical, in at least the sense of (S_m), is by convincing ourselves that the physical reality is at bottom the only one: molecules and neurones are all that there are. And then there might be something about the way mental vocabulary relates to this – relates to the only reality there is – which justifies both (S_p) and (P_p). Perhaps there is some argument that obeying the supervenience constraint is required for conceptual coherence, or at any rate for metaphysical coherence; and perhaps Davidson's argument for (P_p) can be put in a better light than I have allowed. I do not want to deny this possibility. But I do want to point out that once more it is bought at the cost of a highly anti-realist, even idealist, view of the mental. The 'truth' about the mental world is not a matter of how some set of facts actually falls out. It is a matter of how we have to relate this particular vocabulary to the one underlying reality. If we thought like this, then we would begin to assimilate the mental/physical case to the moral/natural case. At any rate, it provides no swift model for arguing that anti-realism is the wrong diagnosis of the (S)/(P) combination in that case.

Why do I say that this is an idealist or anti-realist direction? Because the constraint on our theorising is not explained by any constraint upon the way the facts can fall out. It is constrained by the way we 'must' use the vocabulary, but that 'must' is not itself derived from a theory according to which mental facts and events cannot happen in some given pattern; it is derived from constraints on the way in which we must react to a non-mental, physical world. I regard this as a characteristically idealist pattern: the way the facts have to be is explained ultimately by the way we have to describe them as being. Thus I would say that the explanation of moral supervenience is a paradigmatically anti-realist explanation. By way of contrast, and anticipating example 3, we can notice how there cannot be a strong, analytic, version of the doctrine that colours supervene upon primary properties, precisely because it is so obvious that the only conceptual constraint upon using the colour vocabulary is that you react to perceived colour in the right way. Somebody who thinks that a thing has changed colour, but who is perfectly indifferent to any question of whether it has changed in respect of any primary property (or even who believes that it positively has not done so) is quite within his rights. His eyesight may be defective, but his grasp of the vocabulary need not be so.

Second example

In order to avoid unnecessary complexity, I should enter a caveat here. I am going to take being composed of H_2O as a suitable example of $G^\star$; an example that is of the kind of complete physical or chemical basis which results in stuff being of a certain kind, such as water. I am going to take it that this is known to be the case. So I shall not be interested in the kind of gap, which can in principle open up, in which people might allow that something is H_2O and is water, allow that wateriness supervenes upon the chemical or the physical, but deny that some other specimen of H_2O is water. This is a possible position, because it is possible to disbelieve that the facts registered by something's being H_2O exhaust the physical or chemical facts which may be relevant to its kind. I am going to cut this corner by writing as though it is beyond question that molecular constitution is the right candidate for a complete underlying property – a $G^\star$ property. I don't think that this affects the argument, although it is a complex area and one in which it is easy to mistake one's bearings.

Once more, it is natural to take the various claims involving the relationship of H_2O and water in a metaphysical sense. It is also natural, to me at any rate, to assert (S_m) only if we also assert (N_m), and ($?_m$). Being water supervenes upon being H_2O only because anything made of H_2O has to be water. And if we had an argument that it does not have to be water, perhaps because we imagine a world in which countervailing circumstance makes substances composed of that molecule quite unlike water at the macro-level (and more unlike it than ice or steam), then we would just change the basis for the supervenience. We would have argued for a releasing property, R, and the true basis upon which being water supervenes would be $G^\star$ (being H_2O) and being $\sim R$.

Might someone believe that the (S)/(P) combination arises at some level here? The argument would have to be that in some strong sense it *must* be true that being water supervenes upon physical or chemical constitution; but it need not be true, in this equally strong sense, that H_2O is the particular underlying state. Now I do not think there is any very strong sense in which being water has to be a property underlain by a physical or chemical basis. Of course, *we* are familiar with the idea that any such property must be a matter of chemistry. But there is no good reason for saying that people who fail to realise this are incompetent with the kind term 'water'. They just know less about the true scientific picture of what it is that explains the phenomenologically important, macro-properties of kinds. They are not, in my view, in at all the same boat as persons who fail to respect the supervenience of the moral on the natural. This is because this latter fault breaks up the whole point of moralising. Whereas ignorance of the way in which wateriness is supervenient on the chemical or physical does not at all destroy the point of classifying some stuff as water and other stuff as not. Uneducated people still need to drink and wash. However, it is now commonly held that there is no absolute distinction here: Quine has taught us how fragile any division would be, between conceptual and 'merely' scientific ignorance. So someone might hold that there is an important kind of incompetence, half-conceptual but perhaps half-scientific, which someone would exhibit if he failed to realise the supervenience of being water upon chemistry or physics, and that this is a worse kind of incompetence than any which would be shown by mere failure to realise that it is H_2O which is the relevant molecule. So we might try a notion of 'competently possible worlds' $(_c)$ meaning those which are as a competent person might describe a world as being: then we would have an $(S_c)/(P_c)$ combination. Should this tempt us to an anti-realist theory of 'being water'?

Saying that there are no mixed possible worlds in *this* sense just means that any competent person is going to deny that there are worlds in which some things of a given chemical or physical structure are water, and others are not; but that competent people might allow worlds in which things are H_2O but are not water. The first is a kind of *framework* knowledge, which we might expect everyone to possess; but competence to this degree need not require the *specialist* piece of scientific knowledge, which we might not expect of everyone, and which might even turn out to be false without affecting the framework. We might even suppose that supervenience claims have, characteristically, this framework appearance, and suggest that this is why they do not trail in their wake particular commitments of the (N) form. And now the counterattack against my argument in the case of morals and mind gathers momentum.[1] For if an $(S_c)/(P_c)$ combination works in a harmless case like this, then the shape of that combination cannot in general suggest anti-realism, and something must be wrong in the arguments so far given.

One reaction would be to allow the parallelism, and to grasp the nettle. When I said that we could relax with the $(S_a)/(P_a)$

---

[1] I owe this objection to Michael Smith. I am also greatly indebted to conversations with David Bostock and Elizabeth Fricker.

combination in morals, I tried to explain this by saying that the role of a moral judgment is not to describe further *moral* aspects of reality; it is because the vocabulary must fit the *natural* world in certain ways, that the combination is explicable. I might try the same move here: it is because 'wateriness' is not a further aspect of reality (beyond its containing various stuffs defined in chemical ways) that the combination is permissible at the level of 'competently possible' worlds. But I think this will strike most uncommitted readers as weak: anti-realism has to fight for a place these days even in the philosophy of morals, and is hardly likely to seem the best account of the judgment that I have water in my glass. I think a better reaction is to remember well all that is meant by the notion of a 'competently possible world'. Remembering this enables us to say that an $(S_c)/(P_c)$ combination is harmless, and implies no problem of explanation which is best met by anti-realism. This is because the 'ban on mixed possible worlds' which it gives rise to is explicable purely in terms of *beliefs* of ours – in particular, a belief which we suppose competent people to share. We believe, that is, that no two things could be identical physically without also forming the same stuff or kind *and we believe that all competent people will agree*. Whilst we suppose this, but also suppose that competent people may not agree that if a thing is H_2O then it is water (because this requires a higher level of specialised, as opposed to framework knowledge) then we have 'competently possible' worlds of the two kinds, and the ban on mixed worlds. But this has now been explained purely by the structure of beliefs which can coexist with competence. There is indeed no further inference to a metaphysical conclusion about the status of wateriness, because the explanation which, in the other cases, that inference helps to provide, is here provided without it. To put it another way, we could say that in the moral case as well, when we deal with analytically possible worlds, we are dealing with beliefs we have about competence: in this case the belief that the competent person will not flout supervenience. But this belief is only explained by the further, anti-realist, nature of moralising. If moralising were depicting further, moral aspects of reality, there would be no explanation of the conceptual constraint, and hence of our belief about the shape of a competent morality.

It cannot be overemphasised that my original problem is one of *explanation*. So it does not matter if sometimes an $(S)/(P)$ combination is explained in some ways, and sometimes in others. I do not suppose that there is one uniform pattern of explanation, suitable for all examples and for all strengths of modality (particularly if we flirt with hybrids like the present one). The explanation demanded in the moral case is, according to me, best met by recognising that moralising is an activity which cannot proceed successfully without recognition of the supervenience constraint, but this in turn is best explained by projectivism. In the present case the best explanation of why competent people recognise the supervenience of kinds upon physical or chemical structure is that we live in a culture in which science has found this out. I don't for a moment believe that *this* suggests any metaphysical conclusions. If this is right it carries a small bonus. It means that the argument in the moral case does not depend upon drawing a hard and controversial distinction between 'conceptual' and other kinds of incompetence. It merely requires us to realise that there can be good explanations of our beliefs about the things which reveal incompetence. Anti-realism is one of them, in the case of morals, and awareness of the difference between framework scientific beliefs, and specific realisations of them, is another and works in the case of natural kinds.

Third example

The previous case posed the only real challenge which I know to the original mystery. By contrast the case of colours reinforces the peculiarity in the case of morals. For it would be highly implausible to aim for colour/primary property supervenience as an analytic truth, or one constitutive of competence with a colour vocabulary. Intuitively we feel that it is very nice and satisfying that colours do indeed supervene upon primary properties, and that there would be scientific havoc if they did not. But anybody who believes that they do not (mightn't God live in a world where displays reveal different colours to him, although there are no physical properties of surfaces of the things displayed?) can recognise colours and achieve all the point and subtlety of colour classification for all that.

Recent empirical work casts doubt even on the fact that 'everybody knows', that colours of surfaces are caused by the wavelength of reflected light. Other relational properties may

SIMON BLACKBURN

66matter. So it is wise to be cautious before putting any advanced modal status on supervenience or necessitation claims in this area. Certainly we expect there to be *some* complete primary property story, G★, upon which colour supervenes as a matter of physical necessity. But then we would also immediately accept the corresponding thesis (N_p), and there is no problem about mixed worlds. Similarly if we bravely elevated the supervenience (S) into a metaphysical thesis, there would be no good reason why (N) should not follow suit. (N) will not rise into the realms of analytic necessity, but then neither will (S). So at no level is there a mystery parallel to the one which arose with morals, and with Davidson's position on the mental and the physical. Of course, an (S)/(P) combination could be manufactured at the level of 'competently possible worlds', as in the last example, but once more it would avail nothing, because it would be explained simply by the shape of the beliefs which we have deemed necessary for competence.

IV

I have now said enough by way of exploring the original argument and its near neighbours. It would be nice to conclude with an estimate of the importance of supervenience claims in metaphysics. Here I confess I am pessimistic. It seems to me that (?) is a plausible doctrine, and in every case in which we are dealing with metaphysical or physical necessity, it seems to me that we could cut through talk of supervenience, and talk directly of propositions of the form (N). This makes it clear, for example, that we may be dealing with 'nomological danglers' or necessities which connect together properties of very different kinds, and it may lessen our metaphysical pride to remember that it is one thing to assert such necessities, but quite another thing to have a theory about why we can do so. Like many philosophers, I believe many supervenience claims in varying strengths; perhaps unlike them I see them as part of the problem – in the philosophy of mind, or of secondary properties, or of morals or kinds – and not part of the solution.

REFERENCES

Blackburn, S. 1971. 'Moral Realism', in *Morality and Moral Reasoning*, ed. J. Casey, London: Methuen.

Davidson, D. 1980. 'Mental Events' in *Essays on Actions and Events*, Oxford: Clarendon Press.

Kim, J. 1978. 'Supervenience and Nomological Incommensurables', *American Philosophical Quarterly*, 15: 149–56.

Moore, G. E. 1922. 'The Conception of Intrinsic Value' in *Philosophical Studies*, London: Routledge and Kegan Paul.

4   Indexicals and tense

JEREMY BUTTERFIELD

I

The status of tense

There are two disputes about the status of presentness, and the related notions of pastness, futurity, and their degrees, such as being five days ago. One dispute is about whether these notions are mind-independent. The other is about whether they are ontic; as I shall explain, pastness and future are ontic if, for example, the past is real but the future is only possible. The two disputes sound similar. Philosophers of time have often taken a similar line in both of them. Broad (1938: 308f), Prior (1959; 1968; 1972) and Dummett (1960; 1967) believe that temporal notions are mind-independent and ontic; Russell (1903: sect. 442; 1915), Smart (1949; 1962) and Grunbaum (1968: 7f) believe them to be mind-dependent and not ontic.

I, however, believe that these notions are mind-independent, but not ontic. My reasons for believing them mind-independent are straightforward (see section 2). My reasons for believing them not ontic are complicated: various arguments for their being ontic have to be refuted. I shall confine myself here to refuting one such argument, which is suggested below by the argument for mind-independence. (I dispose of some other arguments elsewhere (1984).) In this section, I shall describe the two disputes.

First, it is convenient to have a single word for presentness, pastness, futurity and their degrees. I shall use 'tense'; so 'tense' is being used here more widely than in grammar, where it relates to verbal inflection. It is also convenient to have a word for those who believe tenses are ontic; and for those, like me, who deny this. I shall call the former 'tensers' and the latter 'detensers'.

In the dispute about mind-independence of tenses, a property or relation is taken as mind-dependent if its holding true of an appropriate item or items – objects, states of affairs, etc. – entails something about minds. So mind-dependence comes in degrees, depending on what is entailed. Those who believe that tenses are mind-dependent have often advocated a strong form: that an item's having a tense entails that some mind truly asserts or judges the item to have that tense. Advocates of mind-independence have gone as far in the opposite direction, holding that an item could have a tense even though at no time does any mind exist anywhere (in the same world). That is, they have claimed that objects, states of affairs, etc., would be present, past, etc., even in a world without minds.

The tenser/detenser dispute, about whether tenses are ontic, needs more explanation. The detenser's view, that they are not ontic, is that the objects, states of affairs, etc. that are located in time form a single reality, no matter how much in the past or future they are. 'Forming a single reality' means two things. First, tenses have no special connection with the notion of truth: sentences about past, present or future are straightforwardly true or false in virtue of the objects, states of affairs, etc., in the past, present or future. Secondly, tenses have no special connection with the notions of fact and complete description. That is, a description of reality which does not specify some time as the present (and thus other times as five days past, five years future, etc.) does not on that account omit some fact or fail to be complete. Each time, object, state of affairs, etc. is simply present relative to itself, five days past relative to something five days later than it, and so on. And accordingly, temporal indexicals, that is, expressions like 'now', 'five days ago' and verbal tenses, are straightforward context-dependent expressions. They simply require time-relative truth-values for the sentence-types in which they occur, or for whatever we consider to be the appropriate truth-value bearer, for example, the proposition expressed. (Where I do not need to be specific about what is the truth-value bearer, I shall call it a statement.)

In effect, the detenser proposes to treat presentness and the other tenses in the way that, as all agree, the spatial notions of being here, being five miles away, etc. should be treated. Thus tensers and detensers agree that – temporal expressions apart – sentences about nearby or spatially distant matters are straightforwardly true or false in virtue of the relevant objects, states of affairs, etc.; and that spatial indexicals like 'here' and 'five miles away' simply require statements to have place-relative truth-values. The detenser proposes a parallel account of time.

If tenses are ontic, there are a number of possibilities, depending on just what connections are made with notions like truth and fact. For example, Prior believed that past and future were species of possibility (1972); and his rejection of the usual possible worlds account of possibility led him to connect tenses with both these notions. In particular, he believed that all sentences referring to objects that do not now exist are neither true nor false (1957: 41f; 1967: 151f); and that even our semantics for such sentences should not refer to these objects – they should be replaced by associated properties, *viz.* their individual essences (Prior and Fine 1977: 122). Other tensers treat the past and future differently, usually taking the past to be real in a sense in which the future is not (Broad 1923: 77; Lloyd 1978; Godfrey-Smith 1978).

A weaker alternative is suggested by McTaggart (1908), and following him, by Dummett (1960). This alternative connects tenses only with the notions of fact and complete description. It accepts that there is an actual past and future, in virtue of which sentences about past and future are straightforwardly true or false. But it claims that a description of this temporarily extended reality omits some facts, is incomplete, unless it specifies which time is present (and so which is five days past, which five years future, etc.)[1]

Detensers must therefore refute various arguments for connecting tenses, in one way or another, with notions like truth and fact. Here I shall confine myself to refuting an argument for the last alternative: an argument which is suggested below.

---

[1] The tenser/detenser dispute is analogous to the dispute over the nature of possible · worlds. The detenser's view is like Lewis' view that other possible worlds are not any kind of construction from entities in the actual world, and that 'actual' is simply a context-dependent expression referring relative to any world to just that world (1973: 84–91). The various tenser views are like actualist responses to Lewis (reviewed in Loux 1979: 48–62). But we need not, of course, take analogous views in the two disputes: I am an actualist as well as a detenser.

II

The mind-independence of tense

Detensers have traditionally held that tenses are mind-dependent. In particular, Reichenbach's and Smart's token-reflexive analyses of temporal indexicals entail a strong mind-dependence claim: that an item's having a tense at a time entails that some mind truly asserts then that the item has that tense.

Thus Reichenbach (1948: 284–7) and Smart (1949: 492) suggest analysing temporal indexicals by relating the items talked about to 'this utterance'. The statement, that is, sentence or proposition, 'The mine is exploding' is analysed as 'The mine's exploding is simultaneous with this utterance'; similarly, 'Five days ago, Reagan was angry' is analysed as 'Reagan's being angry is five days earlier than this utterance': where in the analysanda, 'exploding', 'being' and 'is' are tenseless. Analysans and analysandum are to have the same truth-value relative to all contexts. So on these analyses, if a present-tensed statement (i.e. a statement about the present, whether or not it uses verbal tenses) is true at a time, there is a (true) utterance at that time saying that the item which the statement is about is simultaneous with the utterance. Similarly, if a past-tensed statement is true at a time, there is then a true utterance saying the item is earlier than the utterance.

Now, on any view of tense, an item's having a tense at a time entails the truth then of a suitable tensed statement about the item. (It does not matter whether the statement directly attributes the tense, as in 'Reagan's anger is past', or not, as in 'Reagan was angry'.) And, on the token-reflexive analysis, the truth of this tensed statement entails the existence of an utterance about the item's tense. So the mind-dependence claim above follows.

However, the claim is false. The problem is that there are not utterances at all the times at which items have tenses. Thus the claim means that an item that is not talked about during its existence is never present, and an item that is not talked about five days after its existence is never five days past, and so on: and this is surely wrong (McTaggart 1927: sect. 313; Prior 1967: 11; 1968: 20). Furthermore, the relations between the tenses are disrupted. An item that is never present may be talked about before and after it exists, so that it can be future and past. And an item that is talked about during its existence, so that it is then present, may not be talked about before or after: so that it is never future or past.[2]

This problem does not of course depend on the mind-dependence claim's appeal to utterances, as against say mental judgments (Grunbaum 1968: 19). For, in the same way, there are not judgments at all the times at which items have tenses. Indeed, mind-dependence aside, similar problems will beset any account of tenses, or analysis of temporal indexicals, that replaces times by items for which it may be that at some time no such item exists. For example, one might try to replace times by some kind of event. But provided events involve change, this will not work if, as Shoemaker (1969) and Newton-Smith (1980: 19–24) argue, there can be time without change.

Admittedly, some weaker forms of mind-dependence do not face this problem. Thus it might be held necessary and sufficient for an item to have a tense at a time t that at some time t' perhaps different from t some mind truly asserts or judges that the item has the tense appropriate to t'. On this account, an item will have a tense at all times if it is at some time judged to have the right tense. And there are, of course, yet weaker alternatives. The weakest would be that an item's having a tense entails the existence at some time and place (in the same world) of a mind – whether or not this mind makes a judgment about the item.

But I shall not compare the merits of these alternatives. For I believe even the weakest alternative is false: items *would* be present, past, etc. in a world without minds, though in such a world they could not, of course, be judged to be so, or indeed judged at all. A distinction stressed by Lewy (1976: 9f) is relevant here: *viz.* the distinction between the statements that are true in a world, and those true statements that are expressed in that world. This distinction means that in a world containing only colliding rocks, the statement 'There are rocks' would be true, even though there was no one in the world to express the statement: if it were not true, what sense could we make of the supposition that the world contains rocks? I believe we should extend this distinction to statements with time-relative truth-values, and thus claim the mind-independence of tenses. Thus, in the world with rocks, the statement 'There is now a collision of rocks' is true at some times;

---

[2] The same problem besets the extension of the token-reflexive analysis to complex verbal tenses like the future perfect: cf. Prior (1967: 12).

so collisions are present at those times. And similarly for other tenses.

So far as I can see, a detenser can have only one reason for resisting the mind-independence of tenses.[3] He may want, independently of his being a detenser, to analyse temporal indexicals in terms of others, some of which (like 'this judgment' and perhaps 'I') entail the existence of judgments or minds (cf. McGinn 1983: 17–18, 93). But I think this is a poor reason for resistance. For once we set aside the token-reflexive analysis and its strong form of mind-dependence, temporal indexicals probably cannot be analysed in terms of others – even if we believe tenses are in some sense mind-dependent. For example, I see no way of analysing 'now' in such a way that the truth of 'The mine is now exploding' at a time t entails that at some time a judgment or a mind exists, without *also* entailing that the judgment or mind exists at t. The difficulty is that if the analysandum of 'now' is to induce a time-relative truth-value, it must contain some indexicals; but if it contains an indexical like 'this judgment' or 'I', truths containing 'now' are liable to entail the existence, at the time of truth, of a judgment or mind.

To put the same point in other words: the token-reflexive analysis secured a time-relative truth-value for the analyses of sentences containing temporal indexicals, by making each analysis entail a statement about minds which itself had a time-relative truth-value. On the weaker forms of mind-dependence, the entailed statement about minds (of the form 'at some time, a judgment/mind exists') is to have a time-invariant truth-value. And unless we secure a time-relative truth-value for analyses by letting temporal indexicals occur in them, the analysis is likely to entail time-relative statements about minds.

However, this result – that even if tenses are mind-dependent in one of the weaker senses, temporal indexicals are needed to give analyses time-relative truth-values – raises another question. Does the need for temporal indexicals in analyses support the tenser? This need could hardly lead to a connection between tenses and truth, such as that all sentences referring to future objects are neither true nor false. But what about a connection with facts?

---

[3] Tensers can happily accept my reason for mind-independence. But they also have a deeper reason: to believe tenses both mind-dependent and ontic would tie the notions of truth and fact to the existence of minds in an uncomfortably idealist way.

Might it lead to the existence of perspectival facts, that is, facts that cannot be expressed without temporal indexicals; and thus to a description of reality being incomplete unless it specifies a present time? If so, detensers will have to give up the assumption that analyses can have time-relative truth-values, and follow Quine (1960: 193, 227) in simply suppressing all temporal indexicals in favour of non-indexical expressions like '12 p.m., 1 July 1983'.

I believe that the answer to the above question is No: analyses need temporal indexicals, but this does not support the tenser. The reason is essentially that analyses are required to reflect the epistemic situation of users of the sentences being analysed; and people are in a sense bound to use temporal indexicals. But that does not mean that there are perspectival facts requiring temporal indexicals for their expression. Indeed, non-temporal indexicals, in particular spatial indexicals, must similarly occur in analyses because people are in a sense bound to use such indexicals. Yet no one wishes to infer that a description of reality is incomplete unless it specifies a 'here': nor should we do so in the temporal case.

To substantiate these claims, I shall present two arguments for not replacing indexicals in analyses. The arguments apply not only to temporal indexicals, but also to personal and spatial indexicals like 'I', 'you', 'here' and 'there', which make truth-values relative to persons and places, and to demonstratives like 'this' and 'this F' which make truth-value relative to the ostended object.

III

The ineliminability of indexicals

The first argument assumes that analyses should not convey information that was not available to the speaker of the analysed sentence. It then notes that replacing temporal indexicals by dates, etc. will make some analyses do precisely that. Thus, consider 'It's sunny today' said by someone who does not know the date. Similarly for personal and spatial indexicals and demonstratives; if we replace such expressions by personal proper names, place-names, etc. we risk conveying information that the speaker did not have. Nor is the argument confined to replacements by some kind of standard non-indexical term like dates, personal names, or place-names. It generalises to other non-indexical terms; for someone using an indexical or demonstrative may be unable to supply a non-indexical co-referring term. Perhaps such a person could think of a number of properties, expressible without indexicals, that he believes the indexical's reference to possess. But his belief that these properties apply to the reference may be wrong; even if he is right these properties may also apply to another object. And if either case obtains, the definite description formed from these properties will not (in attributive use) provide a non-indexical co-referring term.

I admit that this argument depends upon rejecting certain description theories of reference. That the speaker can be wrong about the non-indexical properties of the reference of an indexical entails that the reference is not determined as whatever object – if there is one – satisfies the non-indexical properties the speaker believes apply to the reference. But not all description theories are thus rejected; and those that are, really are implausible. For the argument holds that a speaker may be unable to replace an indexical term by a non-indexical one, and accordingly that in analysis one should not make such a substitution: the emphasis is on indexicals, analysis and the individual speaker. On the other hand, a description theory holds that the reference of a singular term (a category taken to include indexicals and proper names) is determined as whatever object satisfies some definite description (not containing any singular terms of course); the association can be in the mind of the speaker or some other person or persons (e.g. experts). The emphasis is on singular terms in general, the determination of reference, and the community as a whole.

As a result, someone who holds a description theory which allows a linguistic division of labour (Putnam 1975: 227), that is, who takes the reference of a singular term to be determined by a (term-less) definite description associated with it by some expert, can accept the argument. He has only to accept that in analysis the aim of reflecting the information available to the speaker should override the aim of presenting the way in which reference is determined. Similarly, someone who holds a description theory, *without* linguistic division of labour, for proper names (but not for indexicals), can accept the argument. For the argument allows that the reference of a proper name (but not of an indexical) is determined by a term-less definite description in the mind of the speaker.

More generally, the argument is clearly compatible with any theory of reference which allows that a speaker cannot provide a wholly non-indexical specification of an indexical's reference, and that this should be reflected in analysis. In particular, the argument does not require that the senses or 'modes of presentation' of indexicals are wholly given by the straightforward rules that 'now' refers to the time of use, 'I' to the speaker, etc.: indexicals can have any sense compatible with their not being eliminated in favour of non-indexicals.[4]

My second argument for the ineliminability of indexicals concerns the explanation of action by propositional attitudes (hereinafter, 'attitudes'). I shall assume that analyses of sentences should respect the contents of attitudes that we attribute using the sentences (embedded in a that-clause, as in 'John believes that ...'); and I shall argue that to explain actions we need to attribute attitudes with indexical contents, that is, contents whose truth-values are not absolute but vary with time, person, place, etc.[5]

At first sight this strategy seems odd. Shouldn't I direct my effort at defending my assumption that analyses should respect the contents of attitudes? After all, the legitimacy of talk about attitudes is questioned (Quine 1960: 219; Churchland 1981). And if it *is* legitimate, the claim that we have attitudes with indexical contents seems trivial, and independent of the explanation of action; if I believe that it's sunny today, doesn't my belief have an indexical content?

My reason for this strategy depends upon distinguishing our everyday practice of attributing attitudes from the more systematic theory of attitudes that some think psychology will produce (e.g. Dennett 1978: xiv–xx; 1981; Fodor 1975; 1981). The objection depends upon concentrating on our everyday practice; and

---

[4] The argument is therefore in no way committed to the idea of direct reference (Kaplan 1978; Schiffer 1978: 200f); I believe this is fortunate (cf. Evans 1982: 65, 81–3, 89f).

[5] The idea that some attitudes have ineliminably indexical contents is the basis of Prior's famous 'Thank goodness that's over' argument against eliminating indexicals (1959) – but I shall not discuss this argument since I agree with McBeath's and Mellor's (1981, 1983) view that it shows ineliminability but does not support the tenser. The connection of the idea with action also goes back some time (Gale 1962); but only recently has the connection been made systematic enough for it not to be dismissed as merely 'pragmatic' (Smart 1962: 264).

my argument will relate equally to some more systematic theory. This shift makes my assumption more plausible; attitudes are *ex hypothesi* acceptable, and one only has to assume that analyses should respect their contents. This shift also puts what I propose to argue in need of argument. There is no question that in our everyday practice we attribute attitudes using indexicals in the that-clause; and, as we have seen, we must do this if our attributions are to respect the information available to the agent. A person can believe that it's sunny today without knowing the date, and perhaps without having any non-indexical beliefs about what the date is. But it seems that someone might envisage a theory that explains actions adequately while attributing only attitudes with non-indexical contents; why, after all, should the notion of content in such a theory be tied to what is available to the agent?

To argue that any theory that explains actions by attitudes must attribute indexical attitudes seems a daunting task. But I believe the work has almost been done already by Perry (1977; 1979). He argues the need for indexical attitudes on the basis of some examples of action–explanation. I want to clarify the assumptions of the argument, and to show how it does not support the tenser. (We will see incidentally that this argument, like the first, allows indexicals to have a sense in addition to the rules that 'now' refers to the time of use, etc.)[6] I shall first present an example of Perry's that suggests the need for temporal indexicals and use it to present a general argument for invoking temporally indexical beliefs in explaining actions. However, this argument does not support the tenser: similar examples and arguments can, I claim, be given for beliefs containing personal and spatial indexicals and demonstratives.

Suppose a Professor – let's call him Rudolf Lingens – has a departmental meeting scheduled for noon on 1 July 1983.[7] He wants to attend; so on that day he works in his office all morning, and at noon he leaves his office and walks down the corridor to the meeting. What explains his action? One might say: his desire to go to the meeting, and his belief that it is to be held down the

---

[6] Some remarks of Perry's (1977: 493; 1979: 7–8, 19) suggest he thinks such senses are excluded.

[7] The Professor and his meeting occur in Perry (1979: sect. 2); the character Rudolf Lingens occurs in Frege's essay, 'The Thought'.

corridor. (Of course, whether he actually has these attitudes cannot be ascertained by considering just this short stretch of behaviour. But suppose for the sake of the example that other pieces of behaviour support the attribution of these attitudes, and the others mentioned below.)

But what explains Lingens leaving his office *at noon on 1 July*? His belief that there is a departmental meeting (which he believes is to be held down the corridor, and which he wants to attend) at noon on 1 July? No. Unless the meeting was arranged at short notice, he will have believed *that* all morning – yet he only acts at noon. Similarly for any other belief to the effect that there is a departmental meeting (down the corridor and worth attending) at time *t*, where '*t*' is some non-indexical description uniquely true of noon, 1 July 1983, or believed by Lingens to be uniquely true of it; for example, 'the moment in 1983 at which the sun is at its highest point in the sky'. Lingens could have any such belief at another time, say 11.30, and yet not act then. The natural suggestion is that in order to act, Lingens needs a temporally indexical belief; for example the belief that there is a departmental meeting (down the corridor and worth attending) *now*; or that there is a departmental meeting (down the corridor, etc.) at noon and it is *now* noon.

I think that two plausible general assumptions about action explanation are at work in this example. The example contrasts Lingens' action with a situation in which he does not act: Lingens sitting still in his office earlier in the morning, say at 11.30. So if we assume, first, that the attitudes that explain an action are sufficient for it, then whatever attitudes explain Lingens' action must be lacking at 11.30.

The example also suggests that at noon and 11.30, Lingens has the same temporally non-indexical attitudes. Or more exactly, it suggests that at noon and 11.30 he has the same attitudes with temporally non-indexical contents that are relevant to the action. (Here, contents are relevant if they have some subject-matter in common with the description, 'leaving Lingens' office at noon', under which the action is explained.) Thus we are to suppose in particular that Lingens believes both at 11.30 and noon that the meeting is to be held down the corridor at noon, and he desires both at 11.30 and noon that he be at the meeting. But differences in irrelevant attitudes are allowed. For example, Lingens may at noon but not 11.30 desire to eat his lunch, or believe Riemann's Hypothesis (since at 11.55 he finished proving it).

Now suppose we also make this second assumption: that attitudes explain an action under a description by their contents being relevant to the explained description. Then it follows from Lingens' relevant temporally non-indexical beliefs being the same at noon and 11.30 that if his action is to be explained by an attitude at all, a temporally indexical attitude, lacking at 11.30, is required. The argument is of course not tied to this example. The two assumptions, about sufficiency and relevance, will prompt a temporally indexical attitude for the explanation of any action where the agent also has the same relevant temporally non-indexical attitudes in a situation of 'no action'.

Admittedly, one can resist this argument by just denying that the actions in question are to be explained solely in terms of the agent's attitudes. That is, one can postulate non-attitudinal differences that explain why the action occurs in one situation but not the other. This line has in fact been taken by Boer and Lycan (1980). They share my denial of perspectival facts; but unlike me they believe that this denial requires all attitudes to have time-independent truth-values. They therefore argue that the agent in examples like that above has a non-indexical *de re* attitude about the time.[8] They recognise of course that such non-indexical attitudes may well be had in a 'no action' situation; but they claim that the difference in behaviour between the two situations is to be explained by differences in the way the time is presented to the agent – differences that are not reflected in the agent's attitudes (1980: 450–2). They agree that this limits the explanatory power of attitudes; but consider this a price worth paying for the avoidance of perspectival facts (1980: 443–6).

I can agree with Boer and Lycan that the explanation of some actions requires more than the agent's attitudes, just because the relevant non-indexical attitudes are insufficient (as shown by comparison with a 'no action' situation) and the agent simply lacks the appropriate indexical attitude. (It does not matter for present purposes whether the non-indexical attitudes are *de re*.) Indeed there might be many such cases, especially on some systematic

---

[8] See pp. 430f. In fact Boer and Lycan concentrate on personally indexical attitudes, which I discuss below; but they say that they would treat temporal indexicals similarly (pp. 433–4). Their view has been developed by Stalnaker (1981).

theory of action whose criteria for attributing attitudes differed from our everyday ones in such a way that indexical attitudes were rarer.

But I deny that I *need* to avoid all temporally indexical attitudes, in order to avoid perspectival facts; Boer and Lycan's price does not have to be paid. The reason is that for many actions, including Lingens' action in the example, there is a straightforward basis for attributing a temporally indexical attitude – in fact a belief – which in no way suggests perspectival facts; and which is likely to be preserved in any systematic theory of action we might develop. (And it is no doubt because of this basis that we were inclined, in the original presentation of the example, to cite an indexical attitude, even though it was not explicitly assumed that there is an explanation in terms of Lingens' attitudes.)

The basis for the attribution is that Lingens is supposed, like the rest of us, to aim to have true beliefs. Since the truth-values of indexical beliefs are liable to vary between the two situations, Lingens will aim to vary his indexical beliefs systematically with situations so as to preserve truth. Thus he will aim to alter his temporally indexical beliefs systematically as time goes by. In particular he will aim to believe that it is now noon, at noon and not at 11.30. How he tries to fulfil this aim can, of course, vary widely: he may believe his watch is reliable and just trust himself to look at it at noon; or he may set an alarm clock for noon. And he may fail in this aim, so that he believes it is noon at say 12.15.[9] But the point remains that Lingens' possession of a temporally indexical belief that he lacks earlier arises directly from belief's aiming at truth, and temporally indexical beliefs changing their truth-values over time.

This, then, is the argument for temporally indexical attitudes. It clearly allows an indexical like 'now' to have a sense other than that given by a rule to the effect that 'now' refers to the time of use. All it requires of temporal indexicals is that they induce a

---

[9] If so, he will (given the other attitudes posited) act at 12.15 rather than at noon. In allowing that Lingens can believe at 12.15 that it is noon, I am implicitly joining Perry (1977: 489; 1979: 15–16) in rejecting the idea of a proposition that can only be believed at a certain time – though it could no doubt be referred to at another time, say as the proposition that someone then believed. If explaining actions required such propositions, the tenser would, I agree, get a foothold. But the literature seems agreed that such propositions are not required (though Perry's attribution of them to Frege is not agreed on; cf. Burge (1979: 428–9)).

time-variable truth-value: that is crucial to the explanation of why agents often have different temporally indexical beliefs at two times, even if there is no reason for them to have different non-indexical beliefs.

I also submit that the idea of perspectival facts gets no support from this argument: how could it get support from such straight-forward considerations about time-variable truth-values and be-lief's aiming at truth? In any case, the argument does not make time *distinctive*. For parallel arguments show the need for personal and spatial indexicals like 'I' and 'here', and for demonstratives like 'this'.

I take 'I' first. To explain Lingens' action, it is not enough to say: (a) Lingens believes that there is now a departmental meeting down the corridor; and (b) Lingens desires that Lingens be at the meeting. After all, we can suppose that a colleague of Lingens who wants Lingens to go to the meeting in his place – and who is therefore staying put in his own office at noon – has these attitudes. Nor can we secure Lingens' leaving his office just by adding further temporally indexical attitudes, such as (c) the desire that Lingens now leave his office, or (d) the belief that Lingens is not now at the meeting; again, we can suppose that the stationary colleague has these attitudes. The natural suggestion is that Lingens needs a personally indexical attitude. The obvious one is (e): Lingens desires that *he* be at the meeting. This together with (a) seems sufficient for action. Another possibility is (f) Lingens believes *he* is Lingens; which seems sufficient when taken together with (a) and (b).

In this example, Lingens' action is again contrasted with a 'no action' situation: the colleague – let's call him Bernard Ortcutt – sitting still in *his* office at noon. We are to suppose that Lingens and Ortcutt have the same personally non-indexical attitudes that are relevant to the action; so that explaining the action apparently requires Lingens to have a personally indexical attitude Ortcutt lacks. Lingens and Ortcutt can of course differ in many attitudes: perhaps only Lingens believes he has a cousin called Ralph. The point is that among all these unshared attitudes only something like the desire that he be at the meeting, or the belief that he is Lingens, seems relevant to the action.

The general argument suggested by this example is parallel to the temporal case. Lingens' action is contrasted with a situation that suggests that all Lingens' relevant personally non-indexical attitudes are not sufficient for action. If we assume that action-explaining attitudes are to be sufficient for, and relevant to, the explained action, a personally indexical attitude is required. I can admit that in some cases the agent may just not have such an attitude, so that explanation will require something other than the agent's attitudes. But in other cases, including our example, there is a straightforward basis for attributing such an attitude. The basis, in our example, is again parallel to the temporal case. We all aim to have true personally (as well as temporally) indexical beliefs. So at noon, Lingens probably believes that he is Lingens, while his stationary colleague across the corridor does not do so. Of course 'I', the personal analogue of 'now', does not as used by each of us vary its reference. But this is analogous to simultaneous utterances of 'now' having the same reference. The basic parallel remains: to secure truth, indexical beliefs, whether temporally or personally indexical, must be adjusted systematically to accommodate the varying reference of indexicals.

Similarly for spatial indexicals and demonstratives.[10] It seems that Lingens' belief that there is now a departmental meeting down the corridor, and his desire that he be at the meeting, are sufficient for action only because of a covert spatial indexical – roughly 'away from here' – in the phrase 'down the corridor'. For if Lingens believes there is now a meeting in Room 505 and desires that he be at the meeting, he need not move. For he may mistakenly believe that he is in Room 505, that is, Room 505 is *here*. (Compare how a colleague of Lingens' in Room 505 who shares this belief and desire with Lingens, will – rightly – not move.) In order to act, then, Lingens apparently needs a spatially indexical attitude, for example, the belief that Room 505 is not here.

This example follows the pattern above. Lingens' action is contrasted with Lingens sitting in his office (or with the colleague

---

[10] It may seem that in extending the argument to places and objects, I am in conflict with Lewis' (1979) account, on which persons and times have special roles. On the basis of his functionalist account of mind (p. 526; pp. 533–4), Lewis proposes that the contents of *all* attitudes are properties, and that believing consists in ascribing a property to oneself, or to a time-slice of oneself. (A proposition, p, with an absolute truth-value, is traded-in for the property 'is an inhabitant of a world in which p is true'.) But there is no conflict here. The special role of persons and times relates to the contexts of having attitudes; only persons at times have attitudes. And that should be distinguished from the contexts in which the attitude's content is true: nothing in Lewis requires the truth-values of contents to be relativised only (and always) to persons and times.

sitting in Room 505), sharing with the active Lingens the desire to attend the meeting, and the belief that the meeting is in Room 505. Given these shared attitudes, what makes Lingens move is apparently his possession of a certain spatially indexical attitude. As before, I can admit that in some cases the agent just lacks the spatially indexical attitude required for action–explanation. But in many cases, including our example, the agent is likely to have such a belief, simply because he adjusts his spatially indexical beliefs to secure truth in the face of the varying reference of 'here'. Yet again, the argument depends only on belief's aiming at truth and indexicals inducing a context-dependent truth-value.

There is a parallel argument for attitudes whose truth-value depends on objects in the agent's environment, rather than on the agent himself and his location in space and time; I dub them 'demonstrative attitudes' since they are typically expressed with demonstratives like 'this'.[11] Thus suppose the door of Lingens' office that opens onto the corridor has a unique property: by mistake, the number '501' was painted on it on the inside. At noon, Lingens gets up and opens the door to leave. Is it enough in explaining this action to cite attitudes of the kind already discussed: say, that Lingens at noon desires that he now be in the corridor, together with the non-indexical belief that the door with '501' painted on the inside opens onto the corridor? It seems not. Lingens could have these attitudes and yet sit still; he could fail to see the door and survey the room in search of it. To act, Lingens apparently needs an attitude referring demonstratively to the door, such as the belief that *this* is the '501' door (and therefore opens onto the corridor).

This example also clearly follows the pattern above. It contrasts Lingens' action – opening the door – with a situation in which he apparently has all the same relevant non-demonstrative attitudes, and in which he does not perform the action. As before, we can admit that Lingens has many attitudes that his stationary counterpart lacks; for example, the belief that the paintwork of the numeral '5' has been scratched. The point is that among all these attitudes only something like the belief that this is the door that

---

[11] My notion of demonstrative attitudes, and my argument for them, is substantially different from Peacocke's (1981). For me, having such an attitude need not entail the existence of what it is about; for him, it must (p. 197). Nothing in my argument favours such methodologically non-solipsist attitudes (cf. Putnam 1975: 220); indeed, I happen to think a methodological solipsist can escape his argument.

opens onto the corridor, seems relevant to the action. The general argument for demonstrative attitudes suggested by this example is parallel to the previous ones. Given the sufficiency and relevance assumptions, demonstrative attitudes are required to explain (by attitudes) any action where the same relevant non-demonstrative attitudes are present in a 'no action' situation. And since agents aim to adjust their demonstrative attitudes to accommodate the varying reference of demonstratives, there is often good reason to attribute demonstrative attitudes that are, as required, not present in the 'no action' situation.

In this example, the situation with which Lingens' action is contrasted is bizarre; Lingens is very likely to see the door and act accordingly. But this just reflects the fact that if a person has an attitude in whose content a currently perceptible and familiar object figures, they are very likely to have the corresponding 'this' attitude. Also, in this example the stationary Lingens does *something*: he looks around the room for the door. But this is essentially a procedure for acquiring the indexical attitudes required for action, such as the belief that this is the '501' door. And there are analogous procedures in the other examples. In the temporal case, Lingens might set an alarm clock for noon; in the personal case, Lingens might get his name (and other personal details) written on the cuff of his sleeve; and in the spatial case, Lingens might get a plan of his building, with a 'You are here' arrow, hung on a wall.

This argument for indexical attitudes applies equally to temporal, personal, spatial and demonstrative indexicals. But it does not of course prevent some indexicals being analysed in terms of others. I believe such an analysis would not give temporal indexicals a special status that supported the tenser. Although temporal indexicals should not be analysed in terms of indexicals like 'this judgment' and 'I', on pain of making tenses mind-dependent, they may well be analysable in terms of other indexicals, such as 'this' (Russell 1940: 108f). And they plainly cannot constitute a set of primitive indexicals, in terms of which others such as 'I', 'here' and 'this' are defined. But a proper treatment of the analysis of indexicals must wait for another time.[12]

---

[12] I would like to thank Martin Davies, Jonathan Lear, Murray McBeath, Colin McGinn, Hugh Mellor, Alasdair Palmer, David Papineau, Tom Pink and Philip Pettit for comments on previous versions.

REFERENCES

Boer, S. and Lycan, W. 1980. 'Who? Me?', *Philosophical Review* 89: 427–66.

Broad, C. 1923. *Scientific Thought*, Cambridge: Cambridge University Press.

1938. *An Examination of McTaggart's Philosophy*, vol. II, part 1. Cambridge: Cambridge University Press.

Burge, T. 1979. 'Sinning against Frege', *Philosophical Review* 88: 398–432.

Butterfield, J. 1984. 'Seeing the Present', *Mind* 93: 161–76.

Churchland, P. 1981. 'Eliminative Materialism and the Propositional Attitudes', *Journal of Philosophy* 78: 67–90.

Dennett, D. 1978. *Brainstorms*, Brighton: Harvester Press.

1981. 'Three Kinds of Intentional Psychology' in *Reduction, Time and Reality*, ed. R. Healey, Cambridge: Cambridge University Press.

Dummett, M. 1960. 'A Defence of McTaggart's Proof of the Unreality of Time', *Philosophical Review* 69: 497–504.

1967. 'The Reality of the Past', *Proceedings of the Aristotelian Society* 69: 239–58.

Evans, G. 1982. *The Varieties of Reference*, Oxford: Clarendon Press.

Fodor, J. 1975. *The Language of Thought*, New York: Crowell Press.

1981. *Representations*, Brighton: Harvester Press.

Gale, R. 1962. 'Tensed Statements', *Philosophical Quarterly* 12: 53–9.

Godfrey-Smith, W. 1978. 'The Generality of Predictions', *American Philosophical Quarterly* 15: 15–25.

Grunbaum, A. 1968. *Modern Science and Zeno's Paradoxes*, London: Allen and Unwin.

Kaplan, D. 1978. 'Dthat', in *Syntax and Semantics* vol. 9, ed. P. Cole, New York: Academic Press.

Lewis, D. 1973. *Counterfactuals*, Oxford: Blackwell.

1979. 'Attitudes *De Dicto* and *De Se*', *Philosophical Review* 88: 513–43.

Lewy, C. 1976. *Meaning and Modality*, Cambridge: Cambridge University Press.

Lloyd, G. 1978. 'Time and Existence', *Philosophy* 53: 215–28.

Loux, M., ed. 1979. *The Possible and the Actual*, Ithaca: Cornell University Press.

McBeath, M. 1983. 'Mellor's Emeritus Headache', *Ratio* 25: 81–8.

McGinn, C. 1983. *The Subjective View*, Oxford: Clarendon Press.

McTaggart, J. 1908. 'The Unreality of Time', *Mind* 18: 457–84.

1927. *The Nature of Existence*, vol. 2, Cambridge: Cambridge University Press.

Mellor, D. 1981. 'Thank Goodness That's Over', *Ratio* 23: 20–30.

1983. 'McBeath's Soluble Aspirin', *Ratio* 25: 89–92.

Newton-Smith, W. 1980. *The Structure of Time*, London: Routledge and Kegan Paul.

Peacocke, C. 1981. 'Demonstrative Thought and Psychological Explanation', *Synthese* 49: 187–217.

Perry, J. 1977. 'Frege on Demonstratives', *Philosophical Review* 86: 474–97.

1979. 'The Problem of the Essential Indexical', *Nous* 13: 3–21.

Prior, A. 1957. *Time and Modality*, Oxford: Clarendon Press.

1959. 'Thank Goodness That's Over', *Philosophy* 34: 12–17.

1967. *Past, Present and Future*, Oxford: Clarendon Press.

1968. *Papers on Time and Tense*, Oxford: Clarendon Press.

1972. 'The Notion of the Present', in *The Study of Time*, ed. J. Fraser, New York: Springer Verlag.

Prior, A. and Fine, K. 1977. *Worlds, Times, Selves*, London: Duckworth.

Putnam, H. 1975. 'The Meaning of "Meaning"', in *Mind Language and Reality*, Cambridge: Cambridge University Press.

Quine, W. 1960. *Word and Object*, Cambridge Mass.: M.I.T.

Reichenbach, H. 1948. *The Elements of Symbolic Logic*, New York: Macmillan.

Russell, B. 1903. *The Principles of Mathematics*, London: Allen and Unwin.

1915. 'On the Experience of Time', *The Monist* 25: 212–33.

1940. *An Inquiry into Meaning and Truth*, London: Allen and Unwin.

Schiffer, S. 1978. 'The Basis of Reference', *Erkenntnis* 13: 171–206.

Shoemaker, S. 1969. 'Time Without Change', *Journal of Philosophy* 66: 363–81.

Smart, J. 1949. 'The River of Time', *Mind* 58: 483–94.

1962. 'Tensed Statements', *Philosophical Quarterly* 12: 264–5.

5   *Arithmetic and fact*

EDWARD CRAIG

Contributors to *Festschriften* usually direct their efforts to particular works or doctrines of the recipient; to offer instead the next instalment of a discussion with a third party may seem out of place. But at least my topic, the nature of arithmetical necessity, is one on which Casimir Lewy thought and published; besides, I hope that he may be amused to see his former students still squabbling away amongst themselves, and pleased to see that the last 20 years have taught us to do it politely.

Chapter XXII of Crispin Wright's recent book *Wittgenstein on the Foundations of Mathematics* is devoted to a paper of mine (Craig 1975); this attention, and the friendly manner of it, would call for a response even if it were not for the fact that his very sophisticated discussion of necessary truth deserves to attract the eye of anyone interested in that subject.

Accordingly, I have two aims in this paper. One is to re-assess my earlier paper in the light of Wright's remarks. This I shall postpone until the last section, by which time it will be possible to see it in proper perspective. My other aim, which I shall attend to first, is to examine and I hope in some respects support and improve on the positive theory of necessary truth offered by Wright. This theory has two components: the doctrine of 'Antecedence to Truth', as he calls it; and what I shall call minimal non-cognitivism or minimal conventionalism. But Wright's view is in one important respect indefinite. For whilst at times (1980: 432) he says explicitly that the Antecedence doctrine is essential to any form of conventionalism (this being the general type of theory he favours), on one occasion (1980: 459–60) he sketches a 'conventionalist prospectus' which appears to consist of the second component alone. I shall argue for the latter approach; minimal non-cognitivism about necessity strikes me as a promising line, but I can find little or no plausibility in 'Antecedence to Truth', and am thankful that it proves to be detachable. On balance, there will be at least as much emphasis on agreement as on disagreement; it was quite consciously that I spoke just now of a *response* and not of a reply. I begin, however, with some remarks on a more general issue which I shall bring to bear on Wright's theory only later: the proper place of imaginability in the theory of knowledge.

I

The imagination, seen as a quasi-perceptual faculty, makes frequent appearances in the history of thought about necessary truth; well known examples are the views of Locke and Hume about the relations of ideas, and Kant's understanding of mathematics. It even has an ability to force its way on to the stage when there is no sign that it has a part. I am thinking in particular of J. S. Mill's ideas about geometry and arithmetic (Mill 1973): he believes that they consist of extremely well confirmed empirical generalisations, and that part of the confirming evidence consists in experiments performed in the imagination. And he appears to have given little thought to the oddity of relying on the imagination, of all things, to provide experimental data for what are to be, in effect, physical laws. The indications are that we had better try to make room for the imagination in our theory of necessary truth, lest it barge in uninvited at an embarrassing moment. Wright and I are agreed about this, as we are about the next point: that we should not ask the imagination to do too much. Thus he writes: 'If, as Craig makes plausible, we are unable to conceive of how any alternative determination might be viable, then that is how things are with us; it is a further, tendentious step to inflate our imaginative limitations into a metaphysical discovery' (Wright 1980: 439–40). It certainly is a further step. In the first place, it is clear that there is a group of possibilities which no argument from premises about what we can and can't imagine could ever rule out. We might, for instance, come to be able to imagine what we can't now imagine, there may be other beings who can imagine what we can't and never will be able to imagine, and so on. The premiss is obtained, as Wright says, quasi-experimentally; the quasi-experiment is done on ourselves, now, and for any logical guarantee we have, that may be as far as it goes. If we close our minds to these possibilities then we make assumptions about our present imaginative capacities for which we have no warrant. But at the same time one thing must not be overlooked: the fact that these are possibilities about *what we cannot at present imagine* gives them a very special epistemological status, because imaginability has a central role to play in making us feel that the world is an intelligible place, transparent to our faculties.

Prima facie it is certainly possible that a theory should have great predictive power whilst asserting the existence of objects or processes which we find ourselves unable to imagine; arguably some current physics actually is like this. Nothing in my previous paper rules this out, nor the further possibility that such a predictively successful theory should include a non-standard arithmetic. Accurate prediction can often be very important to us, so there is always likely to be good reason to adopt the best predictor amongst the available theories, and these reasons might be strong enough to overcome the fact that it contained a 'counter-imaginative' arithmetic.[1] I do therefore regret the overly strong word 'guarantee' in the sentence: 'And if we . . . think in terms of what is a practical possibility, I would have thought that this fact alone was enough to guarantee that a theoretical scheme containing a deviant arithmetic would never be adopted' (Craig 1975: 30). This is too strong for several reasons. First, the call for correct prediction might become so pressing as to outweigh the requirement that a theory make reality intellectually transparent to us; secondly, our concept of intellectual transparency might so change that being 'counter-imaginative' was no longer felt as a serious source of dissatisfaction. Thirdly (perhaps not sharply distinguishable from the second possibility), we might cease to experience intellectual transparency as a virtue.

I cannot claim to know for certain that none of these things will ever happen. On the contrary, I believe that the general movement in the theory of knowledge over the last 150 years has been towards them. But on the other hand one shouldn't just look at

---

[1] I assume here that a deviant arithmetic will be counter-imaginative.

the example of Quantum Physics and suppose that a counter-imaginative arithmetic may be just around the corner. An arithmetic is meant to apply to everything that can be counted; and whereas the admission that the ultimate microscopic constituents of the universe are unimaginable to us is certainly a retreat from the proud picture of the human mind as capable of grasping reality just as it is, it is nothing like so radical or disturbing as the idea that the objects of everyday perception are constantly behaving in ways we cannot even imagine.

The central point is this: the decision to adopt a theory (and especially, because of its generality of application, an arithmetic) which presents reality as imaginable rather than one which does not, is not to be thought of as on a par with the choice between two theories both of which fall into one or the other category. Whether we can achieve imaginable or only predictive theories is the question whether we can insightfully grasp the nature of the world or only learn to 'operate' it, to anticipate and control perceivable events. To abandon imaginability involves a change in our whole conception of our relation to reality, and this gives imaginability special status. But it does not, we must be equally ready to say, make it indispensable, nor does it say anything at all as to whether *what* is imaginable is static; it may have a history, though from its nature it will be a history that is very difficult to tell convincingly.

We must not make too much, then, of unimaginability, but neither must we make too little of it. The second point cannot be argued with the crispness and precision of the first; but it would be a bad mistake (and one that our own philosophical traditions easily make us prey to) to think that imprecise means unimportant. We can't quantify the sense of alienation which would follow the admission that reality was radically counter-imaginative; but we can still see that it would mean thinking of ourselves, and our place in the universe, in a very different way. So although we must not overestimate the force of imaginability as a logical premiss, neither must we underestimate its philosophical weight. Later in the paper I shall suggest a way of putting this point to constructive use.

II

Now to Wright's views about necessity.[2] As I have said, I propose to distinguish two main elements, minimal non-cognitivism and the thesis of 'Antecedence to Truth'. I begin by outlining minimal non-cognitivism, and I start on that by offering a thumbnail character-sketch of a figure whom Wright calls the Cautious Man.[3]

On any question of mere *truth* the Cautious Man cannot be told apart from his bolder colleague, the Normal Man; the distinctive feature of his behaviour is that he will never admit that any truth is *necessary*. Faced with a proof, or an allegedly necessary statement, the Cautious Man will happily say everything *else* that we would (if I may be allowed the assumption that we are Normal Men).[4] He will give the same accounts of the meanings of all the terms involved; he will agree that the allegedly necessary statement is, if not necessary, at any rate *true*, that he feels the greatest confidence that it will always be true, and indeed that he cannot imagine its being otherwise. If what is in question is not a single statement but a proof, he will agree with us that every line is either an axiom or the result of the correct application of one of the rules of inference to an earlier line or lines; he will agree that he can't imagine that sequence of symbols failing to be an admissible result of applying those rules of inference to those premises. But he goes on insisting that, as far as he is concerned, all these things are just truths – he is not disposed to take the step from the un-imaginability of the contrary to their necessity. The limit of his imagination, whatever effect it may have on (for instance) his confidence in their truth, is still just another fact about him, and he sees no reason to take it as a guide to what must of *necessity* be the case.

Wright now introduces a form of conventionalism or non-cognitivism about necessity: the Cautious Man agrees with the Normal Man about all the *facts* of the matter. What he holds back from is a certain decision: he will not commit himself to the policy of treating the unimaginable as necessarily false. So what the Normal Man does when he accepts the necessity of a statement is

---

[2] Principally: Wright 1980, chapters V, XXII, XXIII.
[3] An unabridged version: Wright 1980: 452–6.
[4] There are a few philosophers, of course, who are not Normal.

not recognitional; it is more like the projection on to the world of a fact about himself. In its general outline, then, Wright's theory much resembles a type well known in the field of ethics.

I do not pretend (and neither does Wright) that there are no problems about this view. In the first place, questions arise as to what view it actually is: what does 'treating something as necessarily true/false' amount to? And supposing that preliminary to be out of the way, are we sure that the Cautious Man isn't just an excessive sceptic who relates to the Normal Man just as the global sceptic about physical objects (who won't take the further step although he holds absolutely standard views about what *seems* to be the case) relates to normal people? I shall return to these questions in section IV. They worry Wright as well; but there is one feature of his exposition which worries me far more than it seems to worry him. It is the so-called 'Antecedence to Truth' doctrine.

Since Michael Dummett's well known discussion of Wittgenstein's *Remarks on the Foundation of Mathematics* (Dummett 1959) it has become usual (and it is certainly illuminating) to bear in mind that ascriptions of number to groups of objects are commonly made on the basis of two different kinds of criterion. Sometimes we count the whole group; sometimes we have figures obtained by counting a sub-group and its complementary group separately, and then we usually announce the number of the whole group without recounting, going by what arithmetic tells us about the sum of the two numbers we already have. Correspondingly, there are two different sorts of circumstance either of which is normally sufficient to make us say that a miscount has occurred. One is that a series of counts give, when taken together, a result in conflict with arithmetic; another is that there is a slip in one of the counts, that is, one object is counted twice, something distracts the counter and he goes straight from 'eight' to 'ten' – or anything of this kind. Such slips are events that are in principle perceivable where and when they occur. I shall fall into line with Wright's terminology and call them mistakes 'by operational criteria' or more simply 'operational mistakes'. Interest now centres on the claim that whenever there is a mistake by arithmetical criteria there is always an operational mistake as well. Is it necessarily true? Is it true at all? We shall need to bear two points clearly in mind:

1. However much the perceptual evidence may suggest that *no* operational mistake has occurred, the hypothesis that one (or more) nevertheless has occurred can still in theory be maintained. Two devices are in principle open to us:[5]

(a) We can point out that a complete check of all possible operational mistakes would be infinitely long, and so could never be completed. Further investigation is always possible and may reveal the mistake.

(b) We can claim hallucination, Cartesian demons, or allude to brains in vats. In similar vein, we can claim that something or other was simply overlooked – however carefully our observations may have been conducted.

2. However much the perceptual evidence may suggest that an operational mistake *has* occurred, the contrary can still in theory be maintained. But the position is not quite symmetrical with (1): we are not dealing with an existentially quantified statement ('There was some mistake') but with some particular claim (e.g. 'He said "three" twice', 'he missed Bill out'). So method (a) is not to the point and we shall have to resort to (b).

There is excellent inductive evidence for believing that when counting gives us a result which conflicts with our arithmetic, there has been some operational mistake. People who adopt a deviant arithmetical statement, say $7 + 5 = 13$, will *in fact* (whether of necessity is quite another question) very frequently be confronted by circumstances in which their arithmetic tells them that a mistake has occurred, when operational criteria strongly suggest that it has not. To keep alive the hypothesis that there nevertheless was a mistake they will have to use strategy (a) or – a desperate measure – resort to (b). One might think that there will also be a small number of occasions when their arithmetic does not tell of a mistake, but where by operational criteria some mistake does appear to have occurred, and that they will then be committed to strategy (b) without the option. But this is not quite right. For getting a result in accordance with one's arithmetic doesn't, on anyone's view, guarantee that there was no operational mistake. What it guarantees is that if there was a mistake there was also another, compensatory mistake. And this has the consequence

[5] Compare Wright 1980: 91, central paragraph.

that if our deviant mathematicians find an apparent mistake (by operational criteria) when their arithmetic is satisfied, they can leave this standing and posit *some* further mistake, then keep this (now existentially quantified) claim afloat by employing plan (a). They will, of course, have to be pretty brazen about it: they have to shrug off the fact that virtually every count that fits their arithmetic shows, if they are in a position to investigate it properly, a *prima facie* operational mistake that calls either for the application of (b) or the auxiliary hypothesis of another, exactly compensatory, mistake – which will normally need (a) to keep it going.

Now the doctrine that arithmetic is antecedent to truth says that arithmetic does not codify relationships between *existing* truths about number; it helps to *determine* what these truths are. Prior to the adoption of an arithmetic, claims about whether or not there has been an operational miscount are of indeterminate truth-value; and when one does adopt an arithmetic, which determinate truth-values they acquire depends on which arithmetic it is. So it would be wrong to think that in the above examples, there were – from a point of view arithmetically neutral between the two communities – any determinate facts about whether miscounting had occurred, facts which we acknowledge and the deviants collide with. This is, of course, to be sharply distinguished from the idea that whilst the deviant community are in conflict with the facts in *this* world, nothing has been done to show that they would be in conflict with the facts in *any possible* world.[6] That is a diametrically opposed doctrine which states just what the Antecedence doctrine denies, namely that there are facts about correct and incorrect counting independently of the adoption of any particular arithmetic; it questions only whether those facts are necessary.

So: are the members of the deviant community in conflict with the facts (of *this* world) or are they not? Shall we see their error as the pragmatic one of having opted for a very *inconvenient* arithmetic – as Wright's words sometimes suggest (1980: 426, 430)? If so, can we distinguish that inconvenience from the inconvenience which would undoubtedly result from sticking doggedly to what was just plain *false*? We are asked, in effect, to investigate the

---

[6] Sometimes Wright's language suggests this interpretation (e.g. 1980: 439, bottom of page). But here I assume either aberration on his part, or misreading on mine.

properties of plans (a) and (b), by means of which the members of the alien culture avoid conflict between the 'facts' and the requirements of their arithmetic. Neither, I may say in advance, promises a smooth ride for the proponent of the Antecedence doctrine.

Let us start with (b), the more radical strategy. It is clear that by liberal use of it one can avoid acknowledging any fact at all, and *a fortiori* any fact which might conflict with one's arithmetic, whatever that may be. If the members of the alien culture are allowed this bolthole, no wonder that they can't necessarily be shown that their arithmetic brings them into conflict with fact (see Wright 1980: 91). But the very ease with which the plan succeeds makes it unusable within the terms of the enterprise. If we can show that a belief is not in conflict with the facts by pointing out that, however badly things go, strategy (b) can always be used to sustain it, then no belief (except possibly about what seems to oneself to be the case) can be in conflict with the facts. So the very least we will have to say is that we aren't being told of anything peculiar to logic and arithmetic when they are said to be antecedent to truth. For if 'there has been a miscount' is of indeterminate truth-value pending the adoption of an arithmetic, so will 'the cat is on the mat' be – however things seem, we can always keep it going by pleading persistent mass hallucination, or saying that our observers somehow or other keep 'overlooking' the cat. But the point of the exercise was to account for the differences we feel between those statements we call contingent and those we call necessary. Plan (b) is just not to this purpose.

This is perhaps the moment to make another, similar, point. Wright suggests that one way to reach the Antecedence doctrine is from Wittgenstein's work on rule-following, which he takes to undermine the idea of conflict between statement and fact by undermining the idea that there are objective facts about meanings (Wright 1980: 85–6, 424). I shall not now stick my nose any further than necessary into these issues, some of the most difficult and central facing philosophers today. What I do want to say is that, for our present concerns, they suffer from exactly the same defect as plan (b): if they do anything, they do too much. Whether they do anything, I am not sure; but I know of no version of them which looks, even for a moment, as if it might affect the status of $7 + 5 = 12$ whilst leaving that of 'the cat is on the mat' untouched.

They don't help us to understand the difference between the necessary and the contingent.

So it looks as if strategy (a), relying on the indefinite extensibility of the search for an unspecified counting error, may offer the proponent of Antecedence his best chances. For a start, there is some hope that it may *differentiate* between arithmetical statements and ordinary contingent claims. Our first question must be whether it really is true that a check of all possible operational mistakes in a given count can never be completed. If it isn't true, if the search can be finite, then (a) would have to be supplemented by (b) with all its attendant problems. But *prima facie* it does appear that a finite number of observers observing finite areas of space for a finite length of time (in practice these quantities may be not just finite but actually quite small and manageable) could make all the observations needed. Granted, there is also a *prima facie* case in the other direction: existentially quantified statements often aren't finitely falsifiable. But that seems to be because we can't put limits on *where* to look, or *when* to look, or *what kind of thing* to look for; and it remains to be seen whether these, or anything of similar consequence, obtain in the sort of case we are thinking of.

Suppose we place on the squares of an otherwise empty chess-board some white pawns and some black pawns, and then make three counts, first of white pawns, then of black pawns, then of pawns irrespective of colour. Our results are 5, 7 and 12, so the watching members of the alien culture chorus out: 'You must have miscounted or something'. Now the ways in which a mistake can be made in counting can be fairly easily circumscribed. One can:

(i) Fail to associate a numeral with some item of the relevant group.
(ii) Associate more than one numeral with some item of the relevant group.
(iii) Associate a numeral with some item not belonging to the group.
(iv) Pronounce the numerals in the wrong order.
(v) Repeat a numeral – thus associating it with more than one item.
(vi) Omit a numeral (including: fail to start at 'one').

We also have to cope with the various ways, not strictly involving a *miscount*, in which something relevant could change between the first and third counts. It might be that some item or items disappeared from the group. In the case we are considering this would include:

(i) A pawn moved out of the area in question.
(ii) A pawn disappeared, or turned into an object of a different kind.[7]
(iii) Two or more pawns coalesced.

Or it might be that some item appeared in the group. The possibilities are:

(i) A pawn came into the area in question.
(ii) A pawn simply appeared, or some object of another kind turned into a pawn.
(iii) A pawn split into two pawns.

With that the possibilities seem to be exhausted. There aren't many of them, the three counts won't take long, and the area to be covered can easily be managed if a little spare manpower is available. It seems that if any claims about physical events have finite verification procedures, these do; so given the way counts actually turn out in our world, the members of the deviant community can be forced to activate plan (b) or admit error.

In the light of this I can't accept some things Wright says in this context, for instance: 'It is also hard to see how we should close off a list of possible physical explanations, not involving miscounting, for getting the wrong result' (Wright 1980: 91). If this means that it is hard to see how we could close off a list of possible events which could bring about a counter-arithmetical result, then, as just indicated, what I find hard to see is why we *can't* close it off. If it refers not to those events, but to possible physical explanations of them (e.g. why do drops of mercury coalesce?), it is very likely true. But then it isn't relevant – if a pawn is observed to bifurcate, that is enough; we don't have to settle, or be able to settle, the question how it manages to do so.

---

[7] In the context this should be taken to include changes of colour between black and white.

It is no good responding to this argument by thinking of one or two more entries for the above list. Any convincing reply must give us some reason to believe that the list goes on *indefinitely*. And (to forestall one possible line) that cannot be done simply by pointing out that the list still contains existentially quantified components ('*some* item not belonging to the relevant group', '*some* object of another kind'). These do, in a sense, give rise to an infinite list of possibilities, but that doesn't mean an infinite verification procedure; remember that our observers don't need to know *what* the counter pointed to as he said 'eight'; it is enough if they can see that it wasn't any of the pawns on the board. Come to that, 'There is a cat on the mat' includes infinitely many possibilities ('There is a tabby, a siamese, a black cat with a white patch on its back, etc. on the mat'); so if this is held to entail an infinite verification procedure it does so for every statement, and once again no distinction is made between the contingent and the necessary. So one shouldn't say this unless one is ready with an answer to all the problems that beset strategy (b). For just the same reason, neither should one try: 'There may be ways of going wrong when counting that we just haven't thought of yet'. This is (b) again in disguise. By issuing a completely blank cheque it enables us to hold, or deny, any proposition in the face of any evidence: 'By all known ways of telling whether there is a cat on the mat, there is one there; but perhaps there are ways of going wrong about cats and mats which we just haven't thought of yet'. Like (b), it fails to make any distinction between arithmetical and straightforward contingent truths.

Wright sometimes speaks as if the inductively assured near-certainty that the deviant community will run into trouble was not damaging to the Antecedence doctrine, or at any rate could be easily deflected. He argues (1980: 430–2) that a proof that the proponents of the alternative arithmetic *must* (in any world, not just ours) find themselves asserting things which will be disconfirmed by any sufficiently painstaking investigation, would pose a serious threat to Antecedence. No doubt it would; but if the Antecedence doctrine asserts that, prior to the adoption of an arithmetic, there are no determinate facts to which arithmetic owes allegiance, surely it would be refuted if it were just *de facto* the case that, here and now, the deviants would find themselves in that position. And wouldn't they? That, after all, is what our inductively gained knowledge of the world most strongly suggests. Wright recognises this: 'Of course, if this doubt is correct, it will arise even if propositions standing to deviant arithmetical rules as M stands to $7 + 5 = 13$ are merely always *false* rather than impossible' (Wright 1980: 430). But he goes on: 'But in that case it would be open to the conventionalist to accept the doubt as an elaboration of what he has conceded all along, the undoubted practical superiority of our arithmetic.' It is implied, I take it, that the conventionalist can thus rescue Antecedence, since two pages later the doctrine of the unanswerability of arithmetic to contingent fact is said to be 'the essential conventionalist thesis'. Does the last quotation mean, then, that we can admit the superiority of our present arithmetic just in a *pragmatic* sense – it's more convenient to use – whilst denying that it is superior in respect of conforming to certain *facts* with which an alternative arithmetic would collide? It seems it must, if it is to have anything to do with the salvage of Antecedence. But as we see from the argument of the last few pages, it is anything but clear that that can be done without accepting a similarly pragmatic theory of the most elementary physical descriptions as well and banishing the recognition of facts from one's epistemology entirely. In so far as our choice of contingent statements is answerable to fact, it looks as if our choice of arithmetic is likewise answerable.

The Antecedence doctrine has two components. The first denies that logic and arithmetic are answerable to prior fact; the second affirms that these contingent facts are created or rendered determinate by the adoption of an arithmetic. So far my remarks have been aimed at the first component, but the second isn't without its problems. How is the adoption of an arithmetic supposed to render determinate previously indeterminate truth-values? Or how does it 'sanction our transition from its *seeming* by ordinary criteria that no counting error has occurred to the judgment that it really is the case that there has been no such error'? (Wright 1980: 91.)

Imagine that we have done our three counts and the results are 7, 5 and 12; no miscount, or any other disturbing factor, seems by the perceptual criteria to have occurred. Is it thought that because we have a result which harmonises with our arithmetic we can pass from what seems to have happened to the secure verdict that there was no operational error? Surely not; if the operational criteria aren't good enough, adding the fact that the result doesn't conflict with our arithmetic isn't good enough either. There may have been two (or many) mutually compensatory mistakes; or it could still be maintained – and by someone who used *our* arithmetic – that the right answers were 8, 5 and 13, and the first and third counts only *seemed* to have been right. No determinacy has been achieved; what we have got with the pro-arithmetical outcome is a bit more evidence that nothing went wrong with the counting, and it *can* be treated just like the rest of the evidence is treated by our deviant community.

Suppose, on the other hand, that our results are 7, 5 and 13, and that by operational criteria a miscount does seem to have occurred. Would our arithmetic allow us to pass securely to the judgment that there had in fact been a miscount? Strictly speaking, no; we would still have to allow the possibility that there hadn't been a *miscount*, but that some other disturbance had produced the counter-arithmetical result. The one thing which we could securely assert would be of the nature of 'There was a miscount or something'; we *could* still insist on the 'something', or say that there had been a miscount but not the one which the perceptual criteria had suggested. If we want determinacy we shouldn't agree on an arithmetic – though that might help *a very little* – we should agree to thumb our noses at the Cartesian demon and all his kind.

III

So let us assume what certainly looks to be on the cards: that the 'Antecedence to Truth' doctrine fails. That need not be the total disaster for conventionalism that some of Wright's remarks would suggest. We must remember that our main problem is the nature of necessity, so it is important to bear in mind the distinction between an account of some arithmetical truth and what is going on when we accept it as *true*, and an account of the statement that it is *necessarily* true and what is going on when we accept that. We have to distinguish, in other words, between accepting our arithmetic, which we and the Cautious Man do and the deviant community don't; and accepting that arithmetical truths are necessary, which we and the deviant community do (though of course they aren't the same truths), and the Cautious Man does not.

Keeping these two issues separate, we now reject Antecedence and say that a community using a deviant arithmetic will be just as much in conflict with the facts about counting as someone who denied that I am sitting on a chair would be in conflict with the facts about me and the furniture. But be clear that in saying this we are speaking of what would happen in this world, not of what would happen under any possible circumstances. That is a further judgment which involves not just accepting arithmetic but accepting that it is necessarily true. It is here that epistemological problems become acute, and a non-cognitivist solution correspondingly more appealing.

Now for our theory of this second stage, the attribution of necessity, we can try the form of non-cognitivism proposed by Wright. The Cautious Man and the Normal Man agree on all the facts about the outcome of counting operations, calculations and proofs; they agree as to what they do and don't find imaginable; and because of all this they agree on which arithmetic to adopt. But whereas the Cautious Man leaves it at that, the Normal Man goes on to say that this isn't just what happens but what necessarily happens, what couldn't be otherwise. The non-cognitivist theory consists in the view that this further step is not a matter of the Normal Man's recognition of some different kind of fact to which the Cautious Man is blind; it is a policy which the Normal Man adopts towards propositions when he finds their falsehood unimaginable. Thus we hold a conventionalist, or non-cognitivist[8] theory of necessity whilst avoiding the uncomfortable Antecedence doctrine.

Such a position is *prima facie* quite attractive; its main attraction is to dispense with the idea of a special faculty of the mind which reveals necessity to us. That idea can develop in two ways: either it conceives of the facts which the supposed faculty registers as being facts about external reality, or as facts about the mind itself. Friends of the latter option have normally concentrated on the inner perception of meanings, or – as in Kantian idealism – on the principles in accordance with which the mind constructs the empirical world. Recent history hasn't been kind to such views. To reinstate any of them would call for a Canute-like job on the tides of the twentieth century, and whilst success isn't unthinkable,

---

[8] Of the two I much prefer 'non-cognitivist', since it avoids the irrelevant suggestion that we have a choice in the matter.

the betting must be that the king will end up with wet feet again. The former option, on the other hand, smacks of mystery: how are we to know of necessity in reality unless it affects us, and in some way differently from mere truth? Why should a state of affairs affect us differently for being necessary, as opposed to just being the case? Think of the analogy: what affects my senses is the fact of the tree's being there; it wouldn't affect them any differently if its being there were necessary. 'That', it can be said, 'is just to repeat what is well known, that sight, touch and so on are not sensitive to necessity'. Well, perhaps, but that doesn't in any way help us to understand how a sense could be otherwise in that respect – we have no familiar, well-understood model for such a capacity. So the feeling must start growing that the proponent of the necessity-sensitive faculty is making things too easy for himself to deserve our respect.

Cannot the same be said, though, of the non-cognitivist? He, after all, just announces that we perform this 'projection', that we commit ourselves to this policy. He doesn't say what that comes to, what exactly the policy is to which the Normal Man allegedly commits himself, nor does he tell us why the Normal Man should do it. Is his position any more respectable than that of his cognitivist opponent? I think it is. He is no worse placed over the first question; and I shall suggest that with regard to the second he is better placed, since he can put up a perfectly discussible and not implausible theory.

It may sound strange to say that cognitivist and non-cognitivist are in the same boat as regards the first question: doesn't the issue of a *policy*, and hence of *what* policy, only arise for non-cognitivism? Doesn't it, in fact, *define* non-cognitivism? Here we have to beware of a confusion which our terminology can easily foist on us. There is a pair of views which can be contrasted like this: the words 'is necessary' are not part of a description of a state of affairs, they do not conclude the statement of a *belief*; what they do is signal the adoption of a certain *attitude* or *policy*. Now the confusion is to think that this is the same as saying: attributions of necessity are not cognitive but rather non-cognitive. In the context of this discussion the latter distinction (cognitive/non-cognitive) is rather to be understood in terms of the question: is there a faculty by means of which we *recognise* necessity, or is belief in necessity a psychologically determined consequence of our recognition of facts of another type? The distinction between holding a belief and adopting a policy is not of the essence here – recall that Hume does not have to say that 'A causes B' signals the adoption of a policy rather than the expression of a belief in order to advance a non-cognitivist theory of causality – and so it would be wrong to think that the non-cognitivist has to offer anything more about the 'policy' we adopt than that it is the policy of believing the relevant proposition to be necessarily true. Some, namely those who hold that a belief must have its characteristic outer manifestations, will think that there must be more to be said about this policy, about what those who adopt the belief actually do and hence how they differ outwardly from those who do not. But two points are to be made. First, this is a separate question, because it only arises on the assumption just stated. And secondly, it is a question which can be put to the cognitivist, who certainly takes it that there is a belief in necessity, just as it can be put to the non-cognitivist. If either owes us an answer, both do; and if either gives us one, the other can take it over. The issue is neutral.

When it comes to the second question, why we should think in terms of necessity, commit ourselves to the policy or whatever, the non-cognitivist can draw on the material of section I of this paper. What makes the limits of our imagination so important to us is the fact that they are also the limits within which reality must lie if it is to be intelligible as opposed to merely operable. From the need to find the universe to some degree transparent, not wholly alien to us and our ways of thinking, we rule the unimaginable out of court, decide that it is simply not to come into consideration in the search for truth. Or, if one prefers this way of putting it, we 'project' our incapacities on to the world in the form of a belief that it could not be otherwise. This suggestion should gain in plausibility from an historical observation: when, as in some contemporary philosophical movements, great emphasis is placed on the predictive powers of theories and comparatively little on their ability to render the universe transparent to us, necessity ceases to play any important role. If man's cognitive enterprise is simply that of 'warping his scientific heritage to fit his continuing sensory promptings' (Quine 1961: 46) it is not to be expected that any statement will be absolutely immune from being bent.

There immediately arises the problem that we do not always

treat unimaginability in the same way; we cannot imagine a new colour, for instance, but we don't (do we?) conclude that we know all the shades that are logically possible. Our non-cognitivist, if he makes the suggested appeal to imaginability, will have to tell us why not. But he needn't surrender. If we don't pass from unimaginability to holding it logically necessary that there are no more colours than those known to us, surely that is because an alternative explanation of our inability strikes us as too plausible. We find it too easy to think of the case of a person who sees fewer shades than we do, and too easy to accept that they cannot imagine more shades than they can see – whereupon the application to ourselves becomes hard to resist. A case which has some affinity with this one is that of the number of spatial dimensions: could there, as a matter of logical possibility, be more than three? Many philosophers have thought not, whilst the feeling that our imaginative capacities may be limited by the nature of the space we inhabit has given many others pause. But the question is not nearly so straightforward as it was in the case of colour: we don't know of any beings whose experience of space is two-dimensional, and if there are any it isn't at all clear that we can imagine what their experience is like. Hence, on the present hypothesis, the greater though by no means compulsive attraction of the view that space necessarily has three dimensions. Arithmetic, of course, is in a different boat again. In the case of colour it was easy to imagine experience with a shade or more missing; for that of space we could verbally describe the content of the experience of space with fewer dimensions than ours, and do *something* to represent to ourselves in sensory terms what it might be like. But what it would be to *subtract* a little from our arithmetical experience in order to get some intellectual grasp of the possibility of *adding* to it – that doesn't seem to give a coherent thought at all. An explanation of our inability to imagine the arithmetically deviant along the lines that served for colour and spatial dimensions doesn't get started; so nothing checks our tendency to project our incapacity and suppose that reality just *couldn't be like that*.

Another question arises: this projection, or the commitment to the policy, isn't psychologically automatic, like a Humean 'natural belief'; it depends, for our non-cognitivist, on background considerations which seem to be, to some extent at least, a matter of choice.[9] Shouldn't we then, if we accept this non-cognitivist account of the attribution of necessity to statements, give it up and become Cautious Men? Hume, it is true, didn't counsel us to give up the beliefs in causality, 'body', etc. although he recommended a non-cognitivist view of them; but then he thought them psychologically compulsive, so any such counsel would have been pointless. What then is the position of our non-cognitivist? The example of the Cautious Man strongly suggests that our species could survive the ditching of the concept of necessary truth; and there would not appear to be an insuperable psychological barrier to doing so. Why then should we cling to it?

Some readers will welcome this conclusion, and prefer to see in the foregoing remarks an account of the origin of an illusion, the illusion, namely, that there are necessary truths. Others will experience it as an objection: they will feel that there is a compulsion to believe in necessity, and hence be inclined to reject non-cognitivism, or at least this account of its workings. I would not myself wish to rest an argument on premises about degrees of compulsiveness; but there is a further point which certainly constitutes a *prima facie* objection to our proposals. It claims, in effect, that this account of the attribution of necessity to statements does not explain the *explanandum*, but only something superficially like it.

What I have in mind is this: couldn't the work which this account requires of the concept of necessity be done equally well without it? The idea was that we need to think of the world as being imaginable, so we dismiss the unimaginable out of hand at the beginning, unworried by what data we may encounter during our search. But the requirement that the world be kept imaginable would be satisfied if we held all counter-imaginative propositions to be false; why should they have to be false *of necessity*? Of course, if regarding something as necessary is to be equated with thus ruling it out of court, regardless of what experiences we are called upon to systematise, then the step to necessity will have been taken once we treat the unimaginable in this way. But the equation looks inadmissible. Isn't there, after all, a difference

---

[9] Unless, that is, those who implicitly suggest abandoning the transparency requirement and concentrating wholly on predictive power are proposing something psychologically impossible – which does not seem likely.

between assuming that this world satisfies certain conditions, and holding that any possible world would satisfy them?

Certainly there is.[10] But we can bridge the gap within the spirit of non-cognitivism if we can show a strong motive leading from one to the other. And there is such a motive. For how should we *assume*, that is, decisively adopt regardless of the empirical data, a certain thesis as holding true in our world, without believing that it is true in all possible worlds? If we do not take it to be *necessarily* true, how can we justify our *a priori* acceptance of it as regards the actual world; on what should we base our confidence that this world will not turn out to be one of those admittedly possible worlds in which it is false? Agreed, the two positions are not the same; but they are quickly connected given the slightest wish not to seem wholly arbitrary in one's judgments.

The advantages of non-cognitivism lie in its promise to explain the phenomena by appeal only to propensities of the mind for whose existence there is independent evidence. The approach sketched in this section satisfies that condition, in that it makes use only of unimaginability, the wish to find our habitat intelligible, and the desire not to appear arbitrary in the selection of our beliefs. I do not claim to have shown definitively that it has the other essential property, that of satisfactorily accounting for the *explanandum*; but I do hope to have added weight to Wright's conviction that a non-cognitivist theory of necessity is a discussible and not implausible option.

IV

Looking back, how does all this leave the argument of my earlier paper (Craig 1975)? We may note for a start that there is a

---

[10] Anyone who finds this controversial may like to consider the following two points: (1) if there is no such difference, the non-cognitivist's task becomes easier – there is one obstacle fewer in his way. So if we are testing non-cognitivism, it is a sensible strategy to assume that a difference does exist; (2) in any case, the claim made in the text can be backed up. Imagine a society in which there is a deeply entrenched religious belief to the effect that God would not have placed us in a world so alien that the truth about it was not even imaginable to us; that he would not so have mocked our desire to understand things. Might not its members believe, whatever experience might bring, that what they could not imagine must therefore be false, yet without wishing to extend the inference beyond the *actual* world in which they found themselves? For, they might reason, of course it would have been possible for God to make a world in which there were things or processes which we could not imagine; but from his goodness it is quite certain, however much experience may from time to time suggest the contrary, that he would not have put us in it.

difference between the conventionalist doctrine it purported to refute and minimal non-cognitivism (Wright's theory minus 'Antecedence to Truth'). Both see necessity as something conferred, not discovered. But our 'minimal' theory steers happily clear of the quagmire surrounding the notions of meaning and relationships between meanings; whereas my original target – which might be called Linguistic Conventionalism – held that necessity is a product of a convention applying directly to the sentence in question, and so further determining the meanings of its words and/or the import of its syntax. Unlike the minimal theory, it stuck faithfully by the doom-laden dictum that necessity is truth by virtue of meaning.

Wright, in whose vocabulary 'conventionalism' appears to take in any form of non-cognitivism, suggests at one point that I had 'lumbered the conventionalist with an unplayable position' (1980: 429). Assuming that he did not mean that I had *invented* the position I attacked, he may well be right about this. I hope he is; that the resulting position is unplayable is just what I tried to show.

The importance of the question whether I succeeded or not seems in the meantime to have diminished. The lure of Linguistic Conventionalism lay in its promise to dispense with a special faculty for the recognition of necessity; but that promise is equally fulfilled by any theory which makes the appreciation of necessity non-cognitive. So now the minimal view may appear a much more interesting object than Linguistic Conventionalism; and I indicate my sympathy with that feeling by placing this section at the end of the paper, where it is most easily skipped. In it, these points notwithstanding, I take what I hope may be a last close look at Linguistic Conventionalism and ask, from this new perspective, whether the arguments of the original paper should still be held to dispose of it.

What I argued was that (1) the conventionalist has to say that the two sets of criteria for correct counting could come apart, though in fact they don't. This was the claim that was expressed in the paper as the possibility of (M) (Craig 1975: 12–13).[11] I further

---

[11] For the greater convenience of the reader, I quote the proposition (M): 'There was the best possible perceptual evidence that someone counted a group of boys correctly and made the answer 5, that someone counted a group of girls correctly and made the answer 7, that someone counted the whole group of children correctly and made the answer 13, and that no child joined the groups, or simply appeared in them, during the counting operations.'

argued (2) that the circumstance described by (M) is unimaginable. From that I concluded (3) that (M) is impossible, and therefore (4) Linguistic Conventionalism is false.

Stage (4) is reached by Modus Tollens – enough said; we need to look at the other three. It is conceivable that (2) should be disputed. But Wright was not inclined to do so, and after the efforts of the earlier paper I am disposed to sit back until a serious attempt to imagine the truth of (M) is proposed for discussion. The move from (2) to (3), however, needs more care.

I have hastened to agree that we should not infer any absolute impossibility from the limitations of our own imagination. There are two sources of the idea that such an inference is in order. One is this: the meanings of our terms are transparent to the mind upon inspection, the inspection consists in imaginatively presenting ourselves with their conditions of application, and since we are not liable to error in this process we end up knowing that what *we* mean by *that* sentence could not come out true; nothing could satisfy those conditions. Even such a rough and ready statement is enough to let us see that this cannot nowadays be maintained with a clear conscience, however straightforward it may have appeared to thinkers of earlier times. Is meaning really so transparent? Or is the business of envisaging truth-conditions really so simple? How can we be so confident that we have not overlooked a possibility which, if presented, would strike us as verifying what we had taken till then for a necessary falsehood, and do so without noticeable conflict with the previous meanings of the terms? Alternatively, a second source of support for the inference from the unimaginable to the impossible might be the assumption that our mental powers are perfectly in tune with reality. But as I have said, that can be credible only in a specific philosophical climate, and even in circumstances which render it credible it remains an assumption and not an argument.

Of course, if we see the assumption of necessity as the adoption of a policy towards propositions whose contraries we find unimaginable, none of these objections would apply. So we see no objection to passing from unimaginability to necessity, when the step is taken in-this sense. And our conventionalist can hardly refuse to take it in *some* sense, otherwise it becomes quite unclear what he can be doing. If he emulates the Cautious Man and declines to take unimaginability as grounds for impossibility it becomes doubtful whether there is still a problem for him to solve. Nearly all judgments of necessity are based either on some sort of proof or directly on the unimaginability of the contrary; very few, if any, are a matter of explicit convention about given sentences. Since the last of these is the only necessity which the Cautious Man will admit – he doesn't accept necessity based on proof or immediate unimaginability – this line reduces the scope of the operation almost to vanishing point. Why, we may ask, did he take $7 + 5 = 12$ to be necessary in the first place?

The obstacle facing my argument is now this: the move from (2) to (3) is one that need only be followed by someone who holds that necessity is to be construed in projectivist rather than cognitivist style. But if he so construes the modal concepts why should he be impressed by stage (1)? Why can he not happily say that (M), being unimaginable, is impossible, and leave it at that? Why should he feel any pressure to say that (M) is possible?

If it is the minimal conventionalist we are thinking of, I see no answer to that question. But the Linguistic Conventionalist is not in the same position. He is under pressure to allow that (M) is possible; it results from his adherence to the thesis that necessity is a matter of direct convention which (in accordance with the principles (A) and (B) (Craig 1975: 3, 4)) changes the meaning of the constituent terms of any sentence to which it is applied. Without this change of meaning, he holds, there would be no necessity, since there is no necessity without the convention, and the convention changes the meaning. And this makes him hold that (M), which has been carefully constructed to represent the stage before the convention takes effect, cannot be a necessary falsehood. But this he cannot maintain, and his position falls.

I still believe, therefore, that the earlier paper refuted the theory it attacked. But at the same time I can find a good deal of sympathy for Wright's claim that it did not. What has emerged is how a modification of Linguistic Conventionalism renders it immune to my criticism: drop the doctrine that necessity is truth by virtue of meaning, and all the rest – that necessity is conferred not discovered, that what confers it is the decision to adopt a certain policy towards a particular proposition – walks away scot-free. And someone who feels that the concept of meaning is rather frayed at the edges, that questions of identity of meaning, hence also of slight differences in meaning, cannot be definitively settled, may justifiably think that not a great deal has been lost. What significant difference is there, he will ask, between the theory that insists that necessity-conferring decisions change the meaning of the sentence, and the theory which prefers to say that they don't, or just sees no reason to say that they do?

REFERENCES

Craig, E. J. 1975. 'The Problem of Necessary Truth', in *Meaning, Reference and Necessity*, ed. S. W. Blackburn, Cambridge: Cambridge University Press.

Dummett, M. 1959. 'Wittgenstein's Philosophy of Mathematics' in *Philosophical Review* 68: 324–48.

Mill, J. S. 1973. *A System of Logic*, in *The Collected Works of J. S. Mill*, vol. VII book II, chs. V and VI, Toronto: University of Toronto Press.

Quine, W. V. O. 1961. 'Two Dogmas of Empiricism', in *From a Logical Point of View*, 2nd edn, Cambridge, Mass.: Harvard University Press.

Wright, C. 1980. *Wittgenstein on the Foundations of Mathematics*, London: Duckworth.

6 *Rules, scepticism, proof, Wittgenstein*

IAN HACKING

An essay dedicated to a teacher should say something new or something of deep concern to the teacher, preferably both. This is neither. It is a chapter of my dissertation, written under the direction of Casimir Lewy, examined in 1961 but never published. I was then enamoured of statements like these:

> One would like to say: the proof changes the grammar of our language, changes our concepts. It makes new connexions, and it creates the concept of these connexions. (It does not establish that they are there; they do not exist until it makes them.) (Wittgenstein 1956: 79)

Most philosophers do not share Wittgenstein's inclination, but I did, and still do. But I was never sure of how to express it, and I remain unsure. Part of the difficulty is the need to range over many extremely problematic philosophical domains.

In the years since 1961 one relevant topic has finally been well aired: Wittgenstein's sceptical discussion of rule-following. In brief, and in caricature, it is paradoxically contended that no amount of giving of rules can of itself ever determine the very next application of a rule or a group of rules. We have no trouble using lots of rules, but it is not the rules 'in themselves' that determine what we do. Here are rough similarities with Hume's sceptical problem about induction. We do quite often know what to expect next, on the basis of past experience and using various methods of prediction. But paradoxically neither the experiences nor the methods 'in themselves' give reason for our expectations. Hume relegates the practice of reasonable expectation to associationist psychology.

There are numerous fairly obvious connections between the sceptical problem about rule-following and Wittgenstein's iconoclastic suggestions about proof and concept formation. See Crispin Wright 1980. In 1982 Kripke published his masterly book on rules and private language, stating ideas which, he says in the preface, he had been developing since 1962. There was also an Oxford sequence of talks on the topic (Holzman & Leich 1981).

I am grateful for all this activity, for I find that I have always been in agreement with the best of it, especially the first half of Kripke's monograph. That presents the sceptical problem, and concludes by noting that Wittgenstein's invention of it is a philosophical achievement of the first order, even if one went no further. But the beauty of Kripke's presentation is that he shows how the private language argument arises from the sceptical problem. The connection between the sceptical problem, and Wittgenstein's thoughts about mathematics, is, by comparison, quite shallow. Nevertheless I suspect that, in the future, Wittgenstein scholars will show that the chronological order of Wittgenstein's thoughts is as follows: rather traditional concerns about mathematics ... radical concerns ... scepticism about rule-following ... private language argument ... philosophical psychology. That is mere conjecture, and in any case I am concerned only with the early states of this sequence.

It is an essential feature of sceptical arguments that one can never give real examples. If you state a rule which, it turns out, is indeterminate, then the rule is defective. We may once have believed it to be adequate, but the very fact that we subsequently found it ambiguous shows that we were wrong. That is a tautology, that is, part of what we mean by an adequate rule. Once again we may make a rough comparison with Hume's sceptical problem. As soon as there is any real doubt about what will happen in the near future, we say it is because we have insufficient data or a poor analysis of our methods of inference or schemes for decision. Real doubt is never a ground for philosophical scepticism.

Necessarily, then, I cannot give a real example to illustrate the sceptical problem about rule-following. I hope, however, that variations on one real example may, for some readers, put the sceptical problem in a helpful way. I took the example from J. E. Littlewood's charming book (1953).

Most examples adduced in the discussion about 'following a

rule' have to do with a rule being taken in a nonstandard way, an imaginary bifurcation. I reverse the style of example to make the same point. I take a real bifurcation and imagine that it did not occur. Sadly I choose a chess example. Chess is overworked by philosophers. It does have the merit that its rules are as well codified and understood as any that we know. Here is an obscure one: a game may be drawn if the same position on the board occurs thrice. That is, if on a certain move a player produces the same position for the third time, he has the option of declaring the game drawn. Thus someone who would otherwise lose can force a draw if he can make his opponent keep going around in circles (or else give up the high ground).

Littlewood says that the following difficulty arose in a match played in 1924. What happens if the same position occurs thrice, but with black's rooks interchanged? I have found, experimentally, that some players regard the rule as ambiguous, while others strongly incline to one of the two following alternatives.

One party says that the game is not drawn, because two positions in the course of a game are identical only if numerically identical pieces are on the same squares. This numerical identity interpretation attends to the history of the game.

The other party says that the game is drawn, because chess is a matter of structure on the board, not of the history of the game. One rook is as good as another. We may call this the structural interpretation.

Until 1924 no one noticed anything wrong with the rule, but in 1924 it was observed that the rule is defective. That is how we describe such events. Yet we can use this unusually succinct but historical example to generate some possibilities and create some distinctions. Here are four of many possibilities.

(1) Our situation: The rule is thought to be entirely adequate until move 47 in a certain game during 1924. The 'same position' occurs thrice at that point, but with black's rooks interchanged. Some observers strongly incline to one way of applying the rule, some to the other, but at worst all grudgingly admit that there is an alternative understanding. Move 47 was in no way essential to this realisation. An imaginary example would have done. It happens that an actual match revealed the ambiguity.

(2S) The structural story: Everything proceeds as in (1) until move 47. At that point the player, call him Bok, draws the game by forcing the same position thrice, but with black's rooks interchanged. Everyone agrees that there is a draw. The strategy is so ingenious, and so well defined, that it comes to be called Bok's Salvation, a standard way of escaping from a dire predicament. Subsequent players use Bok's Salvation from time to time, but not very often, for winning players take care to avoid the trap. Commentaries on games will have notes such as this: 'Kt to KB4 (to avoid Bok's Salvation).' In this story no one 'decided' to apply the rule in this way, any more than they 'decide' how to apply the rule for moving a bishop.

(2N) The numerical story: like (1) and (2S) up to 1924, move 47, except that the player is Wit, not Bok. He makes the same moves, aiming at a draw. But at the point where Bok calls a draw, Wit knows that he has forced the same position only twice, because between the first and second occurrences there is only a similar position, one with black's rooks interchanged. The game goes on, Wit loses. No one 'decided' to apply the rule in this way, nor in the future is the rule ever deemed ambiguous.

(3) Split: there are two major chess playing communities, A and Z. Global politics has decreed that for some seven years before 1924 there has been no communication between the two, let alone the chance of playing matches. Détente does not occur until 1936, when players of both worlds eagerly resume competition. It happens that in 1924 events in A proceed exactly as in (2S), while events in Z proceed exactly as in (2N). Moreover events continue in those ways, so that Bok's Salvation becomes standard in A. After détente there is an important match in which the Z player is winning, but the A player sees, to his surprise, that he can force a draw by using Bok's Salvation. He produces the same position for the third time and grimly exclaims, 'draw!' The Z player shouts, 'What?' Pandemonium ensues.

It is easy to coin words to describe (1). At move 47 of the match in 1924 there arose an *unprecedented* situation. It was *distinguishing* in the sense that it served to distinguish two ways to apply the rule. An unprecedented example could be entirely imagined, and also the distinction could have been effected in other ways.

Since the other cases are fictional, there is more latitude for description. As a first proposal I would say that in the cases (2), move 47 should not be called unprecedented for it sets no precedent. Nor is it distinguishing, for no distinction is made. It was only logically possible that move 47 should have been deemed unprecedented and distinguishing. In fact it was not problematic at all.

What of (3)? One way to raise a difficulty is to suppose that A and Z speak different languages, which we may also call A and Z (in the way in which we say that the French speak French). Let the rule about three-occurrence draws be expressed by the sentence a in A and by the sentence z in Z. *Prima facie a* means z, or, more felicitously, a and z express the same rule. No matter what philosophical theory of interpretation you hold, or what realistic practice of interpretation you engage in, you would take that for granted. But after the contretemps of 1936 one could properly (although perhaps not unquestionably) conclude that after all a does not quite mean z. It turns out that a and z do not express the same rule. If b is so to speak the expression for 'same position' in A, and y is so to speak the expression for 'same position' in Z, then b is close in meaning to y, but there is a difference that can be stated precisely.

What about a translator in 1920? He reports that the rules are the same in A and Z. He is right: a and z express the same rule, and b means y. Could one disagree and hold that this is a warranted translation, but one that is mistaken? Since by 1936 b does not mean quite the same thing as y, did not b and y always differ in meaning, although no one noticed? In 1924 did not the people in A reveal a disposition which they would have revealed had the case arisen in 1905, and hence did they not always use a to mean something different from z?

That would be extremely implausible. Different communities do evolve different practices. A ground floor in Britain is a first floor in the United States. Consider an imaginary history of this practice, one in which American usage gradually diverges from British, but was identical in 1776. It would be preposterous to say that Benjamin Franklin meant something different from Richard Price *simply* because Price's successors used the word in one way, and Franklin's in another. Or consider the real history, in which even towards the end of the ninteenth century 'first floor' was ambiguous in much British English, with the British settling on the European usage as definitive only in quite recent times. There was, it seems, no decision made, just a gradual codification. It is clear that in 1936, 'first floor' in American does not mean 'first floor' in British, but we would be entirely wrong to foist this correct interpretation back on to older texts.

All we ought to say about my fictitious chess game is that after 1924, the rule expressed by *a* become *distinct* from that expressed by *z*. I do not think of this as an instantaneous happening at move 47, but rather as an example of two different practices becoming manifest after 1924.

I shall make essential use of (3) later, but for the present I introduce it in order to emphasise that a distinction need not imply *any* ambiguity. Looking back over the history of *A*, we find no more trace of ambiguity than in (2S). There is no ambiguity in the history of *Z* either. There are two distinct rules manifest in 1936. There was only one rule in 1910, and, given our entire imagined history, there is no reason to attribute ambiguity to it.

Cases (2N) and (2S) are more salient to us than is (3). The important point for my understanding of the sceptical argument about rule-following, is that the application of a rule at move 47, in 1924, in (2N), (2S), *A* and *Z* is no different from any other application of a rule. It is in fact misleading to speak of applying a rule. When a competent player makes a move, he does not 'apply a rule'. He moves. A novice may ask, 'Was that in accordance with the rule for castling?' 'Yes', is the answer, but the question does not arise for competent players. One moves. Likewise, Bok moved, and called a draw. Likewise, Wit moved, and his opponent made a move three minutes later. Yet by hypothesis, before the 1924 games began *nothing* existed in the language behaviour (and, I am inclined to say, brains) of Wit and his community that determined he would proceed as in (2N), rather than as Bok in (2S).

It will be objected that Bok, Wit and the whole of *A* and *Z*, are just wrong. They did not notice an ambiguity, but they ought to have! After all, 'same position' just *is* ambiguous. Why? There is no rule that says it is ambiguous. I have even been told by gifted players of chess that the rule is not (really) ambiguous – that if only I had a deep understanding of chess I would see how to apply the rule, uniquely.

At any rate, we are now in a position to state the sceptical doctrine about rules. We observe that in (2N) and (2S) people make moves in what they take to be routine ways, although a novice could ask, 'Is that player following such and such a rule?'

Since, when asked, we reply 'Yes', perhaps with explanation, we may say that the players were following the rules. But it was possible for move 47 to create a situation that was unprecedented and distinguishing. The sceptic says, likewise – the sceptical 'likewise' – *an unprecedented but distinguishing situation could arise in any application of any rule.* There is never anything in the rules themselves that precludes that. We do 'go on', but it is not the rules that make us do that. It is less in the nature of the rules than of ourselves that we go on.

I have deliberately offered an illustration, not the end of an argument. The first half of Kripke's book (1982) in part relieves me of that obligation. I wish instead to use the illustration to connect rule-following with the concept formation idea about proof, conveyed by my opening quotation from Wittgenstein.

For a moment continue my fictions. It is possible to make proofs in chess, although they are not always dignified with the name of proof. Indeed the 'White to mate in three' is a 'problem' in very much the Euclidean sense of problem, that is, find a construction such that ... The solutions may be regarded as proofs, and there are formal arguments about chess, of a more recondite sort, that correspond exactly to our idea of a mathematical proof.

Now consider the following conjecture: 'There does not exist a game in which white has the advantage, and in which black can force a draw by producing the same position thrice.' That conjecture is false, for there are trivial counterexamples. Imagine that they can be eliminated by the clause, 'Except in circumstances C there does not exist ...'. In addition 'having the advantage' is given precise definition.

Finally, consider case (2N), and suppose that in 1920 a mathematician proves the theorem. Likewise suppose then in 1920 someone in Z proves the theorem. In either case the proof is published and admired. It is a 'neat' proof. Moreover suppose that it is in a strong sense a constructive proof: it has an algorithm that tells you how to escape being forced into a draw. It shows not only the theorem is true, but why.

That it is a neat proof does not settle anything. For even in case (2S) someone might have 'proven' the theorem, and then, in 1924, Bok's Salvation provides a counterexample. The experimental physicist and Maxwell scholar C. W. F. Everitt tells me that there is a famous theorem due to James Clerk Maxwell, concerning necessary and sufficient conditions required to build a rigid structure. The theorem has been in the text books for a century. In fact, however, Buckminster Fuller's geodesic domes provide a counterexample. Thus the fact that a theorem is regarded as 'proven' does not guarantee that there will not be a retraction later. However, let us suppose that in case (3) people in Z have been able to prove the theorem since 1920, while people in A have conspicuously failed. Call this (3T).

Recall that in (3) there was no ground, before 1924, for asserting that a and z stated slightly different rules, or that b meant something different from y. But consider the case (3T). It seems to me that we have *prima facie* grounds for saying that a and z express different rules. With the rule expressed by z, the theorem holds, while the theorem is false for the rule expressed by a – as is confirmed, in 1924, by the invention of Bok's Salvation. In this sense, we may say that the proof in Z has fixed the concept, the way in which the rule is applied. The difference could show up in a sufficiently astute translation manual. Note that this does *not* imply that if the theorem had not been proven, the people of Z would have behaved differently in 1924. No, they might well have behaved as in (3). I say only that once they have followed the proof, they are precluded from then behaving like A people. Precluded in the following sense: if they are to admit Bok's Salvation as a viable strategy, they should also admit that their proof had a hole in it. In case (3), the 1924 move 47 could have been unprecedented and distinguishing, but it was not. But in case (3T) that particular precedent and distinction is in a certain sense precluded. Many of Wittgenstein's observations will be recalled here, for example: 'When I said that a proof introduces a new concept, I meant something like: the proof puts a new paradigm among the paradigms of language' (Wittgenstein 1956: 78). It will be said that such remarks are in order for my chess fictions, just because we, who inhabit case (1), see perfectly well that there are two ways of taking the rule. Hence people who prove a theorem, implicitly excluding one of those interpretations, are thereby excluding one interpretation, and thus fixing a concept. Granted: it is only from the standpoint of the sceptical doctrine about following rules that Wittgenstein's *Remarks* can be applied in any generality.

Some will reject the sceptical doctrine. Here I can insist only that it is necessary to make good sense out of Wittgenstein's *Remarks*. To illustrate this I shall take just one forceful, if not succinct, objection to Wittgenstein. It is from Michael Dummett's 1973 British Academy lecture. Wittgenstein, he says:

held that a proof induces us to accept a new criterion for the truth of the conclusion. There is one sense in which this contention is both indisputable and banal. When the proof is given that a cylinder intersects a plane in an ellipse, we acquire a new criterion for a plane figure's being an ellipse: but, in the sense in which this claim is uncontentious, it does nothing to illuminate the nature or role of proof. For all his professed adherence to the maxim that a philosopher should only draw attention to what everybody knows but has overlooked, Wittgenstein did not intend his thesis to be merely trite: he meant to assert that, in accepting the proof, we have modified the meaning of the statement of the theorem, so that, in our example, the adoption of the new criterion for its application modifies the meaning that we attach to the predicate 'ellipse'. To speak of our accepting something new as a ground for applying a predicate as a modification of its meaning would not be, in itself, to go beyond what is banal, save in the use of the word 'meaning': to give substance to the thesis, we have to construe the modification as consisting, not merely in our acceptance of the new criterion, but in the possibility of its yielding a different extension for the predicate from that yielded by the old criteria. The standard view of the effect of the proof is that the new criterion which it provides enables us to recognize as ellipses only figures which could already have been so recognized by the criteria we already had: what the proof establishes is precisely that the new criterion, where applicable, must always agree extensionally with that given by the original definition of 'ellipse'; that is why the proof persuades us to adopt the new test as a criterion. If Wittgenstein's thesis is to be more than a statement of the obvious, it must contradict this standard view: it must be understood as involving that there are, or may be, plane figures formed by the intersection of a cylinder with a plane which could not have been recognized as ellipses before the proof was given (Dummett 1973: 212–13; reprinted in Dummett 1978: 300–1).

I have a proprietary interest in the example. It is not, as one might have inferred, one of Wittgenstein's, but instead comes from my own 1961 dissertation (which Dummett had read for a prize competition).

An ellipse, we recall, is a regular oval with two points inside it called foci: the sum of the distances from any point on the curve to the foci within it is constant. You could draw an ellipse by sticking two pins on a piece of paper, then tying the ends of a thread to the pins. Pulling the thread taut with the point of a pencil and moving

the pencil round, keeping the thread taut all the while, trace out
the oval between the two points. A circle is an ellipse, in which the
foci coincide at the centre.

If a plane intersects a circular cylinder, the curve of intersection
is an ellipse. Call this the ellipse theorem; its proof runs as follows
(see figure 1): Imagine two spheres, equal in radius to the cylinder
and lying in it, one above the plane, and touching it at X, and the
other below, just touching it at Y. Consider any point Z on the
curve of intersection of plane and cylinder. A straight line drawn
on the surface of the cylinder parallel to the axis, but passing
through Z, touches each sphere at one point each, say U and V.
Now ZX and ZU are tangents to the sphere through Z, so
ZX = ZU. Similarly, ZY = ZV. So ZX + ZY = ZU + ZV, which
is a constant.

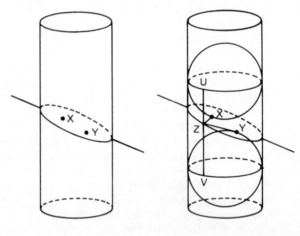

Figure 1

Since Z may be any point on the curve, the curve of intersection
is an ellipse with foci at X and Y. (I first read this proof in Hilbert
and Cohn-Vossen (1956: 9).)

Now let us cast Dummett's objection into a more specific form.
There is a small church near my house, with a small high circular
window. When the sun is shining, at the right time of day, a
roughly oval, bright shape is cast on the floor. This is the
intersection of cylinder and plane, more or less. I have no practical
doubt that someone who did not know the proof of the theorem
might have guessed that this particular shape is an ellipse, marked

with a pencil, and then by trial and error have found foci which would trace out that very shape. It is *not* a consequence of Wittgenstein's doctrine that in any practical sense 'there are' (to quote Dummett again) 'or may be plane figures formed by the intersection of a cylinder with a plane which could not have been recognised as ellipses before the proof was given.' The claim is only that the theorem precludes certain applications of our concepts other than those we do make, but which are consistent with all the definitions of our concepts that exist up to now. 'Precludes', however, is too strong, because we may always retract a proof, believing that we have found a counterexample. One had best say that a proof, accepted and used as a proof, *prima facie* precludes alternatives which, according to the sceptical doctrine, are always logically possible. According to that doctrine, the person who experimentally determines that the shape on the floor is an ellipse is analogous to the chess player in (2S) or (2N). This very example might have been unprecedented and distinguishing. However, if the theorem is proven and used as a theorem, then that possibility is *prima facie* excluded. Notice that my proof provides a non-trivial way to locate one of the two foci (finding the other is trivial). Roll newspaper into a cylinder of the correct dimension, inflate a round balloon so it just fits, dab some wet paint on a bit of the balloon, and note where it touches the floor when held in the cylinder at the right angle. That is far-fetched, but intelligible.

Unfortunately these observations go only a very little way towards explaining Wittgenstein's ideas. I have been concerned with the phenomena that prompt traditional philosophical questions about logical necessity. Why is it that not even God could create a Euclidean world in which planes intersect cylinders but do not thereby form ellipses? Wittgenstein is clearly among those who say it is because of conceptual connections. The theorem has to do with the mark of a concept, not the property of an object. Wittgenstein has the radical (and sceptical) view that such marks are acquired, or formed, by proof. It is essential that such observations, and indeed the problem of logical necessity, arises always in the context of applying a mathematical proposition or proof to some phenomena that can be given independently. Kant's question, 'How is pure mathematics possible?' is really the question of how the application of pure mathematics is possible.

Anwendung is one of the most frequently used words in Wittgenstein's *Remarks*, yet one of the least discussed by commentators.

Secondly there is the much more commonly discussed question of why, how a proof can be compelling. I think this is parallel to the old questions about the possibility of *a priori* knowledge. At any rate, neither the sceptical doctrine about rule-following, nor the doctrine of concept modification by proof, goes any distance towards helping us under 'the hardness of the logical *must*'. That is important, but perhaps less central than is commonly supposed. It happens that when I began I worked from the first edition of Wittgenstein's book, and had to make my own index. *Application, Calculation, Experiment* stand out in that index far more than *Compulsion* and its cognates. I believe that we should look more at application and less at compulsion, if we wish to grasp Wittgenstein's ideas about what he liked to call 'the motley of mathematics'.

In this paper I have had two more limited aims. First, I have used an example of a real ambiguity in a rule of chess to show how an application of a rule may be *unprecedented* and *distinguishing*. Secondly, I have used these terms to state the sceptical doctrine about following a rule: any application of any rule could be unprecedented and distinguishing. Thirdly I have shown how the proof of a theorem may *prima facie* preclude one sort of unprecedented and distinguishing example. Finally I have urged that this is part of what is involved in Wittgenstein's assertion that proofs modify concepts.

REFERENCES

Dummett, M. 1973. 'The Justification of Deduction', *Proceedings of the British Academy* 54: 201–32.
1978. *Truth and Other Enigmas*, London: Duckworth.
Hilbert, D. and Cohn-Vossen, S. 1956. *Geometry and the Imagination*, New York: Chelsea.
Holzman, S. H. and Leich, C. M. (eds.) 1981. *Wittgenstein: To Follow a Rule*, London: Routledge and Kegan Paul.
Kripke, S., 1982. *Wittgenstein: On Rules and Private Language*, Cambridge, Mass.: Harvard University Press.
Littlewood, J. E. 1953. *A Mathematician's Miscellany*, London: Methuen.
Wittgenstein, L. 1956. *Remarks on the Foundations of Mathematics*, Oxford: Blackwell.
Wright, C. 1980. *Wittgenstein on the Foundations of Mathematics*, London: Duckworth.

7   *Propositions, indeterminacy and holism*

DAVID HOLDCROFT

The notion of a *proposition* is central to the kind of analytical philosophy taught and practised by Casimir Lewy with a passion that no one who had the privilege of being his pupil could possibly forget. For him propositions are not linguistic entities, though, of course, sentences can express propositions. This means that there is a very big difference between the kind of linguistic analysis he advocated, and that exemplified by, for instance, Urmson (1950).

However, the notion of a *proposition* has increasingly come under attack. Perhaps the most sustained assault on it has been that mounted by Quine; so I thought it appropriate, as a contribution to this volume, to examine Quine's arguments to see whether the notion of a proposition is discredited by them. I think it is not. But since his arguments constitute a philosophical *tour de force*, I can hope to do no more here than sketch an outline of a reply to them.

After a caveat about the gulf between the aims and methods of logical analysis and those of Quine's pragmatism, section I tries to establish the relevance of Quine's arguments to the existence of propositions, even if, arguably, he has a mistaken view of what philosophers have taken propositions to be. Section II first discusses strategies, both Quine's and my own, and then moves on, by way of illustration of them, to a discussion of Quine's concept of *stimulus meaning*. I question the idea that this is a respectable notion whose virtues reveal the threadbare nature of non-stimulus meaning. In section III the argument to the non-existence of propositions from the indeterminacy of translation (*IT*) is considered and found inconclusive; whilst section IV is devoted to a discussion of Quine's adaptation of Duhem's arguments to show

that theoretical sentences do not *per se* have meaning, and that the
unit of meaning is a theory.

I

Philosophers of an analytic frame of mind have usually desired to
understand the world, but not to change it. In a famous passage
Moore wrote:

I am not at all sceptical as to the *truth* of such propositions as 'The earth
has existed for many years past,' 'Many human bodies have each lived
for many years upon it,' . . .: on the contrary I hold that we all know,
with certainty, many such propositions to be true. But I am very
sceptical as to what, in certain respects, the correct analysis of such
propositions is. (Moore 1925: 216)

From this perspective it is very easy to misunderstand those
philosophers who do not regard it as their business to defend
common sense and to analyse antecedently clear concepts, but
who, on the contrary, argue that 'Putting our house in ontological
order is not a matter of making an already implicit ontology
explicit by sorting and dusting up ordinary language. It is a matter
of devising and imposing' (Quine 1973: 88). For, to argue against
such a philosopher that he has not produced a meaning preserving
translation of, for example, our everyday material object terminology is simply to miss the point of what he is trying to do.

If, as Quine argues, 'There is no place for a prior philosophy'
(Quine 1969: 26), and our overriding concern is to determine what
ontology science is committed to, then it is not surprising that we
should end up suspicious of propositions, treating them as 'half-
entities' without clear identity conditions, not needed for 'official
scientific business' (Quine 1969: 24). But it might be argued that
however sympathetic one is to Quine's project of devising and
imposing, his critique of propositions is vitiated by the fact that he
usually takes a very implausible view of what propositions have
been thought to be, namely, the meaning of a sentence, and, in
particular that of an eternal sentence[1] (Quine 1968: 139; 1970: 2).
Usually philosophers who have written about propositions have

---

[1] An *occasion* sentence is one which commands assent or dissent only if queried after an
appropriate prompting stimulation (Quine 1968: 36). It is contrasted with a *standing*
sentence to which 'the subject may repeat his old assent or dissent unprompted by current
stimulation when we ask him again on later occasions' (*ibid.*) *Eternal* sentences are a
sub-class of the latter, *viz.*, ones that stay forever true or false.

distinguished the meaning of a sentence from the proposition asserted by it (Cartwright 1962; Pollock 1982). However, their arguments have often turned on non-eternal sentences, and so are not directly relevant to Quine's proposals.

Fortunately, there is no need to discuss the merits of Quine's proposal further at this point; particularly since to do so would be to run the risk of getting bogged down in just the sort of analytical argument that I am anxious not to appeal to against Quine. The issue can be avoided because Quine's arguments against propositions do not depend on his own views of what propositions have been thought to be. Rather, they proceed by attacking three assumptions which, as far as I know, any advocate of propositions would wish to make, namely, that a sentence expressing a determinate proposition has a determinate meaning that is separately identifiable, and in principle translatable.

This argument is worth trying to spell out in more detail. Presumably, defenders of propositions would maintain that

(1) Non-observation sentences can express propositions.[2]

Moreover, the defender of propositions would presumably accept that

(2) If a sentence *S* expresses a proposition, then (a) there is a determinate proposition that it expresses, which is (b) separately identifiable.

But if this is so, since it is, at least in part because of the meaning it has that a sentence expresses the proposition it does, it would be difficult to deny that

(3) If *S* expresses a determinate and separately identifiable proposition, then it has (a) a determinate meaning, which (b) is separately identifiable.[3]

---

[2] Arguably it would be better to replace the cumbersome term 'non-observation' by the word 'theoretical', since Quine's arguments often turn on the properties of theoretical sentences. However, this is not clearly so in Quine (1968), and I have preferred to stick to the more cumbersome term.

[3] One could, I hope, subscribe to (3) without wishing to reify meanings. For my purposes the following explanations of 'determinate' and 'separately identifiable' are sufficient. *S* has a determinate meaning if there is, in principle, a correct specification of its meaning, so that of two conflicting hypotheses about its meaning at most one could be right. Whilst *S*'s meaning is separately identifiable if it is possible, in principle, to specify what someone who utters it assertively means by it, without *eo ipso* specifying what he means by the other sentences he utters assertively on the same occasion.

Finally, it would also be difficult to deny that

(4) If *S*, a sentence of *L*, expresses a determinate proposition, then it is in principle possible for there to be a sentence *S'* of some other language *L'* which expresses the same proposition as *S* and *a fortiori* is an exact translation of *S*.

The words 'in principle' are important in (4). There is no need to saddle the defender of propositions with the view that one can always in fact find an exact translation of a sentence *S* in another language, or that one can always express the proposition it expresses in another language. But it is difficult to see what reason he could have for thinking that it is impossible *in principle*.

Given these four claims, the thrust of Quine's argument is clear. He does not attack (1) directly. Rather, he produces arguments, principally *IT* and the Duhemian argument, which are designed to show that the consequents of (3) and (4) are false of non-observation sentences. And if this is so, then the conclusion that non-observation sentences do not express propositions follows trivially. Quine's argument is thus extremely powerful and ingenious, since it casts doubts on the existence of propositions without committing itself to any view as to what they are, or have been taken to be, except, of course, that they satisfy the assumptions (1)–(4).

II

At this point the defender of propositions might draw attention to the limited generality of the conclusion that can be reached by the argument just sketched. It does not show, he might argue, that no sentence expresses a proposition, but only that non-observation sentences do not. Moreover, he might continue, it would be an odd theory of meaning that asserted that *no* sentence has a determinate meaning which is separately identifiable. Surely, unless some occasion sentences at least had such a meaning, language would not be learnable. Hence, Quine's arguments give no reason for thinking that they do not express propositions.

But whilst Quine would indeed agree that at least some occasion sentences have determinate and separately identifiable meanings, he would see no reason to grant that they express propositions. For their meaning, stimulus meaning, is explicable in terms of the concepts of behavioural science, and this obviates the need for any commitment to proposition. Stimulus meaning is scientifically respectable, and sets up a standard which no other candidates for meaning live up to. So why, having granted that some occasion sentences have stimulus meaning, should we make an additional, and dubious, commitment to propositions?

At this point it is worth noting a common strategy in philosophy which consists of first establishing that a certain kind of case is unproblematical, or relatively so, and then taking this sort of case as a standard which all others fail to live up to. For a classical empiricist, knowledge of our impressions is relatively unproblematical, whereas knowledge of almost everything else is, by comparison, highly problematical. Somewhat analogously, for Quine, writing about the theory of meaning, occasion sentences, which have stimulus meaning, are relatively unproblematical by comparison with which the attribution of meaning to terms and to theoretical sentences is highly problematical. Quine illustrates the point by appealing to the plight of the linguist engaged in radical translation of the native sentence 'Gavagai':

> I will grant that the linguist may establish inductively, beyond reasonable doubt, that a certain heathen expression is one to which natives can be prompted to assent by the presence of a rabbit, or reasonable *facsimile*, and not otherwise. The linguist is then warranted in according the native expression the cautious translation 'There's a rabbit,' 'There we have a rabbit', 'Lo! a rabbit,' 'Lo! rabbithood again,' insofar as the differences among these English sentences are counted irrelevant. This much translation can be objective, however exotic the tribe. It recognizes the native expression as in effect a rabbit-heralding sentence. But the linguist's bold further step, in which he imposes his own object-positing pattern without special warrant, is taken when he equates the native expression or any part of it with the *term* 'rabbit'. (Quine 1969: 4)

He goes on to make it clear that the plight of the child learning its first language is strictly analogous (Quine 1969: 7). Just as the linguist has to cross the 'gulf' that divides stimulus meaning from all other kinds of meaning, so does the child.

Now the obvious counter-strategy to adopt to strategies of this sort is to query the credentials of the allegedly unproblematical cases. For if these are bogus, then the attempt to show that other sorts of cases are problematical because they fail to measure up to the unproblematical ones is fatally flawed. So, is stimulus meaning unproblematical?

Quine has given the following explanation of stimulus meaning:

> We may begin by defining the *affirmative* stimulus meaning of a sentence ..., for a given speaker, as the class of all stimulations ... that would prompt his assent. ... We may define the *negative* stimulus meaning similarly with 'assent' and 'dissent' interchanged, and then define the *stimulus meaning* as the ordered pair of the two (Quine 1960: 32).

Perhaps the first question to be asked is whether so-defined stimulus meaning could be of any conceivable use to the linguist engaged in radical translation. Stimulations, conceived of as patterns of ocular irradiation, are about as inaccessible to an observer as anything could be (Davis 1976: 155), except perhaps that auditory, olfactory, gustatory and tactile ones are even more inaccessible. Since, normally, stimulations are not observable outside the laboratory, they surely are not what the linguist or child hypothesises about.

Does Quine, however, really suppose that the child and the linguist do? This passage at least suggests that he does:

> Science itself teaches that there is no clairvoyance; that the only information that can reach our sensory surfaces from external objects must be limited to two-dimensional optical projections and various impacts of air waves on the eardrums and some gaseous reactions in the nasal passages and a few kindred odds and ends. How, the challenge proceeds, could one hope to find out about that external world from such meager traces? In short, if our science were true, how could we know it? (Quine 1973: 2)

What this suggests is that our problem is to construct the external world from the two-dimensional stimulations, impacts of air waves, etc., that we are aware of. But it is surely highly questionable whether we perceive these things at all in ordinary circumstances; if they are the partial causes of our perceptions, they are surely not their objects. However, Quine later introduces a distinction between *reception* and *perception*, and makes it clear that it is not his position that stimulations themselves are perceived: 'Awareness and Gestalt still claim an important place. Sensory receptors operate at the level of reception, and Gestalt operates at the level of perception. The old antagonism was due to the epistemologist's straining toward reception while still requiring awareness, which belongs to perception' (Quine 1973, p. 4). A perception, at the very least, involves an inculcated disposition, as well as a stimulation.

The distinction between reception and perception seems unavoidable, anyway, since, as is well known, the image on the retina can be fixed without uniquely determining the recipient's perception. For instance, in the case of a reversing Necker cube 'the sensory information is constant (the figure may even be stabilised on the retina) and yet the perception changes from moment to moment, as each possible hypothesis comes up for testing' (Gregory 1966: 222). Indeed, it has been claimed that '*all* retinal images are essentially ambiguous since any image could represent any of an infinite set of objects at different orientation' (Gregory 1966: 234). However, once the distinction between perception and reception is granted, it must be concluded that it is not the set of stimulations that prompt assent/dissent that is of interest, but the set of perceptions that do so, since each stimulus pattern is consistent with different perceptions. To remain at the level of stimulations only would be to remain on a level at which one simply did not know what the speaker was assenting to or dissenting from.[4]

The following puzzle then arises. The distinction between reception and perception is Quine's own. But once it is granted, not only is stimulus meaning, as explained, epistemologically useless because, as we already noted, we cannot ordinarily observe stimulations, but it is doubly so, since stimulations are not what determines assent and dissent. So why persist with the notion of stimulus meaning?

One alleged attraction might be that identity conditions for 'X has the same stimulation as Y' are easier to state than the identity conditions for 'X has the same perception as Y'. Quine, however, does not make this implausible claim. In his book (1973) he proposes an account of perceptual similarity which provides a sufficient condition for 'X's perception p is similar to his perception p'', but not a necessary one. He adds, moreover, that the account is one of something which 'is always confined within an individual; the episodes that it relates are episodes in his life, and they are more and less similar for him. One cannot easily give meaning, indeed, to a general objective similarity relation among

---

[4] Davis argues that one reason for preferring to speculate about stimulations, rather than perceptions, is that this is a way of avoiding reading our own object terminology into the native's language (Davis 1976: 156). But the method of analytical hypotheses makes this unavoidable anyway on Quine's account. There seems to be no great virtue in postponing the inevitable.

things in the world' (Quine 1973: 19). But does stimulus similarity fare any better? At the intrasubjective level it does on Quine's account, which defines a pattern of stimulation of a person as a sub-class of his sensory receptors, so that the pattern is realised when all and only those receptors are activated. But, because of the theoretical problems involved in making assumptions about homologies between different persons' sensory receptors, when '... it comes to the intersubjective, however, perhaps the most we can realistically speak of is resemblance and not identity of stimulation patterns. All stimulation patterns should perhaps be viewed as peculiar to individual subjects, and as bearing inter-subjective resemblances, at best, based on approximate homol-ogies of nerve endings' (Quine 1969: 159). The moral is that when we make intersubjective comparisons of stimulations, which given the social nature of language we inevitably must do, we have no well-defined notion of stimulus similarity to apply.[5] So if it is legitimate to complain that traditional theories of meaning do not state precisely the conditions in which utterances by different speakers have the same meaning, it is presumably also legitimate to complain that the conditions in which utterances by different speakers have the same stimulus meaning are not given.

Nor is it obvious that stimulus meaning is determinate in a way that non-stimulus meaning is not. It has often been claimed that translation of the native signs of assent/dissent ought, on Quine's own showing, to involve analytical hypotheses (Hintikka 1968: 71), since the meanings of the signs in question cannot be explained in terms of stimulus meaning. But since analytical hypotheses are the source of indeterminacy, and the explanation of stimulus meaning utilises the notions of *assent* and *dissent*, it follows that stimulus meaning is itself indeterminate. Sur-prisingly, Quine accepts that this is so (Quine 1968: 284), but argues that stimulus meaning is less subject to indeterminacy than 'are the linguist's later adoption of analytical hypotheses, undeter-mined still by what he takes to be the native's sign of assent and dissent, and undetermined still by all the stimulus meanings' (Quine 1968: 284). But it is difficult to see that the indeterminacy, if any, would be less. For though guesses about what are the

---

[5] In practice, Quine argues, we 'usually assume adequately similar stimulation of two subjects by seeing to it that their bodies are reached by similar barrages of outside forces and that the subjects are orientated alike to the stimulus sources' (Quine 1969: 159).

native's signs of assent and dissent can affect one's translation of theoretical sentences, the dependency is surely mutual, since a change in a hypothesis about the meaning of a native theoretical sentence could lead to the revision of a hypothesis about the native's sign of assent.

The claim that hypotheses about the native's sign of assent involve analytical hypotheses is, however, problematical. Normally such hypotheses have to be consistent with our translations of observation sentences, that is, those sentences with stimulus meaning. But such a constraint on hypotheses about the native's sign for assent would not make sense.

Interestingly, there is a tension in Quine's philosophy at this point. For he gives a behaviouristic account of how the sign for assent is learnt which ought, at worst, to be subject to inductive uncertainty, but not to indeterminacy, since no analytical hypotheses are involved.

One of the child's rewarding episodes may be supposed to have included a conspicuous show of red together with the sound 'red' from his own mouth, followed by the sound 'yes' from the parent. In a later episode there is again the color and again the sound 'red'. Such is the partial similarity of the later episode to the earlier. There are of course incidental differences, and one of these just happens to be that the sound 'red' issued from the parent this time, actually with interrogative intent. Anyway the child is moved as usual to heighten the resemblance, so he supplies another element of the earlier episode, the sound 'yes'. Rewarded again, he has learned to say 'yes' in the presence of the colour red and the sound 'red'. Unpleasant episodes will discourage him from saying 'yes' when he hears the sound 'red' in the absence of the color. (Quine 1973: 47)

By language dependent generalisation to other cases, the child learns that 'assent to a sentence entails the same rewards or penalties as repetition of the sentence would entail' (Quine 1973: 48). The spectre of radical indeterminacy hardly seems to arise on this account. Moreover, this example reminds us of the importance for Quine's learning theory of dispositions which involve responses to other sentences, as well as dispositions which involve responses to stimulations. Why should the former dispositions be ignored when we come to consider linguistic items whose meaning cannot be explained solely in terms of stimulus meaning (Dummett 1974; Papineau 1979)? But if, by appeal to such dispositions, the native sign for assent and dissent can be translated, subject only to inductive uncertainty, then presumably many other linguistic items which do not have stimulus meaning can be translated.

One final comment. Whether or not analytical hypotheses are involved in translating the native's sign of assent and dissent – and I have argued that the only coherent alternative is that they are not – it seems clear that stimulus meaning is not determinately translatable. For one cannot say in English, French, or any other natural language, what is the stimulus meaning of a native sentence, for example, 'Gavagai' (see p. 129), since one cannot, using English, report what the native said without using *one* of the sentences in Quine's list. So there simply is no way of reporting what he said which attributes to him the content which is common to all the sentences but specific to none of them.

If stimulus meaning is claimed to have virtues which non-stimulus meaning lacked, in that it has clear intersubjective identity conditions, is determinately specifiable, and is clearly a useful explanatory notion for the theory of language learning, then it seems that it has none of these merits. But it would then hardly be reasonable to claim that non-stimulus meaning was by comparison defective.

Earlier I argued that, in spite of the lack of precision in the concepts involved, the linguist had no option but to speculate about the native's perceptions, since it is these that determine his assent/dissent. The concept of *stimulus meaning* offered the hope that the linguist would be able to commence his enquiries at a more rigorous level by investigating stimulus meaning. But this hope has proved illusory.

III

Obviously *IT* entails the falsity of (4) (cf. section I). But it also entails that no non-observation sentence has a determinate meaning, which, together with (3), (2) and (1) entails that no non-observation sentence expresses a determinate proposition. So if successful, it is a very powerful argument.

Before discussing *IT* it is worth noting that given a holistic theory of meaning of the sort that Quine holds one would expect one's attempts at *exact* translation to fail more often than not. For any significant differences in lexical or grammatical structure between languages would mean that one language introduced meaning determining structure at a point where the other did not, or that they were simply not directly commensurable.[6] But *IT* is committed to more than this; for holistic theories do not *per se* entail that the exact translation of a non-occasion sentence is impossible, but rather that it can occur only in situations, which are, perhaps, not very likely to occur, *viz.*, ones in which all relevant structural factors are reduplicated (Papineau 1979). The difference is that whilst an holistic theory makes exact translation of non-occasion sentences unlikely, *IT* makes it impossible. So *IT* should not be confused with the claim which from a structuralist perspective is something of a commonplace, that exact translation is very much the exception not the rule. Nor, as he has repeatedly pointed out, is Quine claiming no more than that translation of non-occasion sentences involves hypotheses that are undetermined by the data, since this would not itself preclude there being a fact of the matter. For Quine, for instance, physical theory is undetermined; but it is not indeterminate.

Nevertheless, in Quine's view underdetermination is connected with indeterminacy in the special case of the theory of meaning, because of his behaviourism. Given the latter, not only do speakers' dispositions to assent/dissent to sentences, supplemented by other behaviour (Quine 1968: 285) constitute our only *evidence* for the meanings of those sentences, but insofar as there are any objective distinctions to be made about those meanings, they have to be made by reference to those very dispositions. So at the point at which evidence runs out there ceases to be anything objective to make claims about. Thus, Quine has described *IT* as follows:

They (the translations) would be indeterminate in this sense: two translators might develop independent manuals of translation, both of them compatible with all speech behaviour and all dispositions to speech behaviour, and yet one manual would offer translations that the other translator would reject. My position was that either manual could be useful, but as to which was right and which wrong there was no fact of the matter. (Quine 1979: 167)

---

[6] For example, one lexicon may make more distinctions than another. French offers *marron* and *brun* where we have only 'brown'. More interestingly, in French one has to choose between *tu* and *vous*, whereas in English we have only 'you'; and systems of pronouns can vary much more radically than this from our own (Keenan 1978; Catford 1965). It has frequently been argued that where there are such differences exact translation is impossible (Culler 1976, Catford 1965, Keenan 1978); which is not to say that we can't say why it is, or that such structural differences are inevitable.

Now, assuming Quine's theory of stimulus meaning, and his conception of an observation sentence as an occasion sentence that commands community-wide assent/dissent, then it is reasonable to maintain, as Quine does, that the linguist can (i) translate observation sentences, (ii) translate truth-functional connectives, (iii) determine which sentences are stimulus-analytic, and (iv) raise, but not settle, questions of intrasubjective stimulus synonymy of native occasion sentences.

But how, when (i)–(iv) has been done, can the linguist construct a lexicon, and translate non-observation sentences? To the first question Quine's answer is:

He segments heard utterances into conveniently short recurrent parts, and thus compiles a list of native 'words.' Various of these he hypothetically equates to English words and phrases, in such a way as to conform to (i)–(iv). Such are his *analytical hypotheses*, as I call them. (Quine 1960: 68)

Note that analytical hypotheses

exceed anything implicit in any native's dispositions to speech behavior. By bringing out analogies between sentences that have yielded to translation and others they extend the working limits of translation beyond where independent evidence can exist. (Quine 1960: 70)

A famous example of the way in which analytical hypotheses exceed the evidence is described as follows:

Who knows but what the objects to which this term ['gavagai'] applies are not rabbits after all, but mere stages, or brief temporal segments, of rabbits? In either event the stimulus situations that prompt assent to 'Gavagai' would be the same as for 'Rabbit'. Or perhaps the objects to which 'gavagai' applies are all and sundry undetached parts of rabbits; . . . (Quine 1960: 51)

It might seem that differences between these hypotheses would be bound to show up. But Quine argues that that is not so:

If by analytical hypothesis we take 'are the same' as translation of some construction in the jungle language, we may proceed on that basis to question our informant about sameness of gavagais from occasion to occasion and so conclude that gavagais are rabbits and not stages. But if instead we take 'are stages of the same animal' as translation of that jungle construction, we will conclude from the same subsequent questioning of our informant that gavagais are rabbit stages. Both analytical hypotheses may be presumed possible. Both could doubtless be accommodated by compensatory variations in analytical hypotheses concerning other locutions, so as to conform equally to all independently discoverable translations of whole sentences and indeed all speech dispositions of all speakers concerned. (Quine 1960: 72)

However, it has often been pointed out that apart from 'disappointing' examples, such as the translation of *ne . . . rien* into English (Quine 1969: 30), which, incidentally, introduces just the sort of problem to be expected on an holistic theory when one language has more apparent structure than another, Quine gives no detailed example of incompatible translation manuals involving the kind of radical divergences, which would have repercussions throughout the language.[7] Why then should we be confident that it is indeed possible? There is after all a great deal of difference between introducing an *ad hoc* distinction in a particular case, and doing so systematically.

Perhaps one reason for feeling confident that compensatory adjustments always can be made is that we may feel sure that it is possible to give an exhaustive description of what is observable in a portion of space-time, described phenomenologically, by either talking about rabbits or rabbit stages. Note, however, there is no reason to suppose that the two sets of descriptions would differ only by drawing on different lexicons whilst employing the same syntactical devices. For whilst truths about rabbits can be re-expressed as truths about sequences of rabbit stages, a syntax appropriate for set theory is required in the latter case but not the former. Hence unless analytical hypotheses can differ systematically about syntax as well as lexicon, appeal to cases in which there are systematic differences in both is irrelevant. So, as well as 'compensatorily juggling the translation of numerical identity and associated particles' (Quine 1960: 54) is it possible to segment a sentence into as few or many bits as one wishes, devising and imposing syntactical structure?

Certainly, many linguists working within a behaviourist framework in linguistics have tried to show that application of inductive methods gave one determinate surface structure descriptions of utterances (Harris 1960). Moreover, Quine's own account of analogical word learning would seem to assume that surface structure can be learnt inductively: 'Having been directly conditioned to the appropriate use of "Foot" (or "This is my foot") as a

---

[7] The example from Japanese (Quine 1969: 36) raises the question whether the second alternative can be taken generally, so that a classifier can apply to any mass term and a numeral to the result. Presumably it should if the analysis is not *ad hoc*.

sentence, and "Hand" likewise, and "My foot hurts" as a whole, the child might conceivably utter "My hand hurts" on an appropriate occasion, though unaided by previous experience with that actual sentence' (Quine 1960: 9).

However, other passages suggest that Quine does not believe, as some linguists working within a behaviourist framework certainly did, that surface-structure descriptions of syntax are determinate:

in framing his analytical hypotheses the linguist is subject to practical constraints. For he is not, in his finitude, free to assign English sentences to the infinitude of jungle ones in just any way whatever that will fit his supporting evidence; he has to assign them in some way that is manageably systematic with respect to manageably limited set of repeatable speech segments. (Quine 1960: 74)

But the requirement that the linguist should proceed systematically is surely not *just* a practical one. Unless he proceeds systematically he can have no hope of producing a finite description of the native's language with its potential infinity of sentences. Behaviourist learning theory surely must have something to say about the learning of syntax; and the fact that the linguist must proceed systematically itself hardly shows that the behaviourist is mistaken in believing that systematic application of inductive methods will yield determinate results. Moreover, the need to match syntactical distinctions with morphological and phonological ones, let alone with semantical ones, does not lend plausibility to the idea of the radical indeterminacy of surface structure.

However, if descriptions of surface structure are determinate, then it is doubtful whether compensatory juggling with the lexicon will always accommodate non-*ad hoc* alternative translations of 'gavagai'. Suppose a language that on the level of surface structure looks just like English, and whose only difference from English is that it contains the word 'gavagai', but not 'rabbit'. Proceeding rapidly with his translation the linguist sees that he could indeed translate

(5) This is the same gavagai as the one you shot at yesterday, as either (5a) or (5b),

(5a) This is the same rabbit as the one you shot at yesterday,

(5b) This is not the same rabbit stage as the one you shot at yesterday.

But hearing,

(6) Jim and Bill shot at the same gavagai,

uttered in circumstances in which they both shot at the same time at the same rabbit, the linguist would hardly welcome both (6a) and (6b) as alternatives:

(6a) Jim and Bill shot at the same rabbit,
(6b) Jim and Bill shot at a different rabbit stage.

Of course, he could translate the native 'same' by the English word 'same' in (6b) as well as (6a), conjecturing that sometimes it means what we mean by 'same', and sometimes what we mean by 'different'. But if this is compensatory juggling it surely is completely *ad hoc*, and involves further *ad hoc* juggling such as construing the native 'the' as sometimes a definite article, sometimes an indefinite one. The reason why it is *ad hoc* seems clear, *viz.*, that we have a surface structure that accommodates one hypothesis more readily than the other.

So unless syntax is indeterminate, the requirement of system means that the case for *IT* is not proven. Moreover, it is difficult to see how Quine could maintain that syntax is indeterminate whilst, at the same time, giving a behaviourist account of how it is learnt. Recall, in this context, that on Quine's theory there are two sorts of disposition to assent/dissent that are invoked to explain language learning, dispositions to assent to stimulations, and dispositions to respond in certain ways to sentences and other linguistic expressions. This second kind of disposition plays, as we saw, a crucial part in Quine's theory of language learning. But if intralinguistic dispositions are so important, why omit all reference to them in one's account of the data that analytical hypotheses must measure up to? (Papineau 1979: 189). Surely to Quine's list of things (i)–(iv) that the linguist can do relatively unproblematically we must add that the linguist can record (v) dispositions to respond to a given sentence, or linguistic expression, by production of another sentence, or linguistic expression.

Suppose then we have a native sentence which alternative manuals translate into two English sentences which are non-equivalent, in the sense that there are circumstances in which English speakers would assent to the one but not the other. Might it not be that either or both of the manuals has failed to accurately map the set of circumstances in which the natives are disposed to assent to their sentence, on to the set of circumstances in which we are prepared to assent to ours? It is difficult to see how this possibility can be ruled out, since the relevant circumstances include intralinguistic dispositions, and according to (v) these are in principle recordable.[8] But unless this possibility can be ruled out, we would have only competing translations, not a case of indeterminacy.

It could hardly be denied that intralinguistic sentence to sentence connections are important, and, hence, that (v) should be added to the list of things that the linguist can do. Why then should Quine, having insisted on the importance of such connections, fail to stress them when discussing translation? Perhaps because it is difficult to make good behavioural sense of questions such as

(7) Is a Frenchman's disposition to respond to *Bon jour* the same as the Englishman's disposition to respond to 'Good day'?

Since dispositions to respond to sentences are on Quine's account dispositions to respond to sentences of one's own language, interlinguistic comparisons raise very awkward problems indeed.

Anyway, if Quine's theory can yield answers to questions like (7), then the question arises whether divergent translations diverge simply because one of them fails to accord with dispositions of the kind (v), and there is, in principle, a fact of the matter. If, on the other hand, Quine's theory cannot yield an answer to questions like (7), then the theory is surely defective.[9]

The discussion of *IT* to date has not questioned Quine's behaviourism. Given the conclusion of section II about the unsatisfactoriness of the notion of *stimulus meaning*, and the tentative nature of Quine's theory about the learning of sentence to sentence connections, it would be difficult to have confidence in the behaviourist theory of meaning, particularly as it is rooted in what now is generally taken to be a discredited approach to psychology. The implausibility of Quine's behaviourist theory of

---

[8] Of course, in practice, there may be little hope of tracking down divergences.

[9] I am not suggesting that there is an answer to (7) for it is not clear that it is a coherent question. The point is that it has to make sense on Quine's theory if one is to justify the claim that *Bon jour* is responded to by French speakers in a similar way to that in which 'Good day' is by English speakers.

meaning, of course, constitutes the most powerful argument against *IT*. For without the behaviourist theory, one is left without the means of making the crucial link between underdetermination and indeterminacy that is essential to *IT*.

IV

There is another extremely interesting argument, devised by Quine, to show that non-observation sentences do not have separately identifiable meanings. The argument harks back, at least, to Quine (1948), but there is a very clear statement of it in Quine (1970) which I shall follow here (see also Quine 1969).

Quine's argument first claims that the Verification Theory identifies 'the proposition or meaning of a sentence with the information conveyed' (Quine 1970: 5). But, however we understand sensory evidence, there is, Quine argues, a problem in distributing it over separate sentences, and it is at this point that he produces his Duhemian argument:

Suppose an experiment has yielded a result contrary to a theory currently held in some natural science. The theory comprises a whole bundle of conjoint hypotheses, or is resoluble into such a bundle. The most that the experiment shows is that at least one of the hypotheses is false; it does not show which. It is only the theory as a whole, and not any one of the hypotheses, that admits of evidence or counter-evidence in observation and experiment. (Quine 1970: 5)

Quine concedes that an exception can be made for observation sentences because they are individually responsive to observation. But most sentences are not observation sentences, and are learnt 'contextually in ways that generate a fabric of sentences, complexly interconnected' (Quine 1970: 6). The Duhemian argument applies to these sentences. In a later paper Quine sums up the two-stage argument thus:

If we recognize with Peirce that the meaning of a sentence turns purely on what could count as evidence for its truth, and if we recognize with Duhem that theoretical sentences have their evidence not as single sentences but only as larger blocks of theory, then the indeterminacy of translation of theoretical sentences is the natural conclusion. And most sentences, apart from observation sentences, are theoretical. This conclusion, conversely, once it is embraced, seals the fate of any general notion of propositional meaning or, for that matter, state of affairs. (Quine 1971: 80)

If this argument is to apply to the non-observation sentences of everyday life, it is necessary for at least some of them to be on a par with theoretical sentences; but, as the passage quoted makes clear, Quine would be happy with that conclusion.

This argument does not depend on Quine's behavioural theory of meaning, and so reservations about the latter do not affect it. Moreover, the Duhemian argument seems incontrovertible. We do not test hypotheses on their own, but always assume other hypotheses, and make assumptions about initial conditions. So because no observational sentence O is a consequence of a single hypothesis H on its own, we cannot infer $\sim H$ from $\sim O$. This argument is all that Quine needs to scotch the idea of there being a one-to-one correlation between theoretical sentences and the observable states of affairs that confirm/infirm them. Hence, if the Verification Theory really is committed to the existence of such correlations it has been effectively disposed of.

It is true, I believe, that at times Quine may have drawn stronger conclusions from the Duhemian argument than are warranted. For instance, his contention that any sentence may be held true come what may perhaps claims that if a theory containing H implies O, when what is observed is that $\sim O$, then we can always find non-*ad hoc* subsidiary hypotheses which together with H imply $\sim O$; and it might well be questioned whether this is so. But even if Quine is wrong about this, his use of the Duhemian argument to attack the Verification Theory remains unscathed.

It may also be true that sometimes we can

find which hypothesis is responsible for the refutation; or in other words, which part, or group of hypotheses, was necessary for the derivation of the refuted prediction. The fact that such logical dependencies may be discovered is established by the practice of *independence proofs* of axiomatised systems; proofs which show that certain axioms of an axiomatic system cannot be derived from the rest. The more simple of these proofs consist in the construction, or rather in the discovery, of a *model* – a set of things, relations, operations, or functions – which satisfies all the axioms except the *one* whose independence is to be shown: for this one axiom – and therefore for the theory as a whole – the model constitutes a counter example. (Popper 1963: 239)

But this would not show how to pair sets of observations with an individual hypothesis H; at most it shows that there is no connection between H and O, and therefore what is observationally irrelevant to H. Nor would the fact that H was strongly confirmed by O

enable one to uniquely correlate H with O, unless the establishment of a confirming instance of H involved no other assumptions.

It seems that there is no hope of showing that it is possible to pair hypotheses one-to-one with sets of observation sentences. The only response that remains to Quine's argument, therefore, is to question the conclusions he draws from it.

To begin with the derivation of semantic holism, understanding by this the thesis that the meanings of *all* sentences are interconnected, from the Duhemian argument seems to be tenuous.[10] The Duhemian argument shows that theoretical sentences have to be tested in blocks. But that does not show that any such sentence is connected with every other. Quine briefly discusses this point:

> [The scientist's] experiment is prompted by suspicion of one hypothesis, yes; and if the test proves negative he is resolved to reject that hypothesis, but not quite it alone. Along with it he will reject also any which, as he says, imply it. I must not myself now lean on a notion of implication, for I am challenging that notion (or the associated notion of equivalence, which is simply mutual implication). But we do have to recognize that sentences are interconnected by means of associations entrenched in behavior. There are the complex interconnections lately remarked upon: connections of varying strengths that incline us to affirm or deny some sentences when affirming or denying others. Whoever rejects one hypothesis will be led by these habit patterns to reject other sentences with it. (Quine 1970: 7)

But, though this is true, it simply reminds us that, as well as the theory being tested, various background theories are assumed, which is not disputed. But this does not show that *all* sentences belong to one theory. Nor does it seem that all grasp of the idea of individual contribution to the 'meaning' of a theory is lost if we can make sense of the question whether a given hypothesis is independent of the others, or, indeed, of whether its addition to other hypotheses would lead to interesting new predictions. So it may be that what is wrong is not the idea of correlating sentences with something in order to explicate their meaning, but the idea of correlating them directly with sets of observation sentences.

In this connection it is interesting to observe that one of the more systematic attempts to formulate a version of the Verification Theory, that of Schlick, was sensitive to the Duhemian

[10] This is not to say that semantic holism is mistaken; merely that the derivation of a strong form of it from the Duhemian argument is unpersuasive.

considerations adduced by Quine. In spite of this Schlick remained a verificationist. In an early paper he wrote:

Now in the practice of science and life the processes never go on so simply as we have schematically assumed here; into every actual process of verification there always enters an extraordinary number of factual judgements and conceptual propositions in motley confusion, and if the number of verifications were not so great and the mutual combinations of judgements not so manifold, we should never arrive at the high probability inherent, for example, in the judgements that articulate well-founded laws of nature or historical facts. (Schlick 1910: 86)

And he still maintained this much later at a time when he was vigorously defending the Verification Theory:

It is perfectly true that every statement about a physical object or event says *more* than is verified, say, by the once-and-for-all occurrence of an experience. It is presupposed, rather, that this experience took place under quite specific conditions, whose fulfilment can, of course, be tested in turn only by something given; and it is further presupposed that still other and further verifications (after-tests, confirmations) are always possible, which themselves of course reduce to manifestations of some kind in the given. (Schlick 1932: 268)

This means that Schlick could not possibly have subscribed to the view that it is possible to correlate sentences one-by-one with observable states of affairs.

The way in which Schlick's theory was a verification theory was more subtle than this. His theory was essentially a truth condition theory of meaning constrained by three conditions: (i) that the truth conditions must specify logically possible states of affairs; (ii) that a sentence's truth conditions be specifiable on the basis of the contributions made by its constituents; and (iii) that these should, in turn, be explicable by exhibiting circumstances in which sentences containing them are in fact verifiable.[11] What makes the theory a verification theory is thus a constraint on the way in which the meanings of sentence constituents are acquired, not a constraint on the way in which sentences have to be related one-by-one to sets of observation sentences.

Schlick's theory is admittedly sketchy, but it suggests a way of accepting Quine's Duhemian argument without accepting the further conclusion that the meanings of non-occasion sentences are not separately identifiable. For we can, on the one hand,

[11] I have defended this at greater length (Holdcroft 1983).

maintain with Schlick that to specify the meaning of a sentence is to specify its truth conditions, and, on the other hand, agree with Quine, Duhem and Schlick, that a conjecture that a sentence's truth conditions actually obtain inevitably involves assumptions about the truth of other sentences.

It would be very surprising if the Duhemian argument showed that one could not systematically attribute truth conditions to non-observation sentences. And if one could, then such sentences would have separately identifiable truth conditions, not, indeed, in the sense that a theory stipulating a sentence's truth conditions was a theory about just that sentence, but in the sense that the theory stipulated a distinct set of truth conditions to that sentence.

Indeed, if the Duhemian argument showed that it was not possible systematically to attribute truth conditions to non-observation sentences, then it presumably would show that it is not possible systematically to ascribe to non-observation sentences any conditions whatsoever which specified their meaning, or could be used to interpret them, etc. Thus the argument would not only undermine the concept of a proposition, but it would also show that it is not possible to systematically ascribe to sentences sets of conditions which specify their meaning. That would indeed be a radical conclusion.

REFERENCES

Cartwright, R. 1962. 'Propositions', in *Analytical Philosophy*, ed. R. J. Butler, Oxford: Basil Blackwell.

Catford, J. C. 1965. *A Linguistic Theory of Translation*, London: Oxford University Press.

Culler, J. 1976. *Saussure*, London: Fontana/Collins.

Davis, Steven 1976. *Philosophy and Language*, Indianapolis: Bobbs–Merril.

Dummett, M. 1974. 'On the Significance of Quine's Indeterminacy Thesis', *Synthese* 27: 351–97.

Gregory, R. 1966. *Eye and Brain*, London: Weidenfeld and Nicolson.

Harris, Z. S. 1960. *Structural Linguistics*, Chicago: Chicago University Press.

Hintikka, J. 1968. 'Behavioural Criteria of Radical Translation', *Synthese* 19: 69–81.

Holdcroft, David 1983. 'Schlick and the Verification Theory of Meaning', *Revue Internationale de Philosophie*, 37: 47–68.

Keenan, E. 1978. 'Some Logical Problems in Translation', in *Meaning and Translation*, eds. F. Guenthner and M. Guenthner-Reutter, London: Duckworth.

Moore, G. E. 1925. 'A Defence of Common Sense', in *Contemporary British Philosophy*, ed. J. H. Muirhead, (2nd series), London: Allen and Unwin.

Papineau, David 1979. *Theory and Meaning*, Oxford: Clarendon Press.

Pollock, John L. 1982. *Language and Thought*, Princeton: Princeton University Press.

Popper, K. R. 1963. *Conjectures and Refutations*, London: Routledge and Kegan Paul.

Quine, W. V. O. 1948. 'On what there is', *Revue of Metaphysics*. Reprinted in *From a Logical Point of View*, New York, Harper and Row, 1953, pp. 1–19.

1960. *Word and Object*, New York: John Wiley.

1968. 'Replies', *Synthese* 19: 264.

1969. *Ontological Relativity and Other Essays*: New York: Columbia University Press.

1970. *Philosophy of Logic*, Englewood Cliffs: Prentice Hall.

1973. *The Roots of Reference*, La Salle, Illinois: Open Court.

1979. 'Facts of the Matter', in *Essays on the Philosophy of Quine*, eds. R. W. Shahan and Ch. Swoyer, Hassocks: Harvester Press.

Schlick, M. 1910. 'The Nature of Truth in Modern Logic', in *Philosophical Papers*, eds. Henk L. Mulder and Barbara F. B. Van der Velde Schlick, vol. I, 1979, Dordrecht, Reidel.

1932. 'Positivism and Realism', *Philosophical Papers*, eds. Mulder and Schlick, vol. II.

Urmson, J. O. 1950. 'On Grading', *Mind* 59: 145–69.

8   *Names, identity and necessity*

PETER SMITH

I

In *Philosophical Subjects*, Strawson writes in reply to L. J. Cohen:

> Given his general approach, one might have supposed that his view as to
> the semantic contribution made to an utterance by a proper name which,
> in that utterance, designates a particular individual, would be simply that
> and no more: i.e. that the name (non-connotatively) designates that
> particular individual. On this view, the truth-grounds of the utterance, *as
> far as the name is concerned*, turn simply on the denotation which the name
> actually has in that utterance, i.e. on the identity of the individual
> denoted. But from this it follows immediately that a statement in which
> the *same* individual is twice over designated, the two names being
> coupled by the identity-predicate, could not but be true; and that a
> statement in which two different individuals are designated by name, the
> two names being coupled by the identity-predicate, could not but be
> false. For, given the nature of the predicate in such a case (the
> identity-predicate), what fixes the truth-grounds of the statement fixes
> also its truth-value. So the non-contingency of such statements, which
> Cohen denies, is immediately guaranteed (Strawson 1980: 288).

The semantic account of proper names which Strawson here
attributes to Cohen might be characterised as the theory that
names function as mere tags for their referents. On this theory, all
that is required in order to give the significance of a name is a
statement of what, if anything, the name refers to. However,
Strawson does not in fact appeal to this semantic account of names
in its full generality: on the contrary, his argument seems clearly
to require only the supposition that names function as tags *in
identity statements*. It is this, together with an uncontentious
assumption about the significance of the identity-predicate, which
is supposed to entail that a proposition such as the proposition that

Hesperus is Phosphorus is 'non-contingent' – by which, I take it, Strawson means that the proposition is necessarily true if true and necessarily false if false.

But it is surely quite clear that the non-contingency claim *cannot* be inferred in this way from the thesis that names function as tags in identity statements. For a start, note that a counterpart-theoretic treatment of modality is entirely compatible with the restricted tag theory and with the uncontentious assumption that an (unmodalised) identity statement is true just when the singular terms flanking the identity-predicate have the same referent. Yet counterpart theory falsifies the non-contingency claim. For according to Lewis' translation scheme (augmented in the obvious way to incorporate names) the truth-conditions of a claim of the form

(1) $\Box(h = p)$

are given by

(2) $(\forall w)(\forall x)(\forall y)((x$ is a counterpart of h in w
$\qquad\qquad$ & y is a counterpart of p in $w) \supset x = y)$,

where '$\forall w$' is a quantifier over possible worlds and the other quantifiers run over all objects in all worlds (Lewis 1968). If we follow Lewis in *not* requiring the counterpart relation to be one–one, then even if

(3) $h = p$

is true, (2) will still be false and hence (1) must be rejected. Evidently there is nothing here which conflicts with the supposition that 'h' and 'p' function as tags in (3). Further, the names can be functioning as tags in (2) as well, and so (on the counterpart treatment of modality) we will require no *ad hoc* augmentation of the tag theory of names in order to account for their particular role in sentences like (1).

I hasten to add that I hold no special brief for counterpart theory. To begin with, there are familiar grounds for thinking that its characteristic quantifications over possible worlds and over a domain containing non-actual objects commit us to a quite unwelcome degree of ontological inflation. In addition, Feldman and others have drawn attention to problems with Lewis' elucidations of the counterpart relation in terms of cross-world similarity

(Feldman 1971; Hazen 1979). And waiving these rather general difficulties, we might note that the counterpart theory which falsifies (1) apparently also falsifies

(4) $\Box(h = h)$,

for the obvious translation scheme renders (4) analogously to (1), just substituting '*h*' for '*p*' in (2), and hence delivering a falsehood. This consequence of counterpart theory initially looks quite absurd; but perhaps this is not an insurmountable problem. With a modicum of ingenuity we can recast the translation scheme for modal statements involving names so that (1) is still falsified but (4) is not. Or, to adopt a rather more principled approach, we could retain the original translation scheme but shift our attention to a slightly richer language which not only contains a two-place identity-predicate '*I*' but also operators on predicates including the reflection operator 'Ref', which turns a two-place relation '*R*' into a one-place predicate 'Ref *R*' such that 'Ref *Rx*' is satisfied just when '*Rxx*' is (cf. Quine 1960). Then, although counterpart theory does not sustain

(4') $\Box Ihh$,

it does give us

(5) $\Box$Ref *Ih*,

for the latter is equivalent to

(6) $(\forall w)(\forall x)(x$ is a counterpart of h in $w \supset$ Ref $Ix)$

which must be true. And the militant counterpart theorist could now insist that it is (5) which properly captures our very strong intuition of the necessity of self-identity, and that once (5) is distinguished from (4'), or equivalently (4), the falsity of the latter can be tolerated (cf. Forbes 1983: 152). Perhaps this retort is none too convincing: but like the more general difficulties with counterpart theory which we mentioned before, the issues here quite obviously cannot be resolved simply by rehearsing the claim that proper names like '*h*' and '*p*' function as tags in identity statements. In summary then, adherence to the restricted tag theory is not enough by itself to rule out counterpart theory, and hence cannot be enough to underwrite the claim that if Hesperus is Phosphorus then this is necessarily so.

The non-contingency thesis can also be challenged without such a direct appeal to the dubious charms of counterpart theory. Suppose, following Noonan, we introduce the term 'puss' to denote that bodily part of a cat which consists of a cat minus its tail (Noonan 1980: 22). Then pusses can be individuated, counted and re-identified through time; and there would therefore seem to be nothing to bar us from introducing proper names for pusses. Thus we might bestow the name 'Tib' on the puss which is currently a proper part of Tibbles. Tib is evidently not identical with Tibbles: but it seems that she might have been – for Tibbles could have lost her tail and thus been indistinguishable from Tib. Or we could have had the converse situation; that is, Tib's now being identical with the tail-less Tibbles, although she might not have been because Tibbles could have kept her tail. Thus we seem to have here some direct counterexamples to the non-contingency thesis.

But there are problems. For consider the case where Tibbles once had a tail but has now lost it. Then, in pursuing the line of reasoning above, it appears that we are committed to saying

(7) Tibbles once had a tail as a proper part,

(8) Tib is Tibbles

and

(9) Tib, being a puss, never had a tail as a proper part,

and as it stands this offends against Leibniz's Law. One radical solution would be to adopt a Quinean four-dimensional conception of continuants. Then, since there are temporal stages of Tibbles which are not temporal stages of Tib, we can in this case reject (8), strictly interpreted. But, given this conception of continuants, it seems that we can *still* construct counterexamples to the non-contingency thesis. For suppose Tib, treated as a 'space-time worm', is identical with Tibbles; that is, suppose Tibbles never had a tail. It still apparently makes sense to suppose that Tibbles might have had a tail, and then Tib would not have been identical with Tibbles. And conversely, suppose Tib (treated in the same four-dimensional way) is not identical with Tibbles because the latter has some tailed stages: it still seems to make sense to suppose that Tib might have been identical with Tibbles. Further, all this seems quite compatible with the thesis that 'Tib'

and 'Tibbles' function as tags in (unmodalised) identity statements, and with the agreed uncontentious supposition about the
significance of the identity-predicate.

Now again I should hasten to add that I am not an enthusiast for
this sort of argument against the non-contingency thesis. We
might well dispute the four-dimensional conception of continuants latterly invoked. It might perhaps also be argued that there is
a confusion lurking hereabouts between the 'is' of identity and the
'is' of constitution. But what is absolutely clear, without going
into further details, is that the complex issues at stake could not be
settled one way or the other simply by insisting that 'Tib' and
'Tibbles' function as tags in non-modal identity statements. In
other words, adherence to the restricted tag theory of names is
certainly not enough to rule out of court the Tib/Tibbles argument, and hence cannot be enough to secure the non-contingency
thesis.

It is perhaps worth adding one final argument against Strawson,
a variant on the 'ship of Theseus' problem, if only to reinforce the
point that a full defence or critique of the non-contingency thesis
will require an investigation of a tangled web of problems.
Suppose that at time t_1 I tag a particular organism 'h'; and then later
I bestow the tag 'p' on an organism I encounter at time t_2. It turns
out that in fact $h = p$. For this to be the case, it is of course not
necessary that the matter which constitutes h at t_1 is still all to be
found in p (that is, h) at t_2. Indeed, we might suppose that it is
possible in principle for there to be *no* particle of matter in p at t_2
which was contained in h at t_1. But if this is right, there could
apparently be a possible world which diverges from ours after t_1 in
the following way: the later history of h is quite different from that
which obtains in the actual world – in particular, h comes to
consist of matter quite other than that which is involved in h's
actual history. Meanwhile, the material which in the actual world
does constitute p at t_2, though not absorbed into h during its
history, still comes to form an organism which is a particle for
particle replica of p as it is in the actual world for a period around
the time t_2. This is shown diagrammatically in figure 1. The lines
represent the continuity through time of a particular organism.
Now, what are we to say concerning the identity of the second
organism present at time t_2 in the alternative world, the one which
ex hypothesi isn't h? Well, it is constituted of just the same stuff in

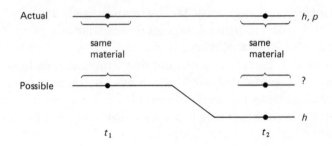

Figure 1

just the same arrangement as the thing dubbed '*p*' in the actual world. So, if we eschew a four-dimensional ontology and allow that an object when present is present in all its parts, why not say that the second organism just is *p* again? But this would mean that, although *h* is actually *p*, it is not necessarily true that *h* is *p* (cf. Nozick 1981: 33–4, 656–9).

Conversely, imagine a world where at t_1 we tag an organism '*h*', and this is later destroyed. Later still, out of new material an organism of the same type is created which is tagged '*p*' at time t_2. Certainly, *h* is not identical with *p*. But it seems that it might have been: for *h*, instead of being destroyed, could have developed into an organism which at t_2 is of the same type and constituted of just the same material, similarly arranged, as *p* in the actual world. So apparently, even if it is false that *h* is *p* in the actual world, this is not necessarily false.

Once more, I need hardly add, I am not positively endorsing this argument against the non-contingency thesis. Obviously it raises complex issues about diachronic identity, about the extent to which (features of) an object's history are essential to its identity, about the pressures towards a Quinean four-dimensional ontology, and so on. But equally clearly these issues cannot be settled by appeal to the idea that names like '*h*' and '*p*' function as tags in identity statements, for *that* was built into the story from the start. So again we see that adherence to the tag theory of names still leaves the acceptability of the non-contingency thesis an open question.

II

Evidently, something is badly amiss with the claim that the non-contingency thesis simply *follows* from the restricted tag theory of names: it is perhaps instructive to see exactly where Strawson has gone wrong.

First, it will be worth trying to give a sharper formulation of the tag theory. So let's begin by examining the suggestion that 'the truth-grounds [of an utterance containing a proper name], as far as the name is concerned, turn simply on the denotation which the name actually has'. The leading idea, presumably, is that the contribution that the presence of a name makes to determining the truth-conditions of a sentence which contains it is that the name locates a particular object on whose properties the truth of the sentence as a whole depends. Now, for present purposes, we may follow convention and abstract from the possibility of ambiguous names which can be used to refer to different individuals in different contexts of use (Kripke 1980: 8–10). With this idealisation, then, Strawson's remark suggests the following thesis:

> If t is a name, then there is an object o (its denotation) such that the truth-condition of any sentence of the form $\mathcal{A}(t)$ is just that o satisfies the condition expressed by $\mathcal{A}(\xi)$.

But this, as it stands, rules out the possibility of vacuous names, for it correlates a denotation with each name. It would seem to be an improvement, therefore, to restrict the thesis so that it no longer applies to a putative name t where $\ulcorner t$ exists$\urcorner$ is false. In other words,

> If t is a name and $\ulcorner(\exists x)(x = t)\urcorner$ is true, then there is an object o such that the truth-condition of a sentence of the form $\mathcal{A}(t)$ is just that o satisfies the condition expressed by $\mathcal{A}(\xi)$.

The notion of a truth-condition deployed here is, however, far from transparent: the obvious way of elucidating it is via the now familiar notion of a truth theory for a language (Peacocke 1975). The suggestion would be that some adequate truth theory for a language L should guarantee that, where t is a non-vacuous name, there is an object o such that just that object must satisfy a certain condition if any given sentence containing a direct, non-quotational occurrence of t is to be true. More formally,

> If t is a name, there will be an adequate truth theory θ for L such that for any direct context $\mathcal{A}(\xi)$ we have

(D) True $(\ulcorner(\exists x)(x = t)\urcorner) \vdash_\theta (\exists o) (\text{True } (\mathscr{A}(t)) \equiv \langle o \rangle \text{ sats } \mathscr{A}(\xi))$

where '$\vdash_\theta$' signifies provability in θ.

However, as Peacocke has in effect pointed out, this condition does not even distinguish names from Russellian descriptions. For suppose t is such a description, for example, '$(\imath y)\ Fy$': then it is easily checked that – so long as the truth theory can deliver correct biconditionals for the Russellian expansions of sentences involving '$(\imath y)\ Fy$' – we will get (D) at least when the description is given wide scope. Hence the condition on names developed above does not even rule out the thesis that names are disguised descriptions marked as having wide scope; so it evidently fails to articulate a conception of names as distinctively *non*-descriptive.

To put the point more briefly and informally: the idea that the 'truth-grounds [of an utterance containing a name] . . . turn simply on the denotation' of the name fails to distinguish proper names from other kinds of expression which also purport to locate a particular object whose properties are peculiarly relevant to the truth or falsity of the whole utterance in which they occur. Thus, in so far as Strawson is trying to capture a view of names which contrasts them with dispositions, his quoted remark stands in clear need of supplementation. But Strawson's only other characterisation of the view of names he is discussing is this: 'the semantic contribution made to an utterance by a proper name which, in that utterance, designates a particular individual, [is] simply that and no more: i.e. that the name (non-connotatively) designates that particular individual'. All the additional work here is being done by the parenthetical 'non-connotatively': yet it is precisely the content of this which a non-descriptive theory of names surely needs to elucidate.

Still, it is perhaps plain enough how Strawson's over-brisk sketch of a view needs to be developed. For contrast two of the ways in which a term t might satisfy the condition (D). One possibility is that the evaluation rules of truth theory θ treat t as descriptive in the sense that they correlate t with a certain predicate; the rules then determine how the truth-condition of $\mathscr{A}(t)$ depends on the satisfaction-conditions of both $\mathscr{A}(\xi)$ and the predicate correlated with t, and do this in such a way that (D) is guaranteed. A second, quite different, possibility is that the evaluation rules are such that *either* we have

$\vdash_\theta \sim$ True $(\ulcorner (\exists x)(x = t) \urcorner)$

or θ delivers something of the form

(D') True $(\mathcal{A}(t)) \equiv \langle a \rangle$ sats $\mathcal{A}(\xi)$,

where 'a' is a metalinguistic name. If the resources of θ include classical logic, then (D) will clearly follow either way. This possibility will be realised if θ either does not evaluate t at all (giving us the first disjunct when the technicalities are right), or assigns an object to t by means of an axiom of the form 't denotes a' which combines with the rules governing the satisfaction relation in standard ways to prove (D'). Now evidently, if t is a Russellian description marked for wide scope, it will satisfy (D) in virtue of being amenable to the first style of truth-theoretic treatment. By contrast, it is plausible to suggest that names as a class are to be treated in the second style, so that the semantic contribution of a (non-vacuous) name in L can be given by a truth-theoretic axiom that just states the denotation of the name. Strawson's remarks can reasonably be interpreted as directed towards this sort of semantic treatment of names.

A more complex truth-theoretic semantics for names might take the form of having *two* axioms governing each name, where the first assigns as denotation the object which the name is (intuitively speaking) used to pick out, and the second assigns – not necessarily as an alternative denotation – some other kind of thing, for example, a Carnapian intension. The theory would then specify, for any style of context in which a name appears, which of the axioms governing the name is to be invoked in order to evaluate the resulting sentence. In the class of contexts with respect to which the truth theory directs that we appeal to the first kind of axiom, we might say that the name there functions as a mere tag. We can in this sort of way make formal sense of what I earlier called the *restricted* tag theory of names, that is, the claim that names function as tags at least in (unmodalised) identity statements.

Our problem now is to understand why Strawson holds that the (restricted) tag theory entails the thesis that a proposition such as the proposition that Hesperus is Phosphorus is non-contingent. Strawson's reasoning is encapsulated in his claim that on the tag theory 'what fixes the truth-grounds of [a statement consisting of two names coupled by the identity-predicate] fixes also its truth-value [so] the non-contingency of such statements is immediately guaranteed'. This suggests the following argument: On the tag theory, the significance of the names, 'Hesperus' and 'Phosphorus' is determined by giving their respective denotations. Suppose that these denotations are the same; suppose, for example, that both names denote Venus. Then, on an obvious assumption about the significance of the identity-predicate, it will follow from the truth theory that 'Hesperus is Phosphorus' is true just if the denotation of 'Hesperus' is identical to the denotation of 'Phosphorus', that is, just if Venus is Venus. But this latter identity is logically guaranteed, so the truth theory guarantees that 'Hesperus is Phosphorus' is true: in other words, it is in this case necessarily true that Hesperus is Phosphorus. Suppose alternatively that the denotations of the two names are distinct: then the truth theory will state that 'Hesperus is Phosphorus' is true just so long as two non-identical objects are identical. But the latter is logically ruled out, so the truth theory here guarantees that 'Hesperus is Phosphorus' is false; in other words, it is in this case necessarily false that Hesperus is Phosphorus. In short, the claim that Hesperus is Phosphorus is necessarily true if true and necessarily false if false. (Note that this argument uses only the assumption that *in identity statements* the significance of a name is determined by its denotation: hence my earlier claims that Strawson in effect needs only the restricted tag theory of names.)

This argument, however, involves at least two bad mistakes. The first of those is slightly more easily seen if we start by considering the leg of the argument which deals with the situation where 'Hesperus' and 'Phosphorus' have distinct denotations. On the tag theory, the axioms of the truth theory governing the two names will have the form

> 'Hesperus' denotes α
> 'Phosphorus' denotes β,

where 'α' and 'β' stand in for singular terms of the theory. From these axioms, together with the obvious evaluation rule for the identity predicate, we will be able to prove in the theory a biconditional of the form

> (T) True ('Hesperus is Phosphorus') $\equiv$ α is β.

Now, from (T) and a supplementary premiss of the form 'α is *not*

β' – which indicates that the names have distinct denotations – it certainly follows that 'Hesperus is Phosphorus' is false. But this goes no way towards showing that, in Strawson's words, what fixes the truth-grounds here also fixes the truth-value. The truth-grounds of 'Hesperus is Phosphorus' are fixed by the truth theory alone; on the other hand, there is no reason at all to suppose that an adequate truth theory need have the resources to prove the supplementary premiss of the form 'α is not β' which is used to fix the truth-value. We must distinguish the claim (a) that, when two names pick out different things, an adequate truth theory will assign what are in fact different denotations to the names, from the claim (b) that, when two names have different denotations, their divergence in denotation must itself be provable within the truth theory. There are no grounds for accepting (b): it is not for *semantic* theory to speak to the issue whether the names 'Shakespeare' and 'Bacon', for example, have distinct denotations. And yet this is what the argument I gave in amplification of Strawson evidently requires. For it is only if the truth theory itself, so to speak, sees the names in question as having divergent denotations that it will be in a position to prove that 'Hesperus is Phosphorus' is true just if two non–identical objects (those divergent denotations) are identical, and thus prove the sentence to be false.

Consider now the other leg of the argument, which deals with the situation where 'Hesperus' and 'Phosphorus' have the same denotation. Given the tag theory, the semantics will again deliver a biconditional of the form (T); and in order to fix the truth-value of 'Hesperus is Phosphorus' we will again normally need a supplementary premiss, this time of the form 'α is β'. And this additional premiss, as before, will be unprovable within the truth theory itself – unless we have the special case where the truth theory actually employs the *same* singular term in place of both 'α' and 'β'. Thus if the truth-theoretic axioms are, for example,

(10) 'Hesperus' denotes Venus
      'Phosphorus' denotes Venus

then we will be able to prove

(11) True ('Hesperus is Phosphorus') $\equiv$ Venus is Venus

and, assuming the resources of the theory encompass first-order logic, we will now be able to deduce the truth-value of 'Hesperus is Phosphorus' from the truth theory itself. So, in this particular case, it will be true that what fixes the truth-grounds also fixes the truth-value. However, it should be noted that this will not hold in general. For we must again distinguish between the claim (a') that when two names in fact pick out the same thing an adequate truth theory will assign the same object as denotation to each name, and the claim (b') that, when two names have the same denotation, the fact that their denotations coincide must itself be provable within the truth theory. It is not an *a priori* requirement on the adequacy of a theory that it satisfy (b'). So, in summary, Strawson is quite wrong to suggest that on the tag theory of names what fixes the truth-grounds of a statement like 'Hesperus is Phosphorus' must inevitably also fix its truth-value.

Further it is arguable – though this raises some contentious issues – that the one case which runs in Strawson's favour, where a truth theory satisfies (b') by explicitly assigning the same denotation to two different names, should in fact be positively avoided. For a truth theory should arguably aim at being interpretative in the sense that the biconditionals of the form 'True $(s) \equiv p$' which it proves should be such that a serious, sincere utterance of the sentence mentioned on the left of a biconditional is interpretable as an expression of a belief whose content is given by the sentence used on the right (McDowell 1977). But a truth theory which employs axiom pairs such as (10), and hence can prove the like of 'Hesperus is Phosphorus', will deliver pairs of biconditionals like

(12) True ('Hesperus moves') $\equiv$ Venus moves
      True ('Phosphorus moves') $\equiv$ Venus moves.

And such pairs should in general *not* feature in a theory which is ideally interpretative – for it just is not normally the case that a pair of co-designative names can be used quite interchangeably without altering the belief which the speaker is best understood as expressing. So, we must in general *not* treat co-designative names in the manner of (10); and thus the provability of the truth of statements like 'Hesperus is Phosphorus' within the truth theory will typically be positively blocked.

Even if we waive this last point, Strawson's first mistake is bad enough: but he compounds the error with a worse one. Suppose, for example that it *is* semantically determined that 'Hesperus is Phosphorus' is true: then, *pace* Strawson, it simply does not follow that the proposition that Hesperus is Phosphorus is necessary. Again, suppose our semantic theory did entail that 'Hesperus is Phosphorus' is false: it likewise would not follow that the proposition that Hesperus is not Phosphorus is necessary. In other words, even if our preferred truth theory which fixes the truth-grounds of the sentence 'Hesperus is Phosphorus' also fixed its truth-value, it still would not necessarily follow that the proposition which the sentence expresses is non-contingent.

The crucial general point here – namely that there is a logical gap between a sentence's being semantically determined to be true and the proposition it expresses being necessary – is made trenchantly by Lewy (1976), who considers as an example the sentence

(13) 'Female fox' means female fox.

Lewy argues that it is quite certain that the proposition expressed by this sentence is contingent; for the phrase 'female fox' might have meant in English something quite different from what it actually does mean. He adds (with trivial changes to numbering and quotational conventions):

Of course, if we state the meaning of the English word 'means', and assume that the sentence (13) is in accordance with the syntax of English, that ''female fox'' is a name of 'female fox' and that 'female fox' has *some* meaning in English, then it will follow that the *sentence* (13), as a sentence of English, always expresses a true proposition. But from this it does *not* follow, and it is *not* true, that the *proposition* (13) is logically necessary .... We must therefore distinguish between saying that a proposition is necessary and that a sentence always expresses a true proposition. From the latter the former does not follow. And notice in particular that although we can deduce that the *sentence* (13) expresses a true proposition from premises which are solely about the English language, it does *not* follow from these premises that the *proposition* (13) is logically necessary (Lewy 1976: 12).

This is, I think, exactly right. And we can make a similar point in our truth-theoretic idiom with respect to sentences like

(14) 'Plato' denotes Plato

or

(15) Something satisfies 'ξ smokes' if and only if it smokes.

To take the first of these examples: if we can deal with the two-place predicate 'denotes' in our truth theory θ, and we assume that "Plato" picks out the name 'Plato', and that 'Plato' is not an empty name, then we will be able to derive as a theorem of θ,

(16) True ("'Plato' denotes Plato') $\equiv$ 'Plato' denotes Plato.

But, given the tag theory of names together with our assumption that 'Plato' is not vacuous, the right-hand side of this is itself a truth-theoretic axiom. Hence, in this case, we have

(17) $\vdash_\theta$ True ("'Plato' denotes Plato').

In other words, (14) is semantically determined to be true. But it obviously expresses a contingent proposition: for that expression 'Plato' might in fact not have denoted the person whom it actually denotes.

It might be objected against this type of argument that semantic claims such as (13) or (14) do after all express necessary truths. The suggestion would be that (14), for example, is properly to be understood as

(14') 'Plato' denotes Plato *in English*

and that this can now be seen to register a *necessary* truth about the English language, since any language in which 'Plato' had a different denotation would not be English. It is, of course, contingent that any particular group speaks English, when that language is defined by the set of its semantic rules; in particular, it is on this view contingent that the English, identified as the inhabitants of a certain region, speak English. However, the basic semantic truth expressed by (14') is, it is claimed, non-contingent.

This objection, despite its recent popularity (Peacocke 1978: 477–8; Davies 1981: 190), seems essentially to be based on a confusion between genuine semantic relations and the set-theoretic constructions discussed by logicians and model theorists. Suppose we begin with a set of objects V and rules for constructing the set S of permissible sequences of elements of V. We may then define a set T by giving axioms, one for each element of V, and suitable derivation rules such that for every sequence s in S we can derive a canonical biconditional of the form

$$s \in T \equiv p$$

where '*p*' holds the place of a sentence of English (which is free from the set-theoretic terms involved in the axioms). So far, of course, all this has not the slightest semantic significance. Imagine now that we call the whole set-theoretic construction 'language *L*', dub *V* the 'vocabulary' of *L*, and call the elements of *S* its 'sentences', and suppose too that we write '*s* is TRUE in *L*' instead of '*s* ∈ *T*'. This still will have no genuine semantic import. For clearly, what injects semantic significance into this kind of set-theoretic construction cannot be a mere change of nomenclature but can only be the supposition that the construction in some sense represents aspects of the actual communicative practice of a speech community. So let us say that the formal language *L* models the actual language of speech community *C* if there is a map *M* (possibly the identity map) from the vocabulary of the language in *C* onto *V* which induces a map *M** from the set of sentences of that language onto *S* such that (roughly) speakers in *C* standardly use a sentence *r* in such a way that their sincere utterances of *r* count as expressing the belief that *p* just when we can derive in *L* the associated biconditional, $M^{\star}(r) \in T \equiv p$.

Now let us suppose further that some elements of *V*, for example *n*, are governed by axioms of *L* with the form

$$\langle n, o \rangle \in D$$

where *o* holds the place of an English designator: and let us also take it that such axioms interact with other axioms within the total construction in such a way as to encourage us to rewrite them in the style '*n* DENOTES *o* in *L*' (this structural role for *D* can be formally described in familiar ways). Again, this constructional detail of *L* has in itself no semantic significance; it only takes on genuine semantic colour if we assume that *L* models the actual language of a particular community *C*. Then we will indeed have the following:

> If *L* models the language of community *C* and ⟨M(*t*), *o*⟩ ∈ *D*, then the term *t* as used in the language of *C* denotes *o*.

If we henceforth assume that *L* deals directly with the vocabulary used in *C* (so we may take *M* to be the identity map), we can recast this conditional in the more suggestive form:

> If *L* models the language of community *C* and *t* DENOTES *o* in *L*, then *t* denotes *o*.

Thus, the formal relation of DENOTATION can be linked to the genuine semantic relation of denotation: but – to come to the crucial point – this of course does *not* mean that the semantic relation has the same modal status as its set-theoretic counterpart.

If we adopt the standard view that it is essential to the identity of a given set that it has the members which it actually has, then it will be necessarily true of D in particular, that it contains the pairs which it is defined as containing by the axioms of L: so if $\langle t, o \rangle \in D$ then it is necessarily true of D that it contains that pair. Or to change the idiom, t will necessarily DENOTE o in L. But, as we have seen, this necessary truth is *not* of intrinsic semantic significance (and the fact that it can feature in a modelling of an actual speech practice no more shows that the real semantic relation of denotation is non-contingent than the fact that other set-theoretic necessities can feature in a mathematical modelling of physical relations shows that those physical relationships are non-contingent). As for the claim that t denotes o as used in community C, that plainly *is* contingent. For it might have been that this term was there used to denote something other than what it actually denotes.

The crucial distinction here is blurred by casual use of such sentences as

(14′) 'Plato' denotes Plato in English.

If, on the one hand, what is meant here is denotation in the actual language of a certain speech community – and this is evidently what is at stake in the context of an interpretative truth theory where we first encountered (14′) – then the sentence expresses a contingent proposition as Lewy has always insisted. If, on the other hand, what is meant is DENOTATION in a formal language which models English, then we do have a necessity. The illusion that there is an interpretation of (14′) on which it is both necessary and also has intrinsic semantic content comes, I suggest, from muddling the two understandings.

I claim, then, that (14) in its originally intended role does indeed express a contingent truth, and likewise for Lewy's favoured example (13). But even if I am quite wrong about this there still remain *other* types of case which establish the required general point that a sentence can be semantically determined to be true and yet express a contingency. Consider, for example, the familiar

(18) I am here now.

If we ignore possible uses of the sentence by God, then this indubitably expresses a contingent proposition on any particular occasion of use: our location is evidently not one of our essential properties. On the other hand, a semantic treatment of (18) which did not radically differentiate it from a sentence like

(19) Peter Smith is in Aberystwyth on July 1, 1983

would involve a hopeless misrepresentation, even if on this particular occasion of its use (18) expresses a truth if and only if (19) does. For such a treatment would, to quote Kaplan, miss

> something essential to our understanding of demonstratives. Intuitively (18) is deeply, and in some sense universally, true. One only need understand the meaning of (18) to know that it cannot be uttered falsely. No such guarantee applies to (19). A [semantic account of sentences involving demonstratives] which does not reflect this intuitive difference between (18) and (19) has bypassed something essential to the logic of demonstratives (Kaplan 1979: 82–3).

Hence, on this plausible view, an adequate semantic theory will deliver the conclusion that (18) always expresses a truth, although the truth it expresses on any occasion will be contingent. So again we find a gap between a sentence's being determined to be true and the proposition it expresses being necessary. And we might add that, given such a case can arise where we have sentences involving demonstratives, and given that the tag theory of names in effect treats names as (so to speak) demonstratives permanently locked to their referents, we should perhaps be prepared for similar cases to arise with sentences involving names.

Hence, in summary: even if we allowed Strawson that it is true to say that what fixes the truth-grounds of 'Hesperus is Phosphorus' also fixes its truth-value, it would plainly be quite unwarranted to infer from this *alone* that the proposition that Hesperus is Phosphorus is non-contingent.

III

Strawson's argument for the non-contingency of the proposition that Hesperus is Phosphorus has been worth labouring over because it frankly presents a version of the still-prevalent idea that straightforward semantic premisses can directly yield substantial modal conclusions. Lewy, of course, has always vigorously dissented from this kind of naive conventionalism about modality; and we have seen that its latest manifestation in Strawson's remarks involves one of the same confusions that Lewy discerned in earlier forms of conventionalism. In the rest of the paper, I want briefly to bring related objections to bear against Kripke's most recent reflections on his notion of rigid designation. For what I have called the non-contingency thesis is now specially associated with Kripke and with his claim that proper names are rigid designators. But the latter claim about names is presumably intended to be a distinctively semantic one; so it seems that here again semantic reflections are supposed to yield modal conclusions in just the direct way which Lewy thinks is unavailable.

In the Preface which Kripke wrote for the book *Naming and Necessity*, he complains that his doctrine of rigidity has been confused with a point about scope. He insists that his doctrine is *not* simply a claim about how names and descriptions respectively embed in modal contexts, a claim which could be understood as reflecting the scope conventions governing the two sorts of expressions. For the doctrine applies equally to such unmodalised sentences as

(20) Aristotle was fond of dogs,

for which questions of scope obviously cannot arise. Kripke writes:

A proper understanding of this statement involves an understanding both of the (extensionally correct) conditions under which it is in fact true, *and* of the conditions under which a counterfactual course of history, resembling the actual course in some respects but not in others, would be correctly (partially) described by (20). Presumably everyone agrees that there is a certain man – the philosopher we call 'Aristotle' – such that, as a matter of fact, (20) is true if and only if *he* was fond of dogs. The thesis of rigid designation is simply – subtle points aside – that the same paradigm applies to the truth conditions of (20) as it describes *counterfactual* situations. That is, (20) truly describes a counterfactual situation if and only if the same aforementioned man would have been fond of dogs, had that situation obtained (Kripke 1980: 6).

This is, however, less than ideally clear – as Dummett has remarked *in extenso* (1981: 557–603).

Just what does Kripke mean when he talks of the truth-conditions of (20) 'as it describes a counterfactual situation'? For a plain, unmodified occurrence of the sentence is surely simply true or false of the *actual* world. It is only when we embed it, with suitable syntactic changes, into a modal context as in

> (21) If he hadn't been bitten as a child, Aristotle would have been fond of dogs

that we get an occurrence of the sentence which could plausibly be said to describe a counterfactual situation. Hence, the unsympathetic might well conclude, if the doctrine of rigidity is a claim about how names function when describing counterfactual situations, it cannot be anything but a claim about how names function inside modal contexts – and so Kripke's insistence that the issue of rigidity makes sense as applied to simple sentences like (20) is quite misplaced.

There is, however, a more sympathetic reading of Kripke which does indeed give him a coherent point that distinguishes the role of names in contexts like (20) from the corresponding role of descriptions in equally direct sentences like

> (22) The greatest philosopher of antiquity was fond of dogs.

The point may be crudely put as follows. It is semantically fixed that the denotation of the name 'Aristotle' is the particular man Aristotle; but it is not in the same way semantically determined that the denotation of the description 'the greatest philosopher of antiquity' is this or that particular person. As things are, the description (let us suppose) properly locates Aristotle. But the world could have gone differently; and then the description – consistently with its still being governed by the same semantic rules – would have denoted someone other than Aristotle. Thus we might say that so long as the sentence (20) retains the same semantic content it could only have been used in a counterfactual situation to speak of Aristotle himself: while the sentence (22) could have been used to speak of some other person (whoever in that counterfactual situation it is who fits the description).

The point can be put a trifle more formally if we again invoke ideas already deployed in section II. Let us say that the term *t* is a designator in the language *L* (at least according to the truth theory θ) if

(D) True ($\ulcorner(\exists x)(x = t)\urcorner$) $\vdash_\theta$ ($\exists o$)(True($\mathcal{A}(t)$) $\equiv$ $\langle o \rangle$ sats $\mathcal{A}(\xi)$)

for any direct context $\mathcal{A}(\xi)$. This, to repeat, captures the idea that – in the non-empty case where $\ulcorner(\exists x)(x = t)\urcorner$ is true – there will be some object whose satisfaction of the condition expressed by $\mathcal{A}(\xi)$ will be semantically required if $\mathcal{A}(t)$ is to be true. Now, our semantic theory may proceed with respect to a particular term t by offering an axiom which directly associates t with the particular object in question, so that we can prove

(D′) True ($\mathcal{A}(t)$) $\equiv$ $\langle a \rangle$ sats $\mathcal{A}(\xi)$

for some metalinguistic constant 'a'. In this case, where t is a tag in the sense we elucidated before, θ may be said to semantically fix the denotation of t. And then t could not have been used by L-speakers to denote something other than its actual denotation without at the same time rendering θ's axiom for t false. On the other hand, if t is a descriptive designator then, with suitable co-operation from the world, it could have been used by L-speakers in a counterfactual situation to pick out something other than the thing which actually satisfies the description in the world as it is, compatibly with θ still giving an adequate semantic account of the function of t.

It seems, then, that a sympathetic interpretation of Kripke's quoted remarks would identify the thesis that names are rigid designators (as he presently understands it) with the claim that the denotation of a name is semantically fixed. This certainly gives us a thesis which has immediate application to an unmodalised sentence like (20), and which also serves – as Kripke wants – to demarcate names from descriptions marked as taking wide scope. The problem is to understand how the rigidity thesis is now supposed to be related to the non-contingency thesis which it famously was intended to sustain. For the idea that the denotation of a name is semantically fixed is embodied in the tag theory. And how are we supposed to get from a version of the tag theory as premiss back to the non-contingency thesis as conclusion? The apparently attractive quick route taken by Strawson turned out to be doubly fallacious: Kripke does not develop any explicit alternative.

It might be argued that, once it is granted that names function as tags in basic unmodalised sentences like (20), it *must* also be granted that they continue to so function in the richer contexts governed by modal operators. And if we *do* take names as tags which retain their normal function in modal contexts, then this means that 'It is necessary that Hesperus is Phosphorus' will have the same truth-value as 'It is necessary that Hesperus is Phosphorus' (since co-designative names will obviously be intersubstitutable *salva veritate* in contexts where they function as tags). So, on a plausible assumption, we will indeed get at least one half of the non-contingency thesis.

But what grounds could there possibly be for holding that the fact that names operate as tags in simple sentences will guarantee that they do so in modal contexts? David Smith avers that 'this should be immediately obvious, since a pure referrer has no descriptive content in virtue of which the expression might have a variable designation with respect to the different factualities in different possible worlds' (1984: 190–1). This will not do. To mention just one difficulty: suppose it were similarly argued that a name must continue to function as a tag preserving its normal reference even in belief contexts, for it has no descriptive content in virtue of which the expression might have a variable significance with respect to different belief worlds. Evidently *this* argument is hopeless, if only because it overlooks the possibility that names in belief contexts have a quasi-quotational occurrence and thus do not retain their normal significance for that reason. In this way, a name can function non-standardly on certain occurrences without its needing to have descriptive content. Given the *prima facie* possibility of regarding modal contexts as likewise analysable as involving a paratactic construction – given, that is, that we might parse 'It is necessary that Hesperus is Phosphorus' thus:

(23) Hesperus is Phosphorus
     That is necessarily true

where the second, asserted, sentence ascribes the modal property of being necessarily true to the referent of the demonstrative – it can hardly be said to be *obvious* that modal operators do not again create quasi-quotational contexts where names therefore do not continue to function as tags for their normal references.

To repeat, Kripke's latest remarks about rigid designation intimate a picture of names as operating as non-descriptive tags at least in unmodalised contexts like (20). But there is, I maintain, no route from the *restricted* tag theory back to the desired non-contingency thesis. So does Kripke intend simply to assert an unrestricted tag theory that applies to modal and non-modal contexts alike? As just remarked, this would indeed deliver at least half the non-contingency thesis. But no one tempted by the sort of considerations against the thesis outlined in section I is going to be persuaded of the error of his ways by a bald assertion, without any further defence, that names just *do* still behave as tags in modal contexts – for that would seem to come far too close to simply begging every question at issue. So, in summary, the general prognosis for the project of getting support for the non-contingency thesis from elementary semantic premises about names looks bleak – a conclusion which those who have learnt from Lewy's criticisms of naive conventionalism will hardly find surprising.

REFERENCES

Davies, M. 1981. *Meaning, Quantification, Necessity*, London: Routledge and Kegan Paul.
Dummett, M. 1981. *The Interpretation of Frege's Philosophy*, London: Duckworth.
Feldman, F. 1971. 'Counterparts', *Journal of Philosophy* 68: 406–9.
Forbes, G. 1983. 'More on Counterpart Theory', *Analysis* 43: 149–52.
Hazen, A. 1979. 'Counterpart-Theoretic Semantics for Modal Logic', *Journal of Philosophy* 76: 319–38.
Kaplan, D. 1979. 'On the Logic of Demonstratives', *Journal of Philosophical Logic* 8: 81–98.
Kripke, S. 1980. *Naming and Necessity*, Oxford: Basil Blackwell.
Lewis, D. 1968. 'Counterpart Theory and Quantified Modal Logic', *Journal of Philosophy* 65: 113–26.
Lewy, C. 1976. *Meaning and Modality*, Cambridge: Cambridge University Press.
McDowell, J. 1977. 'On the Sense and Reference of a Proper Name', *Mind* 86: 159–85.
Noonan, H. 1980. *Objects and Identity*, The Hague: Martinus Nijhoff.
Nozick, R. 1981. *Philosophical Explanations*, Oxford: Clarendon Press.
Peacocke, C. 1975. 'Proper Names, Reference and Rigid Designation', in *Meaning, Reference and Necessity*, ed. Simon Blackburn, Cambridge: Cambridge University Press.
    1978. 'Necessity and Truth-Theories', *Journal of Philosophical Logic* 7: 473–500.

Quine, W. V. O. 1960. 'Variables Explained Away', *Proceedings of the American Philosophical Society* 104: 343–7. Reprinted in Quine's *Selected Logic Papers*, pp. 227–35, New York: Random House.

Smith, A. D. 1984. 'Rigidity and Scope', *Mind* 93: 177–93.

Strawson, P. F. 1980. 'Reply to Cohen, Geach and Quine', in *Philosophical Studies*, ed. Zak van Straaten, Oxford: Clarendon Press.

9   *In defence of the Conventional Wisdom*

CRISPIN WRIGHT

My concern is with Lewy's arguments against a conventionalist conception of logical necessity (1976).[1] I first became familiar with these arguments, or ancestors of them, when I attended Lewy's 'Philosophical Analysis' lectures as a student of Moral Sciences at Cambridge in 1963. Then, they seemed to me devastating. It is with mixed feelings that I find that this is no longer my response to them: it is good, if it is true, that some form of conventionalism may be defensible – but I should have liked my first teacher of philosophy, to whom my debt is so great, to be, as he always seemed in tutorials, conclusively correct.

I

Lewy's arguments revolve around three propositions discussed by John Wisdom (1938),[2] which he formulates, somewhat differently from Wisdom, as

(1) 'Vixen' means the same as 'female fox'
(2) 'Vixen' means female fox
(3) The concept of being a vixen is identical with the concept of being a female fox

Wisdom's claim was that (1)–(3), while they might serve different purposes in context, nevertheless make the same 'factual claims'. Apparently, then, since (3) entails (whether or not it is entailed by)

(4) Necessarily: all and only vixens are female foxes

---

[1] See especially chapter 5.
[2] Reprinted in Wisdom (1953).

Wisdom intended to hold that the truth of judgments attributing necessary truth to a proposition (*ascriptions of necessity*) may be constituted by conventional, metalinguistic facts. This is what Lewy denies.

Lewy's strategy is to argue that (3) neither entails nor is entailed by either (1) or (2). First thoughts suggest that this has got to be an appropriate strategy, whatever exactly 'makes the same factual claims as' is supposed to mean. But a very vague, second thought is that there may be a risk of some subtle question-begging, within the context of discussion of conventionalism, in relying on what are, if the conventionalist is right, presumably *conventionally established* entailment relations. One of the things I aim to do is to clarify what force attaches to this vague worry. For the moment, let us review Lewy's arguments.

That (3) entails neither (1) nor (2) is straightforwardly established, Lewy believes, by two reflections. First (1) and (2) are both contingent, whereas (3) is necessarily true. Hence an entailment from (3) to either (1) or (2) would involve, contraposing, the possibility of entailment from a contingent to a necessarily false proposition. Secondly, (1) and (2) both entail that 'vixen' has a meaning in English, whereas (3) entails nothing at all about English and would be true, indeed, if no such language existed.

Are these reflections conclusive? Well, it might be felt unobvious whether (1) and (2) do *entail* anything about English – there could, for example, be a language other than English which happened to contain the expressions 'vixen' and 'female fox' of which (1) and (2) happened to be true. No doubt the reply to this would be that (1) and (2) are elliptical: that the occurrences of 'means' which they contain must be understood as short for 'means in English'.[3] That response, however, does not allay a complementary doubt whether the truth of the proposition expressed by (3) *is* independent of the existence of the English language, since an argument is wanted – and Lewy gives none – that the conceptual ingredients of that proposition would so much as exist if English did not. In any case, from the point of view of a conventionalist of Wisdom's sort, the flat claim that (1) and (2)

---

[3] This particular move carries a severe risk. If the present stock of conventions for the use of expressions in English turns out, on analysis of the criteria of identity for languages, to be *constitutive* of that tongue, then (1) and (2), so disambiguated, would hold necessarily. The effect of that would be entirely to undermine Lewy's arguments, as any reader already familiar with them will immediately realise.

have consequences which (3) does not is merely question-begging: Lewy needs to present an *account* of the content of (3) which independently corroborates his claim.

The first reflection, too, may seem not quite water-tight. The natural explanation of why a (false) contingent P cannot entail a necessarily false Q is that, being contingent, P will be true in certain possible circumstances C, under which, given the rogue entailment, Q would also have to hold – which is absurd since necessary falsehood is exactly falsehood in all possible circumstances. But that is to presuppose that the entailment from P to Q would continue to hold under C; for which the most obvious supporting thesis would be the claim that when an entailment holds, it holds necessarily and so in all possible circumstances. It appears to want argument, however, that this claim is reasonable in the present context: for – so a simple-minded thought runs – if entailment relations are generated by convention, and if we might have had alternative conventions, then entailment relations could have been different too. I shall return to this (pp. 175–6).

The main battery of Lewy's arguments, however, are directed against the existence of any entailment from (1) and (2) to (3). Actually one argument only (1976: 52) is precisely so directed. The others (1976: 54–8) concern rather the existence of entailment from (1), or from (2), to

(5) There is no vixen which is not a female fox.

The justification for this shift, Lewy claims, is that Wisdom confuses 'higher order necessary propositions' – ascriptions of necessity, modal propositions generally, and propositions like (3), offering analyses of concepts and so entailing propositions of the former sort – with 'first order necessary propositions' like (5) (1976: 53). Hence, in order to refute Wisdom, it is necessary to show that neither type of necessary proposition is rendered true by linguistic convention. (In regarding modal propositions generally as, if true, necessarily true, Lewy intends to be endorsing the adequacy of C. I. Lewis' system S5.) Actually it is plausible that, whether or not Wisdom was confused about the matter, what the conventionalist *ought* to be advancing is a thesis about the meanings of the modal operators in the first instance; and that what he has to say will therefore bear only consequentially on 'first-order' necessary propositions. But Lewy's giving so much attention to the relations of (1) and (2) with (5) is, as he is well aware, amply justified by the reflection that to show that (5) is not entailed by (1), or by (2), is to show the same about (3). Hence Lewy's strategy seems perfectly adapted both to address Wisdom's equivocal formulations and to confront a more sharply defined conventionalism concerning the meanings of sentences whose principal operator is modal.

Consider first the relation between (1) and (3). How can Lewy show that it is not *in virtue of* the truth of (1) that (3) holds – that, in Wisdom's terms, the 'factual claims' effected by the two are different? The evident difficulty is that (3) and (5) are – presumably – necessarily true and are hence *strictly implied*, in the sense of C. I. Lewis, by any proposition whatever. So Lewy needs to explain a relation narrower than strict implication whose obtaining between (1) and (3), say, justifies saying that they make the same 'factual claims', that (3) holds true *because* (1) does.

His proposal is that we should require a strict implication from (1) to (3) to be *formal*: more specifically, Wisdom, Lewy proposes, is right about the relation between (1) and (3) only if (a) (1) strictly implies (3), and (b) any proposition of the same form as (1) strictly implies the corresponding proposition of the form of (3).

When both these conditions are met for a pair of propositions, Lewy characterises the relation between them as that the first *justifies* the second; his proposal is accordingly that what Wisdom requires is that (1) and (2) each *justifies* (3).[4]

Let us defer discussion of the merits of this proposal in order speedily to review how Lewy puts it to work. Clearly (1) justifies (3) only if

(1′) 'Vixen' means the same as 'male fox'

strictly implies

(3′) The concept of being a vixen is identical with the concept of being a male fox.

But (3′) strictly implies

(4′) Necessarily: all and only vixens are male foxes.

---

[4] Lewy gives no general account of justification in chapter 5, illustrating his intentions only by stipulations specifically related to (1)–(3). The general account eventually offered in chapter 8 diverges importantly from the proposal which I have just attributed to Lewy in the text; an explanation of this divergence will be offered in section II below.

Given, then, that any proposition of the form 'necessarily: . . .' is, if true, necessarily true and, if false, necessarily false, and that a contingent proposition cannot strictly imply a necessarily false one, it follows that (3') is also necessarily false and is therefore not strictly implied by (1'), which is contingent. Hence (1) does not justify (3). And an exactly parallel argument would serve to establish that (2) does not justify (3).

Two points are noteworthy. First, Lewy's play with (4') and the principle of the necessity of modal propositions generally is at this point inessential, since, Wisdom's concern having been, *inter alia*, to clarify the nature of necessity, he would presumably have been quite content to grant the necessary truth of (3), and the necessary falsehood of (3') without further ado. Secondly, that there can be no *strict implication* from a contingent proposition to a necessarily false one is – notwithstanding the reservation above about the corresponding claim concerning entailment – compelling. For since 'P strictly implies Q' is defined as the necessitation of '$P \supset Q$', that is of '$-PVQ$', it follows – at least for those who do not share the qualms of the 'Relevantists' about disjunctive syllogism – that when Q is necessarily false, the strict implication of Q by P will require the necessary falsehood of P also. Hence someone who wished to hold that this is not a feature of entailment proper would be committed to denying, what is usually accepted by everyone, that if strict implication and entailment do not coincide, the latter is at least a proper sub-relation of the former. In fact it is clear that more would have to be denied, *viz.* that the entailment of Q by P involves the necessitation of the ordinary conditional 'if P then Q' (whatever that is). Otherwise that conditional will hold true in the counterfactual circumstances in which the contingently false P holds true – and then Q will have to hold as well, contrary to the hypothesis of its necessary falsehood. To sever that connection between entailment and the ordinary conditional, however, is, I think, to sever one's grip on the 'intuitive' notion of entailment altogether.

What then of the earlier 'simple-minded thought'? Two points are worth emphasis. First, the contingency, if they are contingent, of the 'conventions' which we employ, does not immediately force us, if it is indeed coherent to try, to consider as lying within the scope of the 'possibility' operator states of affairs in which different conventions are used; rather we may, perhaps ought to, allow our *actual* conventions to determine the extent of the logically possible. If we do, there will be no question of entailment relations which hold in the actual world failing under the hypothesis that some proposition contingently false in the actual world is true. (More of this when we discuss reiterated modalities in section III.) Secondly, and more straightforwardly, there is, in any case, no evident reason why a world in which the contingently false P held true would *have* to be a world in which the putative *actual* entailment from P to a necessarily false Q ceased to obtain; on the contrary, the contingency of P presumably involves exactly the possibility of its truth *within* the existing conventions for possibility, when, *a fortiori*, all actual entailment relations will continue to hold. For this reason, if for no other, the 'simple-minded thought' was beside the point. I conclude that Lewy has indeed shown both that (3) *entails* neither (1) nor (2), and that neither (1) nor (2) justifies (3).

Lewy proceeds to apply the notion of *justification* to the question of whether (1) or (2) may be viewed as making the same 'factual claims' as (5), constructing no less than five 'proofs' that (1') does not strictly imply

(5') There is no vixen which is not a male fox,

each of which exploits only the contingency of (1') and so may easily be adapted into a proof that (2') does not strictly imply (5'). Only completely uncontroversial properties of strict implication are involved in these various proofs. In particular no higher-order premises about the modal status of modal propositions are involved. Since justification is clearly a transitive relation,[5] and the necessitation of P will invariably justify P, it follows that neither (1) nor (2) justifies either (4), or its consequence, the necessitation of (5). The interested reader should refer to the details of Lewy's chapter.

II

Will Lewy's arguments generalise? The goal of an appropriate generalisation would be the conclusion that, no matter what true

---

[5] For if every proposition of the form, '. . .', strictly implies a corresponding proposition of the form '---'; and every proposition of the form, '---', strictly implies a corresponding proposition of the form, '-.-.', then, by transitivity of strict implication, every proposition of the form, '. . .', strictly implies a corresponding proposition of the form, '-.-.'.

statement of the form 'necessarily *P*' we take, it will neither entail nor be justified by any proposition(s) which, mentioning expressions occurring in *P*, describe conventionally assigned aspects of their use. At first sight – and with an assumption – the generalisation looks straightforward. On the one hand, neither *P* nor, assuming that necessary propositions hold necessarily (the assumption in question), 'necessarily *P*' will entail any such metalinguistic propositions which, since they state conventions, are presumably contingent. On the other hand, no such proposition(s) can justify *P*, nor, *a fortiori*, 'necessarily *P*', since under appropriate substitutions *P* will be transformed into a necessarily false proposition while the resulting metalinguistic propositions will remain contingent. So Lewy's strategy of argument might well be thought to indicate a global independence of modal propositions from linguistic conventions; the only question would be whether some interesting form of conventionalism could survive the particular form of independence – no entailment one way, no justification the other – involved.

That question sub-divides into two. There is the question of whether justification provides a satisfactory account of Wisdom's intuitive 'makes the same factual claims as', that is, whether when *P* justifies *Q*, circumstances conferring truth on *P* may properly be regarded as constituting the truth of *Q*. And there is the question of whether, if the answer to the first question is affirmative, conventionalism about necessity has to be, in the manner endorsed by Wisdom, a (broadly speaking) reductive thesis about necessary statements and explicit metalinguistic conventions. About the latter I shall have only a few, very cursory things to say, largely at the end of the paper. The best approach to the former will be, as it turns out, to take a harder look at the prospects of generalising Lewy's argument.

One seemingly immediate obstacle is the explicit play with the principle: if *P* is necessary, then it is necessary that *P* is necessary (the *S4 principle*), which the generalisation involves. Once again, in the context of a discussion of conventionalism, is there not more than a *soupçon* of question-begging about recourse to such a principle? After all, if convention begets necessity, *necessary* necessity would have to be the offspring, so it seems, of *necessary* convention. And what could that mean? However, Lewy devotes a section of his chapter to argument for the S4 principle (1976:

58–64); accordingly the question of whether its role in his arguments, and in the suggested generalisation, is question-begging, is
best deferred till we review the case he makes for the principle in
section III.

A more serious obstacle to generalisation of Lewy's argument is
that it simply isn't true that no contingent, metalinguistic propo-
sition(s) of the appropriate type can justify a necessarily true one.
We need at this point to be more specific about the notion of
sameness of *form* used in characterising Lewy's proposal earlier.
But now we encounter a certain awkwardness. What Lewy
actually says in the substantive discussion of Wisdom in chapter 5
is that he will count, for example, (1) as justifying (3) just in case
any proposition of the form: '– – –' means the same as '. . .',
strictly implies the corresponding proposition of the form: the
concept of being a – – – is identical with the concept of being a
. . ., where the dashes and dots are to be respectively replaced by
the same word/expression. However, when he comes to attempt
a generalisation of the notion of justification in chapter 8 (1976:
99–101), Lewy offers: P justifies Q if and only if P strictly implies
Q *and* only logical or semantical expressions occur essentially in
sentences which express the propositions P and Q respectively.
The notion of 'essential' occurrence to which Lewy is here
appealing is that of Quine (1966: 73ff): roughly, a particular
sub-sentential expression occurs *essentially* in a given sentence just
in case its uniform replacement in that sentence by occurrences of
another sub-sentential expression of appropriate type is liable to
change the truth-value of the sentence. Now, the evident effect of
Lewy's generalisation is that unless we are concerned with expressions of convention in which only logical or semantical
expressions occur essentially, and with sentences expressing
necessary propositions, or ascriptions of necessity, in which only
logical or semantical expressions occur essentially, there is no
question of justification obtaining. And none of the original
(1)–(3) passes this test. Accordingly this generalisation cannot
have been what Lewy had in mind when he found it appropriate to
argue *in detail* that neither (1), nor (2) justifies (3). So far as I can
see, the generalisation which subserves the discussion of chapter 5
is rather that given by clauses (a) and (b) above, where sameness of
form is characterised as follows:

> Q is of the same form as P just in case Q may be arrived at
> from P by uniform substitution for non-logical and non-
> semantical vocabulary occurring in P,

where semantical vocabulary is understood to include such expressions as 'means', 'means the same as', 'the concept of being a',
etc., and uniform substitution is required to involve, in addition to
the usual understanding of it, substitution of the same expression
for both used *and* mentioned occurrences of an expression. At any
rate, this account so perfectly fits the substance of Lewy's discussion that there is no reason to hesitate to proceed in terms of it.

What is clear is that if a contingent P is to justify a necessarily
true Q, and that if the latter coincides in form with a necessarily
false R, then the same substitution which transforms Q into R had
better transform P into a necessary falsehood; alternatively, if the
question was of justification of Q by a set of conventions,
$P_1 \ldots P_n$, then the relevant substitutions in the latter had better
supply the materials for a necessarily false conjunction. But that is
not a difficult situation to contrive. Consider for example

(6) All and only objects characterised by 'vixen' are charac-
    terised by 'female fox'
(7) All and only vixens are characterised by 'vixen'
(8) All and only female foxes are characterised by 'female fox'
(9) All and only vixens are female foxes.

Clearly $\{(6)–(8)\}$ strictly implies (9). Further, each of $\{(6)–(8)\}$ is
contingent (if (1) and (2) are) and may, with whatever propriety
the description is applied to (1) and (2), be regarded as expressive
of linguistic convention. For its part, (9) is necessarily true. The
substitution of 'male fox' for 'female fox' in all occurrences of the
latter (both used and mentioned) in (6)–(9) is form-preserving in
the sense proposed, and transforms both (9) and the conjunction
of $\{(6)–(8)\}$ into necessary falsehoods, so that the strict implication
survives the substitution. Indeed, the strict implication is always
going to survive such a substitution, since the pattern of inference
is valid purely formally. So we are empowered to conclude that a
necessary truth may after all be justified by a contingency (a
conjunction of contingencies). More to the point in the present
context, the contingent truth in question may conjoin nothing
but propositions each of which may plausibly be regarded as

expressive of a conventional feature of English whose suspension may easily be envisaged.

How ought a proponent of Lewy to respond to this example? It is true, of course, that there is no suggestion of a converse entailment of {(6)–(8)} by (9). But there cannot be a decisive anti-conventionalist point to be made out of that or Lewy's chapter should have been very much briefer and need have included no discussion of putative truth-conferring relations *from* convention *to* necessity. A better response would be that the obtaining of justification between certain conventionally true propositions and a necessarily true one is only required, by Lewy's strategy of argument, to be a *necessary* condition for the appro-priateness of a conventionalist view of the latter's necessity. Wisdom's choices, (1) and (2), fail this necessary condition in connection with (3). However, that {(6)–(8)} meet the condition with respect to (9) is no evident ground for the conclusion that the truth of (9) is conventional: that conclusion would require a corresponding *sufficiency* condition – and no argument has been given for thinking that justification sustains such a condition.

One thing that makes this response possible is that Lewy himself says virtually nothing to explain why he thinks that a convention, or set of conventions, justifying a necessary prop-osition, or an ascription of necessity, is a satisfactory explication of what the conventionalists had in mind when they spoke of identity of 'factual claims', or of necessary propositions 'owing their truth to' or 'being based on' linguistic conventions. (For the cynical reader, indeed, perhaps the most striking feature of justification would be its well-adaptedness to the task of construing Wisdom's specific assertions so as to render them most easily confounded.) Nevertheless there is some point to the response. If the truth of (9) were actually constituted by the obtaining of the three conven-tions {(6)–(8)}, then – notwithstanding the fact that, since (9) does not entail {(6)–(8)}, it could be true when they were not – the suspension of any of those conventions could be expected *ceteris paribus* to undermine the truth of (9). A rough parallel: if what in fact entitles me to a tax rebate is the occurrence of an error in the calculation of my mortgage repayment, then – notwithstanding the fact that I could be entitled to a tax rebate for quite other reasons – the supposition that there has been no error will *ceteris paribus* enjoin the supposition that I am no longer entitled to the rebate. In general terms, the point is this: whatever exact account it might be appropriate to offer in a particular case of what it is for Q to 'owe its truth' to the truth of P, or for P to 'constitute' the truth of Q, it will be, plausibly, a necessary condition on such a relation obtaining that, as it were, the smallest adjustments sufficing to undermine the truth of P will suffice to undermine the truth of Q also. For if that were not so, the truth of Q would be otherwise determined, and so scarcely constituted by, or owing to, that of P. Vague as this idea may be, it seems plain that the situation is quite otherwise with {(6)–(8)} and (9). For envisage the requisite 'smallest' adjustment: suppose that two but only two of {(6)–(8)} enjoy the status of conventions for English, and that matters otherwise differ *only* in ways consequential upon this difference. The result is that so far from describing a world in which (9) ceases to hold, we have a world, rather, in which either the third convention is complied with, though not specifically acknowledged, or a world in which the conventions for the use of 'vixen' and 'female fox' are inconsistent. If, for instance, (7) and (8) were accepted, the situation would not be that the truth, *a fortiori* the necessity, of (9) would then wait on our acceptance of (6). Rather, the necessity of (9) would then ordain our acceptance of (6) – and that shows that the truth of (9) is in no way constituted by the truth of {(6)–(8)}.

Lewy takes it that Wisdom's claim that necessary propositions/ascriptions of necessity are, in effect, tantamount to linguistic conventions, asserts a coincidence in truth-conditions between such propositions and explicit statements of linguistic convention. Hence the strategy of his counter-argument: to show that there is no such coincidence in truth-conditions, because propositions in the two classes are mutually independent. A quite different interpretation of Wisdom, maybe in better keeping with the Wittgensteinian pedigree of his ideas, would be that the traditional notion of logical necessity is a *confusion* erected upon a misunderstanding of the role of what we mistakenly regard as necessarily true propositions – roughly, their role as *rules of description*. Whatever merit this thought may have, it can at least be said on its behalf that articulation of a rule for the use of certain expressions need not involve *mention* of those expressions; definitions given by *using* the defined expressions – most typically, ostensive definitions – are actually standard form, indeed it is hard to imagine any other use for a sentence like 'A vixen is a female fox'. At any rate, if this was Wisdom's intention, then Lewy's whole discussion rests upon a misunderstanding: he faces an opponent whose project is not to account for what makes it true that a proposition is necessary, but to dismantle a faulty construction which we have placed on a large class of propositions.

That is one form of conventionalism which might be offered in response to our earlier question whether varieties exist which could survive the success of Lewy's manoeuvres. That Lewy himself considers no such interpretation of Wisdom inevitably somewhat qualifies the force of his discussion. But there may seem another reason for discontent with the way things have so far gone, even if we suppose Lewy's discussion is perfectly faithful to Wisdom's general intention. We have seen that the notion of justification will not subserve Lewy's independence claim in general, that it is possible for a set of propositions of the sort which Lewy seems willing to count as linguistic conventions to justify a necessary proposition. What seems to have emerged above, however, is that Lewy is right in spirit, if not in detail. No convention, or set of conventions, for the use of expressions in the formulation of a necessary proposition P can *constitute* the truth of P provided that relation is taken to involve – as seems intuitively compelling – that the truth of P could be undermined by waiver of those conventions. The dissatisfaction comes with the realisation that this is really a terribly simple thought: we trounce the conventionalist because we have lumbered him with what appears to be the hopelessly ill-considered claim that the truth of a necessary proposition – a proposition which is to hold true in all thinkable circumstances – can be constituted by a state of affairs – the currency of certain linguistic conventions – which might not have obtained. No need then for argument of the degree of sophistication which Lewy develops to knock the conventionalist down: on the assumption that the conventionalist is a respecter of the intuitive notion of necessity, we simply confront him with the thought that the intuitive notion has it that a *necessary* proposition would have to hold true in any possible circumstances, including circumstances in which standard conventions for the use of expressions featuring in its formulation had lapsed. Can it really be correct that Lewy's Wisdom – henceforth the *reductive conventionalist* – must cave in so easily?

I don't think so. However, the simple objection doesn't touch on reductive conventionalism with respect to ascriptions of necessity in general unless the S4 principle holds;[6] for only then can we confront the contingency of our conventions with the necessity of propositions of the form 'necessarily *P*', in the requisite manner. Accordingly I shall devote the next section to a review of arguments for the S4 principle, and to consideration of the reductive conventionalist's best response to them.

III

It's worth emphasising how apparently powerful is the extended objection which the S4 principle enables us to make out of the simple objection. The power lies in tolerance by the extended objection of very various conventionalist formulations. The promise is of a generalised 'Conventionalistic Fallacy', appropriately enough, in view of the very Moorean character of Lewy's methodology and concerns. But there is an important contrast with the Naturalistic Fallacy argument. Moore's arguments establish at most that there is no interesting analytically reductive relationship between moral statements and naturalistic ones (however exactly the latter class should be demarcated). If he is right, naturalistic concepts cannot form a sufficient basis for the *analysis* of moral judgments. But a form of naturalism which can make out some *other* sort of truth-conferring relationship by the natural on the moral is outside the remit of Moore's considerations. In particular, the claim that the truth of moral judgments *supervenes* upon certain natural facts – meaning by that that sufficient change in the latter is necessarily apt to generate changes in the former, *and* that change in the former necessitates change in the latter, where these necessities are both conceptual – is quite consistent with Moore's having been right about the analytic isolation, so to

---

[6] Exception: the objection bears directly, it would seem, on any ascription of necessity entailed by a proposition, like (3), which is free of modal vocabulary but whose necessity the conventionalist may be presumed to grant. For if, as conceded to Lewy above, a necessarily false proposition cannot be entailed by a contingently false one, then – assuming that entailment is contrapositive, and that the negation of a necessarily false/contingently false proposition is respectively necessarily true/contingently true – it follows that a necessary proposition cannot entail a contingent one. Notice, though, that in order to infer that anything entailed by a necessary proposition is itself necessary, we now need the lemma that every true proposition is determinately either necessary or contingent. And there is some question whether that lemma will be acceptable to conventionalism; see below, pp. 185–6.

speak, of moral judgments; and, if true, is quite sufficient to frustrate the non-naturalism which Moore wished to infer. But no such loophole is left open by the Conventionalistic Fallacy. In the presence of the S4 principle, supervenience of necessity upon convention would appear to be excluded by the simple reflection that no amount of change in linguistic convention can be apt to generate changes in which truths hold necessarily; and that, indeed, the very idea of *change* in the range of necessary truths is now excluded. More generally: if it is of the essence of any necessity-respecting conventionalism (contrast the alternative interpretation of Wisdom briefly canvassed above) that it will somehow construe necessity as created by *us*, then it seems very unclear how the conventionalist can avoid the admission that the facts in which the necessity of a proposition consists can be anything but contingent. After all, presumably the relevant creative acts might not have occurred. So the S4 principle is bound, it seems, to make trouble for even the most weakly reductive forms of conventionalism: forms which accept merely that a necessary condition for the truth of 'necessarily *P*' is the occurrence of some sort of human performance. At least, such trouble seems inevitable so long as the conventionalist respects the intuitive conception of necessity to the extent of allowing that a necessary proposition will hold true in any coherently conceivable state of affairs.

Lewy gives two reasons for thinking that the S4 principle holds (1976: 60–1). First, whenever it can be known at all that *P* holds necessarily, it can be known *a priori*. (He is prescinding, of course, from consideration of the putative species of necessity lionised in the writings on natural kinds of such authors as Putnam and Kripke.) Secondly, unless the necessitation of (5), say, is itself necessary, then it is presumably contingent. And hence a vixen which is not a female fox, 'though not an *actual* possibility, is a *possible* possibility. And this is absurd.' Lewy himself reposes more confidence in the second argument – which he ventures is 'conclusive' – mistrusting the epistemological character of the first. In fact, however, neither argument is decisive, and each involves large assumptions.

Let us scrutinise the second argument more carefully. How exactly does it follow, if we reject the S4 principle, that male vixens, or round squares, while not actually possible, are possibly possible? And what ground is there for Lewy's direct conclusion that that result is absurd? Set out more explicitly, the first part of Lewy's argument will run:

(a) It is not necessarily true that: it is necessarily true that there are no round squares
(b) It is contingently true that: it is necessarily true that there are no round squares
(c) It is possibly not true that: it is necessarily true that there are no round squares
(d) It is possibly true that: it is not necessarily true that there are no round squares
(e) It is possibly true that: it is contingently true that there are no round squares
(f) It is possibly true that: it is possibly not true that there are no round squares
(g) It is possibly true that: it is possibly true that there are round squares.

It is notable that the moves from (a) to (b) and from (d) to (e), presuppose that every true proposition is determinately either necessarily true or contingent. And the same presupposition, or rather its consequence, that every true proposition is determinately either necessary or not, is involved in the whole strategy of Lewy's argument; otherwise success in eliciting absurd consequences from (a) would provide no reason for deleting, as Lewy wishes, rather than doubling its initial negation. Lewy, however, provides no reason for accepting either presupposition (various things which he says of the stronger suggest that he regards it as merely obvious). And, in the context of an attempt to get an impartial view of the S4 principle, with the prospect of using it to mount an objection against conventionalism, his argument seems tendentious as a result. At any rate, to suppose that there is reason to believe in general determinacy in modal status is to suppose, since we lack any effective method for ascertaining in general what the modal status of a proposition is, that *what confers* a proposition's modal status upon it cannot be assumed to be anything which human beings must be able to get to know about. And that is in open contravention of the spirit of the conventionalist's approach, that it is *we* who – presumably self-consciously, or at least potentially self-consciously – determine the extension of necessary truth.

Even if we pass that reservation by, however, it remains unclear for what reason Lewy simply dismisses (g) as absurd. A likely train of thought might be as follows. Any possibility represents a state of affairs which the actual world might have exemplified. Accordingly, if (g) is true, it might actually have been a possibility that there be round squares: the world might have been such that no *conceptual* objection could have been mounted against a believer in round squares. But it seems impossible to give any sort of constructive account of what such a world would be like, of what could prevent the obvious conceptual considerations from getting a grip (Wright 1980: 366). So why should we believe in any such possibility? Only that, of course, is a weaker conclusion than was sought for: we cannot elicit an argument for the *truth* of the S4 principle from the reflection that there is no reason to believe in the possible possibility of round squares; what is required is that there *is* no such possible possibility.

There is a temptation, though, to take the train of thought on a stage. The actual world, (g) implies, might have been a world in which round squares were possible. Suppose that had been so. Then, if every possibility represents a state of affairs which the actual world might have exemplified, it follows in turn that the actual world might actually have contained round squares. And that surely is absurd.

We have begged the question. We have, in effect, carried out a thought experiment in which the world is transformed through two successive possible states: first into an intermediary state alleged to be already possible, and then into a state possible relative to its intermediary predecessor. But to suppose that we might, as it were, travel with *the actual world* through two such states is just to refuse to take seriously the relativity of the second alleged possibility: it is to suppose, in effect, that any state of affairs which can be obtained by successive relatively possible transformations of the actual world is already possible *tout court*. That may seem an intuitively attractive assumption, but it is hardly an independent argument: the principle, 'if it is possible that it is possible that *P*, then it is possible that *P'*', is merely an equivalent of the S4 principle (and the conception that the notion of relative possibility is, in the relevant sense, empty marks a tacit acceptance of the Leibnizian idea of a unitary all-embracing realm of possibilia which, as we shall shortly see, is tailor-made for the S4 principle). To put matters another way: the argument fails because it discloses no reason why the conventionalist should accept the transitivity, among possible worlds, of the relation: . . . can be transformed into. . . .[7]

An element of question-begging is also involved in Lewy's first 'epistemological' argument, at least if that argument is unpacked along the most natural lines. The argument evidently presupposes that whatever it is possible to know *a priori* holds necessarily true.[8] And the plausibility of this thought is owing, presumably, to the consideration that the feasibility, at least in principle, of an act of *a priori* cognition cannot depend on any contingent features of the world; hence the truth of a proposition which it is possible so to know cannot depend upon contingencies either. However, to suppose that the feasibility, in principle, of an act of *a priori* cognition has no contingent pre-conditions is to suppose that it has no *conventional* pre-conditions, that *a priori* knowledge is in no way informed by convention. The conventionalist could hardly accept that.

The standard justification for the S4 principle, beloved of introductory modal logic textbooks, is as suggested a moment ago, by appeal to the conception of Leibniz. Consider then an array of all possible worlds, including the actual world, and let necessity/possibility consist in truth in all/some possible worlds respectively. More specifically, let us have, for any world k

(i) 'Nec P' is true in world k iff 'P' is true in every world
(ii) 'Poss P' is true in world k iff 'P' is true in some world.

Clearly if P is true in every world then, by (i) 'Nec P' is also, holding in whatever world k we care to choose. But in that case 'Nec Nec P' likewise holds in whatever world we care to choose; and an exactly parallel thought yields that 'Nec Poss P' holds in whatever world we care to choose whenever P is true in some world.

So long as it's granted that the conception of a range of all

---

[7] No reason, that is, why, in the jargon, he should accept that the *accessibility relation* among possible worlds is transitive.

[8] Lewy prescinds from consideration of Kripke's suggestion that certain sorts of contingent propositions may be knowable *a priori*; see, for example, Kripke (1979: 54–7).

possible worlds, and the meaning of quantification over them, are sufficiently definite, it must be unobjectionable that these stipulations succeed both in conferring a sense upon reiterated applications of 'Nec' and in establishing a sense of that operator by which all modalities hold necessarily. No telling consideration has been presented, however, why this way of looking at necessity is especially commendable, still less inescapable. Indeed the suspicion lingers that the Leibnizian conception rather grandly begs the question against conventionalism: how can necessity consist in truth in *all* possible worlds if it's generated by conventions which might have been otherwise?

Let us try to formulate that suspicion more sharply. The Leibnizian conception has two essential ingredients: the analysis of necessity as consisting in truth in all possible worlds, and the notion of a comprehensive domain of possible worlds over which the quantifiers in the recursions for 'Nec' and 'Poss' are to range. What the complaint comes to is that, from a conventionalist point of view, these two ingredients are in tension. If there is to be a single, comprehensive domain of possible worlds, it will presumably have to include worlds in which – from the conventionalist point of view – alternative necessity-generating conventions operate; there will accordingly be no reason to suppose that *any* propositions turn out necessarily true in accordance with the recursion given for 'Nec'. In that case, to be sure, the S4 principle will still hold; but there will be no question of basing the argument of the Conventionalistic Fallacy upon it, since there will be no material – no necessary propositions – to which it can be applied. Conversely, if we insist both on the recursion for 'Nec' and on having some necessary truths, the domain of possible worlds had better be restricted to those in which our *actual* necessity-generating conventions operate; for it is only in that restricted range that we can guarantee the truth of their products. But in that case the S4 principle will be established *only* for this restricted domain; as a result, it will be merely illicit to argue from the principle, so established, that necessary statements would retain the status of necessity in worlds in which different conventions operated, in the manner of the argument of the Conventionalist Fallacy.

The position at which we arrive, then, is that Lewy's two arguments for the S4 principle variously beg the question; and that, from a conventionalist point of view, Leibnizian ideas support the principle only at the cost either of doing away with necessary truth or of restricting the application of the S4 principle to worlds governed by our actual linguistic conventions – so that the principle no longer subserves the argument of the Conventionalist Fallacy. For all that we have seen, then, a strict form of reductive conventionalism may yet be a defensible position: ascriptions of necessity, it may still be held, 'owe their truth' to, or 'make the same factual claims' as, explicit statements of linguistic convention. At least, no *refutation* of this position is so far to hand;[9] whether it can be attractively motivated is another matter.

IV

It will occur to the alert reader that the strategem of construing necessary truth as truth in all worlds in which our present linguistic conventions operate would not merely defuse the Conventionalistic Fallacy in its general form but would also deflect the original very simple objection against reductive conventionalism with respect to 'first-order' necessary propositions. For if that is how necessity is construed, then it simply no longer follows from the necessity of a proposition that it would still hold true in circumstances in which different conventions operated for the constituents in its sentential expression. The fact is, however, that the simple objection still seems right: intuitively, nothing seems more certain than that there would have been no round squares even if the words 'round' and 'square' had been assigned whatever use you please. Our ordinary conception of necessary truth is indeed that of truth in *all* possible worlds, irrespective of changes in linguistic convention. And what the simple objection seems to bring out conclusively is that this conception will not marry any form of reductive conventionalism about the truth-conditions of propositions accepted as holding necessarily. Nevertheless, there is, I think, some room for manoeuvre: a perspective on the situation may be possible whereby the reductive conventionalist may accept both the unrestrictedness of the intuitive idea of necessity and the S4 principle without damage to his position.

---

[9] But cf. the qualification in fn. 6.

The basic point is simple enough. It is, presumably, uncontroversial that, of the following pair of counterfactual conditionals,

(10) If 'red' had meant what 'blue' now means, the sky would have been red;

(11) If 'red' had meant what 'blue' now means, the sky would have been blue,

the first is false while the second is true.[10] Clearly, then, in talking of certain hypothetical states of affairs in which other linguistic conventions operate, what it may truly be said would then have been the case is determined by the conventions which we *actually* have. Not only that, but what it would *then* have been true to say is determined by the same conventions. If that is not immediately obvious, reflect on the equivalence of: 'It would have been the case that P' with 'It would have been true to say that P', and the consequent equivalence of (10) and (11) respectively with

(12) If 'red' had meant what 'blue' now means, it would have been true to say that the sky was red;

(13) If 'red' had meant what 'blue' now means, it would have been true to say that the sky was blue.

While it is unclear how the claim might be proved, it is thus at least strongly suggested that the following convention governs our talk of *all* hypothetical states of affairs:

(C) What it is true to say *of* a hypothetical state of affairs, and what it is true to say would be true to say *in* a hypothetical state of affairs, is to be determined by reference to our actual linguistic conventions, even if those are not the conventions that would then obtain.

Convention (C) amounts to a convention for *rigidity*, in Kripke's sense (1979: 48–9), of *meaning* (rigid *designation* is a foreseeable corollary for expressions, if there are any, whose meaning is a function of the objects which they designate). I call it a convention with no solid supporting argument but the thought that it would be extremely difficult to show it to be anything else. Perhaps

---

[10] This point is made (with a different example) in the discussion of the S4 principle in Wright (1980: 366–7). But the role of the point there is quite different. Indeed the conception of conventionalism which dominates that book is quite different from the variety espoused by Lewy's Wisdom; see section V below.

alternatives would be complex to operate and inconvenient but, at least on superficial inspection, our practice could have been, when talking of hypothetical circumstances in which linguistic conventions were different, to *use* the different conventions hypothesised. In that case (10) would rightly be regarded as true, and (11) as false.[11]

If (C) does indeed govern our discourse, and is correctly viewed as a convention, there is an important consequence for our present concerns. Simply: (C) would enjoin that any proposition whose truth is generated purely by our present conventions for the vocabulary in its sentential expression, and which involves only use, not mention, of the elements of that vocabulary, will remain assertible even under the hypothesis of a change in those conventions. Moreover, (C) will require us to say that the proposition would still be true even if the relevant conventions were different. Hence *if* it is true that it is conventions for the use of 'vixen', 'fox' and 'female', etc. which somehow constitute the truth of the proposition that (necessarily) all and only vixens are female foxes, convention (C) will require the assertibility of such propositions as:

> (14) Even if we had not had the convention that all and only objects characterised by 'vixen' are characterised by 'female fox', it would still have been (necessarily) true that all and only vixens are female foxes.

And it is exactly the acceptability of such propositions which constitutes the heart both of the simple objection and of its generalisation in the Conventionalistic Fallacy.

This consequence is, I think, something which gives some substance to the very vague feeling, voiced early in section I, that the conventionalist cannot really be engaged by arguments concerning entailment and independence. The simple objection distils the quintessence of any such argument: if necessarily true propositions are somehow tantamount to statements of convention, or if, more vaguely, necessity is somehow constituted by, or even merely not independent of, convention – whatever the right account of

[11] Stephen Read has called my attention to a similarity between the distinction between 'of' and 'in', used in the formation of (C), and that between 'of' and 'on' drawn by Prior (1976: 207–8); and to a parallel between the use Prior makes of his distinction between 'possibly-true' and 'possible' and the use made here of (C).

'somehow tantamount', 'somehow constituted', etc. – we are surely entitled to expect a certain *co-variance*: hypothetical variation in convention ought to be associated with hypothetical variation in necessity. And the seemingly unexceptionable character of propositions like (14) apparently confounds that expectation. The reason why these reflections are not decisive, why indeed they do amount to a subtle form of question-begging, is that the foregoing reflections put the conventionalist in a position to place the following construction upon the situation. In effect, the force of the objection depends upon our assent to propositions like (14) being something which is *rationally demanded* of us. But there is now a case for saying that the acceptability of such propositions is, rather, *itself* conventional. That we accept them as true is a consequence not of intellection that necessity and linguistic convention are independent but merely reflects the dominance of the general convention (C): *all* hypothetical states of affairs are to be described in accordance with our actual linguistic conventions. Thus the correct perspective, the conventionalist will urge, on propositions like (14) is not that they give the lie to the claim of co-variance but that they bring out how convention (C) *masks* co-variance: in its presence, the constitutive relations between convention and necessity cannot be described by means of what would otherwise be the most natural form of description, *viz*. the sort of conditionals which, like

> (15) If we had not had the convention that all and only objects characterised by 'vixen' are characterised by 'female fox', it might not have been true that all and only vixens are female foxes.

controvert propositions like (14).

There is a notable parallel here with the debate concerning the possible supervenience of value judgments upon certain very general features of human attitude and response. Suppose, if I may be forgiven a hackneyed example, that each of us fears and deplores the prospect of a frontal lobotomy, despite knowing that afterwards we should pass our days in a state of steady contentment, judging our lives most fortunate and scornful of our previous misgivings. What we *now* want to say is that the potential erased by such surgery is itself of value, and that a responsive life which journeys through highs and lows takes a better course than one that stands still on an anaesthetic plateau; and we want to say this in the teeth of our recognition that it would no longer be our view if our lives were, in the way envisaged, of the latter sort. So it looks as though we commit ourselves to a certain *autonomy* of value, in tension with the relevant sort of supervenience claim: one form of life can be of greater value than another, even though everyone might live lives of the latter sort and judge them best. And that commitment in turn generates a commitment to explain how it is that our natural judgments and responses have the appropriate cognitive dignity. The supervenience theorist, for his part, has the task of justifying his reluctance to undergo lobotomy. More specifically, his problem is to entitle himself to such a judgment as

> (16) Even if, after lobotomy, we were all to judge our lives most excellent, and the sort of life which we were then no longer able to live most dreadful, it would still be true that life of the latter sort is of greatly superior value,

without commitment to an autonomy inconsistent with supervenience. The manoeuvre parallel to the invocation of convention (C) then comes with the suggestion that we operate with something like the convention

> (V) How it is correct to appraise a hypothetical state of affairs, and what appraisal it would be correct to offer in that state of affairs, is to be settled (may be settled?) by reference to our actual evaluative responses and attitudes, even if those are not the responses and attitudes which we would then have.[12]

Accordingly, the supervenience theorist may suggest, the explanation of the acceptability of a proposition like (16) is not that the supervenience thesis is false, but that convention (V) requires (allows?) rigidity of evaluative criteria and so works to mask the sort of co-variance which the claim of supervenience leads one to expect. We suffer, in consequence, no commitment to anything which it might be proper to describe as the autonomy of value by our willingness to accept such propositions.

The supervenience theorist (evaluative relativist), like Lewy's

---

[12] As Hilary Putnam might have joked: 'So we should rely on *someone else*'s evaluative responses?'.

Wisdom, maintains a broadly-speaking reductive claim: both are keen to deny a certain multiplicity of *genres* of states of affairs, with a view to solving, or simplifying, certain epistemological issues. And reductive theses of whatever exact formulation must, it seems, issue in some sort of co-variance claims, naturally cast in the form of the claimed truth of certain kinds of subjunctive conditional: if things in the reductive class had been/were to be different in thus and such ways, things in the reduced class could have been/be correspondingly different. What has emerged is that, at least in these two cases, the reductive thesis need not be sunk by the received unacceptability of the relevant conditionals. Another form of explanation of that unacceptability may be possible than the absence of the requisite co-variance, in terms of the presence of a dominant convention, prescribing some form of rigidity, which bids us reject the conditionals which would otherwise be adequate to express the co-variance.

So far only scant attention has been given to an aspect of Lewy's polemic in which he places great confidence: his recourse to the so-called 'translation argument' to controvert Wisdom's claims about (1)–(3) (Lewy 1976: 57–8; 64–6). It is worth considering how the reductive conventionalist may now respond to this. What Lewy's considerations about the proper translation of sentences like (1)–(3), or *mutatis mutandis*, (6)–(9) tend to suggest is that, whereas linguistic conventions are specific with respect to the vocabulary of a particular language, the necessity of propositions is *international*, as it were – and so presumably cannot be constituted by parochial facts of any sort. But the last part of that, the conventionalist ought now to reply, is a *non sequitur*. Everyone can agree – whatever they think of Lewy's tendency to talk of propositions as though they were the universal currency of conceptual exchange – that necessity is 'international' at least in the sense that its preservation supplies a constraint on correct translation. Let us suppose then, with the conventionalist, that it *is* conventions concerning 'round', 'square', etc. which generate the necessity that there are no round squares. Since it is necessarily true, it will be a constraint upon the translation of the latter proposition into French, say, both that the result involve an articulation of ingredient vocabulary which appropriately corresponds to 'round', 'square', etc. *and* that it express a necessary truth. So – still assuming the correctness of the conventionalist view – the very feasibility of an adequate translation will depend upon the existence of appropriate conventions governing the use of the relevant French vocabulary; otherwise a suitable necessity-expressing French counterpart of the English formulation will not exist. Accordingly there is no need, in order to do justice to the 'international' character of necessary truth, to recognise any necessity which is not generated by convention.

A different point which the considerations about translation suggest is the correctness of the claim, for example, that even if English had not existed, it would still have been (necessarily) true that there are no round squares. But that particular orthodoxy is something which the conventionalist will now seek to explain by reference to convention (C); the point breaks no new ground.

If the foregoing reflections are correct, then Lewy's Wisdom can at least fight a draw – unless, of course, better moves can be conjured against him than any so far canvassed. But the obvious worry is whether the defensive strategy supplied is not a little *too* powerful. If the status assigned by orthodoxy to subjunctive conditionals of the appropriate kind is not to the point, what *is* to be the appropriate form of expression of the conventionalists' co-variance claim? – what independently checkable statements will he recognise his co-variance claim as involving? And if no such class of statements comes to hand, what can there be to be said *for* reductive conventionalism in the first place? The form of response which the conventionalist needs to make is clear: he must adduce considerations which tend to suggest that, of the two presented explanations of the acceptability of propositions like (14) – the autonomy of necessity with respect to linguistic convention, and the operation of (something close to) convention (C) – the latter is superior. His opponent, for his part, must adduce considerations which suggest the opposite. But if neither protagonist can deliver, the effect of the play with convention (C) which we have had the conventionalist make will be properly described, so it seems to me, not so much as a rebuttal of the objections against which it was directed, as an annihilation of the very content of the dispute. One conclusion is that, so far from enhancing the prospects of belief in the autonomy of necessity, Lewy's discussion, for all its clarity of focus and admirable rigour, ultimately achieves nothing to disturb the suspicion that there may be, between him and Wisdom, no substantial matter of debate.

V

Apart from a cursory acknowledgment that Wisdom may have intended an iconoclastic view, our concern has been exclusively with 'necessity-respecting' forms of reductive conventionalism. So it's worth stressing, finally, that conventionalism may retain its respect for the intuitive notion of necessary truth while ceasing to be reductive at all. The thesis on which Lewy concentrates – typically expressed during the thirties and forties as the claim that necessity is 'really verbal'[13] – was doubtless a product of the cross-fertilisation of the Positivists' ideas by the then contemporary teachings of Wittgenstein. Whatever its origin, it needs to be sharply distinguished from another thesis, central to Wittgenstein's later philosophy of logic and mathematics, which would also naturally be described as the claim that necessary statements are conventions, *viz.* the thesis that the acceptability of a statement *as* necessary is a matter of convention. This is not a reductive thesis: there is no suggestion that necessary propositions, or ascriptions of necessity are somehow tantamount to explicit statements of linguistic convention, nor even that their truth supervenes on that of statements of the latter sort. Rather the claim is that the (formerly) orthodox belief in the objectivity of necessary truth and in our capacity for a purely rational intellection of it, is mistaken; that a contrast needs to be drawn between the rationally constrained character of our acceptance of prototypical matters of 'hard fact' and a comparative absence of objective constraint in our arriving at judgments about which propositions hold necessarily.

On the face of it, this view seems utterly unattractive, for we *feel* no such absence of constraint – good proofs, after all, are described as *cogent*. That such reservations are not really to the point emerges when we compare Wittgenstein's claim with the corresponding claim in the theory of value that ethical, or aesthetic, judgments serve not to express real fact but to *project* aspects of our feelings and responses. Perhaps the least controversial kind of example of a type of judgment about which a projective view would be our antecedent prejudice would be judgments about what is *funny*; and that prejudice is, of course,

---

[13] Cf. Malcolm (1940). Whatever the proper interpretation of Wisdom, there is, I think, no doubt that Malcolm held the position which Lewy attacks.

quite at home with the acknowledgment that assent to such judgments may be something not given voluntarily but elicited irresistibly from us.

Why Wittgenstein held such a position about necessity, and how best it should be formulated and considered, are questions about which I have already indulged my curiosity at considerable length elsewhere.[14] I shall not add to that discussion now, except to record the beliefs that the issue is of fundamental philosophical importance – not least because analytical philosophers have tended to think of necessary truth as their stock-in-trade while simultaneously seeing themselves as seekers after *knowledge* – and that Wittgenstein's position admits of profoundly based and powerful support. Above all, it should be realised that cognitive realism about necessity is not the only alternative to the scepticism about the concept favoured by (Quinean) empiricism.

REFERENCES

Kripke, S. 1972. 'Naming and Necessity', in *Semantics of Natural Language*, eds. O. Davidson and O. Harman, Dordrecht: Reidel.
1979. *Naming and Necessity*, Oxford: Blackwell.
Lewy, C. 1976. *Meaning and Modality*, Cambridge: Cambridge University Press.
Malcolm, N. 1940. 'Are Necessary Propositions Really Verbal?', *Mind* 49: 189–203.
Prior, A. N. 1976. *Papers in Logic and Ethics*, eds. A. Kenny and P. T. Geach, London: Duckworth.
Quine, W. V. O. 1966. *The Ways of Paradox and Other Essays*, New York: Random House.
Wisdom, J. 1938. 'Metaphysics and Verification', *Mind*, 47: 452–98.
1953. *Philosophy and Psychoanalysis*, Oxford: Clarendon.
Wright, C. 1980. *Wittgenstein on the Foundations of Mathematics*, London: Duckworth.
Forthcoming, 'Inventing logical necessity', *Language, Mind and Logic*, ed. J. Butterfield.

[14] See Wright (1980: *passim*), but especially Part 3, 'Necessity', chapters XXI–XXIII; also Wright (forthcoming).

Bibliography of the publications of Casimir Lewy

1937. 'Some Remarks on Analysis', *Analysis* 5: 1–5.

1938a. 'A Note on Empirical Propositions', *Analysis* 5: 51–5.

1938b. 'On the "Justification" of Induction', *Analysis* 6: 87–90.

1939. 'Some Notes on Assertion', *Analysis* 7: 20–4. Reprinted in *Philosophy and Analysis*, ed. M. Macdonald, Oxford: Blackwell, 1954, pp. 120–4.

1940. 'Logical Necessity', *The Philosophical Review* 49: 62–8.

1943. 'Is the Notion of Disembodied Existence Self-Contradictory?' *Proceedings of the Aristotelian Society* 43: 59–78.

1944. 'On the Relation of Some Empirical Propositions to their Evidence', *Mind* 53: 289–313.

1946a. 'Entailment and Empirical Propositions', *Mind* 55: 74–8.

1946b. 'The Terminology of Sense-Data', *Mind* 55: 166–9.

1946c. 'Equivalence and Identity', *Mind* 55: 223–33.

1946d. 'Why are the Calculuses of Logic and Arithmetic Applicable to Reality?' *Aristotelian Society Supplementary Vol.* 20: 30–9.

1947a. 'Critical Notice of Arthur Pap: The *a priori* in Physical Theory', *Mind* 56: 271–5.

1947b. 'Truth and Significance', *Analysis* 8: 24–7. Reprinted in *Philosophy and Analysis*, ed. M. Macdonald, Oxford: Blackwell, 1954, pp. 242–5.

1949. 'Critical Notice of Rudolf Carnap: Meaning and Necessity', *Mind* 58: 228–38.

1950. 'Entailment and Necessary Propositions', *Philosophical Analysis*, ed. M. Black, Ithaca, New York: Cornell University Press, pp. 195–210.

1953. 'The Notion of Infinity', *Aristotelian Society Supplementary Vol.* 27: 45–52.

1958. 'Entailment', *Aristotelian Society Supplementary Vol.* 32: 123–42.

1959. 'Bibliography of the Writings of C. D. Broad', *The Philosophy of*

C. D. Broad ed. P. A. Schilpp, New York: Tudor Publishing Company, pp. 831–52.

1962. G. E. Moore: *Commonplace Book 1919–1953*, edited by C. Lewy, London: Allen and Unwin.

1964a. 'Entailment and Propositional Identity', *Proceedings of the Aristotelian Society* 64: 107–22.

1964b. 'G. E. Moore on the Naturalistic Fallacy' (Dawes Hicks Lecture), *Proceedings of the British Academy* 50: 251–62. Reprinted in *Studies in the Philosophy of Thought and Action*, ed. P. F. Strawson, Oxford: Oxford University Press, 1968, pp. 134–46.

1966. G. E. Moore: *Lectures on Philosophy*, edited by C. Lewy, London: Allen and Unwin.

1967a. 'A Note on the Text of the *Tractatus*'. *Mind* 76: 416–23.

1967b. 'George Edward Moore', *Encyclopaedia Britannica* 15: 817.

1975. C. D. Broad: *Leibniz*, edited by C. Lewy. Cambridge: Cambridge University Press.

1976a. '*Mind* under G. E. Moore 1921–1947', *Mind* 85: 37–46.

1976b. *Meaning and Modality*. Cambridge: Cambridge University Press.

1978. C. D. Broad: *Kant, an Introduction*, edited by C. Lewy. Cambridge: Cambridge University Press.

Shorter book-reviews have not been included in this bibliography.

Notes on the contributors

J. E. J. Altham is Lecturer in the University of Cambridge, where he is a fellow of Gonville and Caius College. He was a pupil and then a research student of Lewy 1960–5. He is the author of *The Logic of Plurality* (Cambridge University Press, 1971) and now works mainly in ethics and political philosophy.

Thomas Baldwin is a lecturer at the University of York (U.K.). He was a pupil and then a research student of Lewy 1965–9. At present he is working on a critical account of G. E. Moore's philosophy.

Simon Blackburn is Fellow and Tutor at Pembroke College, Oxford. He studied under Lewy 1962–7. He is the author of *Reason and Prediction* (Cambridge: Cambridge University Press, 1973) and *Spreading the Word* (Oxford: Oxford University Press, 1984).

Jeremy Butterfield is Assistant Lecturer in the University of Cambridge. He was a pupil of Lewy 1973–6. His main interest is the philosophy of space and time.

Edward Craig is Lecturer in the University of Cambridge and a Fellow of Churchill College. He was a pupil of Lewy, first as an undergraduate and then as a graduate, from 1960 to 1966. His publications include *David Hume: Eine Einführung in seine Philosophie* (Frankfurt: Klostermann), and various journal articles, mostly in the area of epistemology.

Ian Hacking teaches at the Institute for the History and Philosophy of Science and Technology, Toronto. He was a pupil and then a research student of Lewy 1956–61. He is the author of *Why Does Language Matter to Philosophy?* (Cambridge: Cambridge University Press, 1975), *Representing and Intervening*, (Cambridge: Cambridge University Press, 1983) and books on probability.

David Holdcroft teaches at the University of Leeds. He was a pupil and then a research student of Lewy 1956–60. He is the author of *Words and Deeds* (Oxford: Clarendon Press, 1978), and various journal articles, mostly on the philosophy of language.

Peter Smith teaches at the University College of Wales. After taking a degree in mathematics he was a pupil and then a research student of Lewy 1965–70. His journal articles are mostly on the philosophy of mind and philosophical logic.

Crispin Wright holds the Chair of Logic and Metaphysics at the University of St Andrews. He was an undergraduate pupil of Lewy 1961–4. He is the author of *Wittgenstein on the Foundations of Mathematics* (London: Duckworth, 1980), *Frege's Conception of Numbers as Objects* (Aberdeen: Scots Philosophical Monographs, 1983), and various articles on the philosophy of language.

Index of names